The Culture Industry, Information and Capitalism

The Culture Industry, Information and Capitalism

César Bolaño
Universidade Federal de Sergipe, Brazil

Translated by

John Penney

palgrave
macmillan

Published in 2000 as *Indústria Cultural, Informação e Capitalismo* by HUCITEC, ISBN 85-271-0525-X
In 2013 as *Industria Cultural, Información y Capitalismo* by GEDISA, ISBN 978-84-9784-754-4

This edition first published 2015 by
PALGRAVE MACMILLAN

Palgrave Macmillan in the UK is an imprint of Macmillan Publishers Limited, registered in England, company number 785998, of Houndmills, Basingstoke, Hampshire RG21 6XS.

Palgrave Macmillan in the US is a division of St Martin's Press LLC, 175 Fifth Avenue, New York, NY 10010.

Palgrave Macmillan is the global academic imprint of the above companies and has companies and representatives throughout the world.

Palgrave® and Macmillan® are registered trademarks in the United States, the United Kingdom, Europe and other countries.

ISBN 978-1-137-48076-7

This book is printed on paper suitable for recycling and made from fully managed and sustained forest sources. Logging, pulping and manufacturing processes are expected to conform to the environmental regulations of the country of origin.

A catalogue record for this book is available from the British Library.

Library of Congress Cataloging-in-Publication Data
Bolaño, César.
[Industria cultural, información y capitalismo. English]
The culture industry, information and capitalism / César Bolaño.
pages cm
Summary: "This study shares the tendency, which has been widely maintained in Europe over recent years, to approach the problems of communication and the culture industry with the tools of economic theory. The oldest approaches to the mass communications media have often been criticized, and basically viewed from the standpoint of political domination and ideological reproduction. The critical aspect of the communication and culture economy, by contrast, is that attention has been focused on investigating the functions of the media in the process of capital accumulation, thereby prioritizing the problems of advertising and the mass communications media as a privileged locus for the accumulation of capital at the current stage of capitalist development. Drawing on Marxist theory and concepts, as well as on various theoretical contributions developed by prominent political economists, Bolaño develops a unique approach to understanding the culture industry, offering an interesting intervention in debates surrounding media and communication." — Provided by publisher.
ISBN 978-1-137-48076-7 (hardback)
1. Politics and culture. 2. Communication—Political aspects. 3. Political culture. I. Bolaño, César. Industria cultural, información y capitalismo. II. Bolaño, César. Industria cultural, información y capitalismo. English. III. Title.
JA75.7.B6513 2015
306.2—dc23 2015002146

Contents

Figures and Tables

Figures

Tables

Foreword

It is an especially appropriate time for César Bolaño's book *The Culture Industry, Information and Capitalism* to be published in English. The book is an extension of his previous work, a dissection of the Brazilian television industry, which formed the foundations for his discussion of a general theory of communication, which is rich in analysis and insights that return us to the heart of Marxist theory.

Thus, this book is consistent with the recent call by some scholars for a reinvigoration of Marxist analysis (see, e.g., Terry Eagleton's *Why Marx Was Right*, 2011). This return to classic Marxist analysis has also been a recent trend for some scholars who study the political economy of communications (PEC). While most critical PEC scholarship draws on Marxist theory and practice, a few media scholars and/or sociologists have emphasized the need to use Marxist theory more explicitly and return to classic themes and concepts to explain the evolution of media and communications. Christian Fuchs (2008) has been especially active in these efforts, while John Bellamy Foster represents a sociologist who uses Marxist theory to study environmental and media issues (see McChesney et al., 1998).

Other examples would include the attention to labour, media and information, with a number of recent collections devoted to these issues (e.g. McKercher and Mosco, 2007). The evolution of digital technology has also been studied using Marxist theory. Digital labour has been analysed in a number of studies (e.g. Fuchs, 2014), and is the focus of a recent special issue of *Triple C: Communication, Capitalism & Critique*. In this issue, entitled "Philosophers of the World Unite! Theorising Digital Labour and Virtual Work – Definitions, Dimensions and Forms", the editors explain that it "aims to contribute to building a theoretical framework for the critical analysis of digital labour, virtual work, and related concepts that can initiate further debates, inform empirical studies, and inspire social struggles connected to work and labour in and beyond digital capitalism". Critical Marxist theory has also been used to look at big data and cloud technology (Mosco, 2014), as well as the policies and politics surrounding digitization (Burkart, 2014). Important historical perspectives on the digitization process have been offered as well, with reminders that "new" media technologies often present a good deal of continuity, especially in terms of corporate involvement, commercialization and commodification (see, e.g., Wu, 2010, for a historical overview of corporate intervention in new media development). Meanwhile, other classic concepts have been revived, such as the concept of the commons, which several media scholars have recently integrated into their analysis of the current media climate (see especially Murdock, 2011).

In this volume, Bolaño develops an approach to understanding the culture industry that draws on Marxist theory and concepts, as well as on various theoretical contributions developed by Latin American, European and North American political economists. His proposals may challenge some of these theories; however, it is important that such debates take place, in order to continue building and refining this approach to understanding media and communication.

Indeed, PEC is no longer a marginal approach to media and communication studies, but crucial to understanding the growth and global expansion of media and information industries. Consequently, more researchers have turned to this perspective as a necessary and logical way to study these developments. The study of the political economy of the media and communications continues to attract communication researchers around the world. For instance, Bolaño refers to the Political Economy section of the International Association for Media and Communication Research (IAMCR) as one of the inspirations for his work. The section has grown dramatically over the last decade or so, attracting numerous scholars from all over the world. It is also appropriate that the section leadership has recently shifted from US/British scholars to representatives from Portugal and (currently) Mexico.

The growth of PEC is not so surprising given the growing importance of the media and its industrial development within an expanding international market system. In other words, a careful analysis of capitalism, its structures, the consequences of those structures and the contradictions that abound is more than ever relevant and needed. As Jean Paul Sartre once said, "Marxism remains the philosophy of our time because we have not gone beyond the circumstances which engendered it" (1963, p. 30).

This book is part of the recent reinvigoration of Marxist analysis, but it is also important for other reasons. PEC has often been limited by the relative absence of voices from non-Western scholars. This is partially due to language differences, but it has also been influenced by the "blind spots" of Western PEC, as well as the political economy of the global academic publishing business. In his introduction, Bolaño refers to the global PEC as a "melting-pot of many different research traditions". This volume promises to add more ingredients and additional spice to this melting pot and should contribute significantly to the broadening and refinement of the global study of PEC.

Janet Wasko
University of Oregon

Janet Wasko is the Knight Chair for Communication Research at the University of Oregon in Eugene, Oregon, USA. She is the author, co-author or editor of 19 books, including *Understanding Disney: The Manufacture of Fantasy* and *How Hollywood Works*. Her research and teaching focus on the political economy of media, especially the political economy of film, as well as issues relating to democracy and media. She currently serves as the President of the International Association for Media and Communication Research.

References

Eagleton, T. (2011). *Why Marx Was Right*. London: Yale University Press.

Fuchs, C. (2008). *Internet and Society: Social Theory in the Information Age*. New York: Routledge.

Fuchs, C. (2014). *Digital Labour and Karl Marx*. New York: Routledge.

McChesney, R. W., E. M. Wood & J. B. Foster. (Eds.). (1998). *Capitalism and the Information Age*. New York: Monthly Review.

Mosco, V. (2014). *To the Cloud: Big Data in a Turbulent World*. New York: Paradigm Publishers.

Murdock, G. (2011). "Political Economies as Moral Economies: Commodities, Gifts and Public Goods." In J. Wasko, G. Murdock & H. Sousa (Eds.), *The Handbook of Political Economy of Communications* (p. 331–357). Malden, MA: Wiley Blackwell.

Sartre, J. P. (1963). *Search for a Method*. New York: Alfred Knopf.

Wu, T. (2010). *The Master Switch: The Rise and Fall of Information Empires*. New York: Vintage.

Acknowledgements

I acknowledge institutional support from CAPES under the PICD programme. As part of my doctoral project I spent one year in Paris under the CAPES-COFECUB N° 94/88 Cooperation Agreement (1990 programme). In this respect I am grateful for the support given to me by the Economics Institute of Campinas State University (UNICAMP) Public Policies Studies Nucleus, especially by its director, Dr Sonia Draibe. I am also indebted to Dr Bruno Theret, who supervised my attachment at the Institut de Recherche et d'Information Socio-Economique – Travail et Société, University of Paris, Dauphine (Paris IX).

Special gratitude is also due to Dr João Manuel Cardoso de Mello and to Professor Liana Maria Lafayette Aureliano da Silva, who provided me with unfailing support from the time I began my studies on the economy of communication and culture in the early 1980s. Furthermore, I cannot fail to mention my dear friend Vinicius Dantas, who provided the main incentive for me to publish the first edition of this book. Thanks are due to my translator, John Penney, and to my colleague Ancizar Narvaez Montoya (Universidad Pedagógica Nacional de Colombia), who translated the original text for the Spanish-language edition on which the English translation is based.

For the English edition, I would like to add especial thanks to some colleagues not referred after, like Janet Wasko, whose outstanding role in the IAMCR/AIERI/AIECS Political Economy Section has been essential for the ongoing unification of PEC. It is impossible to made references to my many Ibero American colleagues, but I must mention in particular Pedro Jorge Braumann (Portugal), Délia Crovi (Argentina), Francisco Sierra (Spain) and, in Brazil, Ruy Sardinha Lopes, my late partner Valerio Cruz Brittos, and all my colleagues from the Sergipe Federal University. These and countless other colleagues have stood by me in the construction of the Latin American PEC. Finally, I must also thank the Ford Foundation, which funded the translation into English.

Note to the English Edition

This book has a long history. My initial studies in the field of political economy in the early 1980s resulted in an earlier work first published in 1988, titled *The Brazilian Television Market* (Bolaño, 1988). This first venture into the field of study that would later become Brazil's PEC sought to address the constitution of the television oligopoly, the dynamic core of Brazil's cultural industry. In it, the theoretical influences that I had imbibed at the School of Communication and Arts of São Paulo University (Univerisity of Sao Paulo) and UNICAMP blended with critiques of political economy, Brazilian sociology, the Frankfurt School, São Paulo Marxism, Latin American structuralism and heterodox microeconomics.

With my knowledge of this paradigmatic case of a genuine media oligopoly, and drawing upon a broad conceptual framework, I decided to formulate a more general Marxist theory of communication that progressed beyond mere critical theories of a sociological nature (e.g. Frankfurt School and dependency theories). This theory of communication was, I believe, unusual in that it was rooted in Marx's greatest work, *Capital*. The theoretical basis was thus laid for a critique of the epistemology of communication, currently enjoying renewed development. This present second study was completed in 1993, revised in 1997 and published in Brazil in 2000 as *Indústria Cultural, Informação e Capitalismo* (Bolaño, 2000).

Four years later, the revised and expanded second edition of *The Brazilian Television Market* (Bolaño, 2004), in line with the developments described in the above book, further expanded the framework of the oligopoly theory and incorporated neo-Schumpeterian School analytical tools. Both books were published in Spanish in 2013 – *El Mercado Brasileño de Televisión* in Argentina and *Industria Cultural, Información y Capitalismo* in Spain. A chapter was added on the political economy of the internet, not contained in the original Portuguese-language edition. The 2013 version in Spanish was the basis for the English translation.

The present book is therefore a work that has matured over the years, during which I devoted myself to deeper study of the themes contained therein. I have, for example, prepared a set of articles (perhaps the basis for a future book?) in which I develop a hypothesis about the third industrial revolution, understood as a process of subsumption of intellectual labour, substantially influenced by the theory presented here.

My interest in the subject has been sharpened by contact with different PEC schools of whose existence I was initially unaware.

In Latin America different authors worked during the 1980s in relative isolation (like me) with limited contact with, or knowledge of, the North American, European or even each other's schools. Older Latin American dependency or cultural imperialism theories in effect formed the critical cultural mass that was to give rise to the subcontinent's PEC. As Mariano Zarowsky (2013) argues, Latin American critical thinking via Armand Mattelart (following his return to Europe) was also to have considerable influence on European, and especially French, PEC at the time of its inception. In fact, the first European contributions emerged at the end of the 1970s, almost at the same time as those spawned in Latin America.

But dependency and cultural imperialism theories were not initially PEC as such, but rather a sociologically based critical perspective influenced by the Frankfurt School and Latin American structuralism in addition to theories of dependency. The Latin American School interacted with key English-speaking authors, strongly influenced by Herbert Schiller or the new American left (with the pioneering works of Baran and Sweezy), and also with those who played leading roles in the Political Economy and other sessions of the International Association for Media and Communication Research (IAMCR) and countless others who, in reality, together constituted the first school of PEC at the global level.

The Latin American PEC acknowledges this critical heritage and its limitations, and sets itself the task of conducting a "critical retreat" back to the work of Marx aimed at securing more substantial support for a general theory of communication. All the aforementioned authors belong to the generation that distinguished itself in the struggle for the New World Information and Communication Order (NOMIC) and for national communication policies. As we now know, these efforts were aborted with the withdrawal of the USA from UNESCO, and these authors are generally regarded, in the work conducted in the 1980s that gave rise to the Latin American PEC, as belonging to the broader field of critical thinking, predominantly Marxist but not Marxian, that is, not affiliated with the so-called "orthodoxy of method".

The work of these authors was not widely known in Brazil during my early years of academic training (the 1970s and 1980s). The classics of communicational thought were of course well known and the Frankfurt School was thoroughly studied. At the same time, we were still in thrall of the events of May 1968, the revolutionary movements in Latin America and the struggle against military dictatorships – where popular and alternative communication significantly increased – while remaining fully aware of the basic reforms and the writings of Paulo Freire, Augusto Boal, Lenin and Gramsci.

While youth showed solidarity with the peoples of Africa and Asia and the decolonization struggle, acknowledged the existence of "Patria Grande" (Great Homeland, a loose political idea of Hispanic American integration) and espoused vague third-world views, discussion of NOMIC failed to impact Brazilian communication students. It was only in 1992, with the first (refounding) congress of the Latin American Association of Communication Researchers (ALAIC), and the IAMCR congress in the Brazilian cities of Embu-Guaçu and Guaruja respectively, that the subject began to emerge from the shadows. My original draft of the present book, which was to lead to the first edition in Portuguese, was already written at that time. However, its ideas and form, from the initial formulation of its leading question, resonating in a Marxist framework in the far-off 1980s, did not change in a material way, even in the final version (1997).

As a result of my year's academic attachment in France – when my theoretical proposal was firmly entrenched, but the text had not been completed – the book makes an internal and external critique of the French School of Economy of Communication and Culture. I also included the outcome of my researches into the so-called Latin American PEC literature, as well as references to relevant Latin American, European and North American studies, in an effort to determine where my proposal fitted into this field of study. While I did not exhaustively research the PEC at the international level, I chose to select a small group of interlocutors in order to give visibility to my own argument.

I discuss the work of certain key English-language authors, but I cannot lay claim to critical completeness in this respect. I make reference of course to the founding work of Baran and Sweezy, Schiller and especially Dallas Smythe. I focus exclusively on the latter's celebrated 1977 article, republished in Spain in a well-known collection edited by Richeri. In this respect, my aim was to throw light on the difference between mine and Smythe's definition of "audience as merchandise", focusing on the misconceived idea of the work of the culture-consuming public.

In short, there can be no doubting the major influence of Smythe and the American school in the constitution of the field of PEC. In addition to the above-mentioned authors, many others contributed to the worldwide expansion of this area of studies. These include Vincent Mosco, Janet Wasko, Andrew Calabrese, Manjunat Pendakur, Joseph Starubhaar,

John Sinclair and many others that I have had the pleasure of meeting, since 1992, at the Political Economy sessions of the IAMCR. These were also attended by leading British PEC authors such as Nicholas Garnham, Graham Murdock, Peter Golding and other Europeans (Pascal Preston and Helena Sousa).

The list of contributors to PEC is too long to give here, although it is an important list at a moment like the present when once again, under the aegis of the IAMCR Political Economy session, the PEC is unifying worldwide, stretching beyond the confines of North America and Britain. While it is not of course the purpose of this book to map this development, there can be no doubt that the global PEC is a melting pot of many different research traditions, with diverse backgrounds, intellectual influences, academic environments, economic situations, and national and regional policies, all of which obviously influence the work of the authors in this field.

This book originated on the periphery of capitalism. Publishing it in English is hopefully a way of bringing to the international debate a somewhat eccentric perspective, demonstrating the vitality of the field and highlighting the existence of other possibilities for dialogue and potentially innovative approaches, perhaps by authors cited in the book who publish little or nothing in English. This dialogue will necessarily entail an extensive review of English-language literature in the area, which is outside the scope of this work, but which I have in mind for the future.

Global unification of PEC is part of the broader epistemological struggle of Marxist and critical thinking in communication. This broader perspective was precisely the inspiration behind this book in the latter half of the 1980s. A quarter of a century later many important steps have been taken at the institutional, theoretical and epistemological levels and in terms of our knowledge of empirical reality.

It is notable that even as late as 1996, a core book such as that by Vincent Mosco (perhaps the most quoted author today as a synthesizer of all previous thought on the subject, concerned with the renewal and redirectioning of PEC as a global theoretical framework) failed to cite any Latin American PEC author in his bibliography.

However, an important article by Janet Wasko (2014) can be taken as a starting point for a comprehensive worldwide review of the literature in this field. This author presents, in addition to an overview of the history and theoretical foundations of PEC and its most significant debates, a long list of current topics, authors, trends and major ongoing dialogues.

A collective review of the literature would certainly serve worldwide to ensure a more symmetrical approach to PEC unification as a respected discipline. It would also reposition PEC at the heart of the communication area, understood in the present book as the "science of mediation". From the time of the old mass communication research, right through to studies on cyberspace, social networks, information theory, semiotics, language and Latin American cultural studies, it is the concept of mediation (on which there is, of course, no consensus) that effectively pulls PEC together regardless of the many areas of dispute.

Careful examination of the concept of mediation in the pages of this book will reveal that it is indeed an alternative that highlights work and its subordination to capital movement in order to explain the specificities of communication typical of 20th-century capitalism, which exist to the present day. Enric Marin and Josep Tresseras, in a little-known work published only in Catalan in the late 1980s, turn to the magnificent work of Ferruccio Rossi-Landi to define communication as follows: "the communicative dimension of social production resulting from communication work [...] assumes the mediating function that makes possible the indissoluble unity between experience and awareness of the human subject – in other words, the transition from objectivity to subjectivity, from the 'social being to awareness' " (Tresseras & Marin, 1987, p. 75).

This definition chimes fully with my own perspective, but we must emphasize that Rossi-Landi (1968), by developing the theme of language as work, does so in terms of homology in order to preserve, unlike many others, including self-styled Marxists, the separation between symbolic production and (economic) production value. Of course, as Marin and Tresseras explain, supported this time by Raymond Williams (father of cultural studies and grandfather of European PEC), poetry can constitute "goods" in the more prosaic sense of the term, and cars can be "signs", among other things. Always a matter of matter!

But beyond homology, there is real confusion. This can contaminate much theory, when for example communicational work is not only useful but also productive, benefiting, in the strictest sense, the capital invested in the cultural and communication industries. In this case, not only does capital subsume work but, by the same token, economics (capitalist) subsume culture. Mediation thus becomes much more complex, since the mediating function of all linguistic work is at the service of capital (private and total) without losing its fundamental purpose. In this way the contradiction is established and popular culture becomes mass culture – the root cause of so many misconceptions and prejudices.

I hope readers will consider this book as a first step towards a broader critique of the epistemology of communication. The goal is to present a theoretical framework as a basis upon which a careful analysis of all the previous theories can be made at some later time. Although I have touched on this in the following pages, it was not my main intention to offer such an analysis. A study of the enormous repository of work in English in particular needs to be left for another occasion.

I appreciate the opportunity given to me, with the publication of this book, to participate in this process.

Introduction

This study shares the tendency, which has been widely maintained in Europe over recent years, to approach the problems of communication and the Culture Industry with the tools of economic theory. With regard to the Marxist analyses which adopt this approach, the oldest approaches to the mass communications media have often been criticized, basically viewed from the standpoint of political domination and ideological reproduction. The criticism of the communication and culture economy, by contrast, is that attention has been focused on investigating the functions of the media in the process of capital accumulation, prioritizing the problems of advertising and the mass communications media as a privileged locus for the accumulation of capital at the current stage of capitalist development.

I also share the more recent perspective regarding the criticism generally raised of the shortcomings of previous political approaches. However, I defend the need for an understanding of the phenomenon of the state in order to explain both its functions in the process of capital accumulation and those related to the ideological reproduction of the system. But this means that, leaving aside the more or less key inconsistencies of each of the specific approaches at the theoretical level at which these problems are usually discussed, one cannot speak seriously about two general alternatives of analysis, but rather of two different perspectives whose complementarity, although not immediate, presents the possibility of being defined in terms of regulation. Based on this discussion, a tableau of analyses may be extracted to aid the study of specific cases.

Prior to this it is possible to seek to reach, at a more abstract level, the essential complementarity, as opposed to the apparent lack of complementarity between two different logics which determine the need for constituting an instance of mediation such as the state – one defined by the requirements of the state and the other derived from the demands of capital. I maintain that this is possible, by displacing the discussion to the level of form, as Blanke, Jürgens and Kastendiek did in their explanation of the state based on capital, following in the footsteps of Paschukanis and the discussion of the method adopted by authors such as Rodolski or Zélèny. This is basically what I seek to do in Chapter 1. In our case it is only necessary to define, at this higher level of abstraction, the most simple and general concept of information, firstly taking the ratio of interchange as a complete communicative action as posited by Habermas, then verifying what occurs with the concept when its link to capital is considered. In this way I believe that it is possible to define the different specific forms of information under capitalism, and its contradictions with regard to mercantile relations, to the relationship between capital and labour and, finally, to capitalist competition.

For the purposes of this study, it is important to discuss more specifically the two general forms of information related to mass communication, that is the advertising form and the propaganda form, whose contradictions are related to, although not to be confused with, the conflicts of interest between the state and capital in terms of communication with the masses. Based on this we may return to the question of the function of the Culture Industry in the processes of capital accumulation and ideological reproduction of the system within the framework of monopoly capitalism, thus going back to how this question is generally framed.

The logical development of the concept of information and its contradictions is also insufficient for focusing on the Culture Industry, which requires, inter alia, a subsequent historical analysis linked to the discussion on the constitution of "lifestyles" which meet the different needs for reproduction of the system. Although a complete historical analysis of the genesis and development of capitalist cultural production cannot be made within the limits of this study, the general themes and events which seem to me to be the most important to this focused approach will be examined; these could in due course be analysed more systematically in another context. It is also of interest to show how the contradictions of information materialize in classical capitalism, in what Habermas called the "bourgeois public sphere".

Chapter 2 aims to define the theoretical-historical elements necessary for the complete particularization of the Culture Industry, which represents the new form of materialization of the contradictions of information in the historical situation of monopoly capitalism. In Chapter 3, the main Marxist approaches to this theme will be classified according to their emphasis on the advertising or propaganda function. In Chapter 4 I will make a critical examination of the French school of the communication and culture economy. In Chapter 5 I will attempt to propose an alternative analytic framework to serve as a starting point for empirical studies.

This framework is a regulationist type analytical model whose link, in epistemological terms, to the more general proposal formulated in the first two chapters of this study is explained in Bolaño (1996a). In the present context I only need to state that the theoretical strategy adopted offers a step towards the derivation of the regulation based on the definition of advertising and propaganda as general and contradictory forms inherent in capitalist information, which at the level of the analysis of competition consists of two global functions concerning the differences between the interests of capital and the capitalist state with regard to mass communication. This requires a discussion of the mechanism which guarantees the compatibility and effectiveness of the two in relation to, respectively, the process of capital accumulation and the ideological reproduction of the system. Based on this implicit function-regulation dynamics I will build, in Chapter 5, an analytical framework for addressing specific cases.

However, a derivationist strategy will only permit an approach to the subject of the Culture Industry based on a unidirectional perspective of the determination of the advertising and propaganda functions exercised upon it by the state and capital. In order for the process to reach the masses, and for class communication to appear effectively as mass communication, the mediation facility must also respond to the psychological or psychosocial needs of the public. Thus, using the terminology of Habermas, the Culture Industry must efficiently substitute internal mechanisms of symbolic reproduction of the lifeworld, to be able to colonize it in favour of capital and the state, thus guaranteeing its task of mediation.

It is interesting to note that it is precisely this consideration of the theme of social mediation which explains the importance, in the general theoretical framework proposed here, of our contribution to the communication and culture economy, especially in relation to the French school. Moreover, our analysis is essentially focused on making clear the specifics of the cultural product, the work processes involved in it and the specific forms of valorization of capital in this sector, together with demonstrating the need for and the centrality of the analysis of competition, an area to which the French school has assigned little importance.

In fact, it is the competitive strategies of the television companies, for example, constrained by their situation in a given market structure, which will define a specific pattern of cultural production, and which will also allow in turn the building of a bridge between the competitive strategies of companies focused on what I have called the "broadened sector of 'differentiated' consumer goods" market and the strategies aimed at what Bourdieu calls a "distinctive" public, and which will be in an enhanced position to sell to the advertising market a "differentiated" type of merchandise tailored to the audience.

The mechanism of mediation, historically constituted as an "institutionalized compromise", to use the expression of the school of regulation, capable of resolving from within, and evidentially always in a provisional form, the advertising-propaganda-programming contradiction, is the Culture Industry. This arose together with monopolistic capitalism, but only appeared in its complete form, as an integrated system, after the Second World War. At that time the two models – commercial and public service television – came into being on a nationwide basis, signifying the adoption of two different historically determined solutions, which to some degree and for some time after resolved the tensions in the system between the demands of advertising and those of propaganda, as well as between the imperatives of the state and those of capital in relation to mass communication. The regulation-crisis-regulation dynamic was obviously in full swing.

From the viewpoint of capital, the European solution was only acceptable as a provisional solution, at a moment when important factors of a political nature gave priority to propaganda mechanisms over those of advertising, with a view to maintaining social equilibrium and assisting the post-war reconstruction efforts, similar to what had occurred previously with radio. However, the perpetuation of this type of organization limited the involvement of capital, on one hand by impeding the full development in general of the advertising sector which was crucial to the process of capital accumulation under monopolistic capitalism, and on the other hand by closing an area of investment of growing interest for big business despite the growing importance of the television medium to advanced capitalism.

Privatization at the time was a recurrent theme throughout Europe. The "mixed" system was established in England in 1954. From the outset, Luxemburg's private TV system represented a constant threat to the stability of the state systems of neighbouring countries. From the 1970s the subject took a dramatic turn, with the economic crisis, undermining the bases of the welfare state, reviving the neoliberal argument. Meanwhile, the advent of the new communication technologies constantly weakened national television systems, and international competition began to make inroads into a sector which was starting to attract the keen attention of big business.

Furthermore, especially after the events of May 1968 in France, civil society itself began to raise key questions about state involvement in the public sector. The legitimacy of the "state system" came under threat (at least in the form in which it was structured, especially in France and Italy). Such reactions showed that under monopolistic capitalism there is indeed space for civil institutions (public educational establishments, trade unions, political parties, different types of associations etc.), which are capable of significantly depleting the manipulative power of the media. All these factors together were to provide fuel for the great debate on the reform of the audiovisual sector, which culminated with the emergence of an important market sector in Europe's main countries, reversing the situation which had hitherto reigned since the Second World War.

It should be emphasized that this process was by no means confined to Europe. The internationalization of competition in the TV sector and the interest shown by new, big financial concerns keen to exploit fast-emerging technological developments (e.g. integration of telecommunications and audiovisual sector) threatened the oligopolitical structures in the countries with commercial systems. This was the case, for example, in Latin America, where relations between the state and business in the Culture Industry were of particular importance at a time when efforts to consolidate democracy in the region entailed demands for broad discussion on the democratization of information and the ideal structure of social communication systems.

The current trend appears to involve the consolidation of a small group of oligopolitical big businesses which operate on a global scale, linked in different ways to national groups and state companies which are striving to remain competitive by adapting to the new conditions. Increasing international competition in the sector, the profound changes occurring as a result of the development of new communications technologies and the advance of segmented television, the increasingly widespread deregulation processes, all provide new ingredients which add to the complexity of the problem and underline the urgent need for the introduction of a broad theoretical and analytical scheme to fully address the many different issues involved. I am convinced that constructing this scheme is necessarily a collective and interdisciplinary task. This study endeavours to make a small contribution in this respect.

This book contains the essential parts of my doctoral thesis "Business, State, Culture Industry", defended in April, 1993 in the Economics Institute of the State University of Campinas (IE-UNICAMP). As part of a wider project of the study of the political economy of communication, beginning with an analysis of the Brazilian television market (Bolaño, 1988), this book is confined to a theoretical discussion within the area of Marxism, although it also contains references to authors who are external to this approach. At any rate, the critical potential of the theoretical alternative proposed here in relation to the conventional, neoclassical and functionalist approaches to the economics and sociology of communication, as well as to the postmodern authors and the theoreticians of the so-called information society, will be established in the course of my analysis. Chapter 1 points particularly to the possibility of subsequent theoretical developments leading towards a general critique of traditional and postmodern theories of communication.

1
The Contradictions of Information

The greatest difficulty in constructing a Marxist theory of mass communication under capitalism is the fact that the few references by Marx pertinent to the subject are clearly insufficient for such an undertaking. Apart from the historical references to the revolution in transport systems, a product of capitalist expansion which, together with other factors, would provide mechanized production with "enormous power to quickly expand by leaps and bounds" (*Capital*, Volume I*), and his statement that the "development of ocean navigation and of the means of communication generally has swept away the technical basis on which seasonal work was really supported" (ibid.), Marx's main reference to the subject in Volume I is in the section on "Division of Labour in Manufacture, and Division of Labour in Society". The famous reference to the town-country antithesis is followed by the comment that

> [...] the number and density of the population [are] a necessary condition for the division of labour in society. Nevertheless, this density is more or less relative. A relatively thinly populated country, with well-developed means of communication, has a denser population than a more numerously populated country, with badly-developed means of communication.
>
> (Ibid.)

In the third volume, Marx also makes repeated references to the subject of transport (and telegraph communications), asserting for example that "the chief means of reducing the time of circulation is improved communications" (*Capital*, Volume III). But the main references are to be found in Volume II. Already in Chapter 1 ("The Circuit of Money Capital"), he states that

> there are certain independent branches of industry in which the product of the productive process is not a new material product or a commodity. Among these only the communications industry, whether engaged in transportation proper of goods and passengers, or in the mere transmission of communications, letters, telegrams, etc., is economically important.
>
> (*Capital*, Volume II)

He goes on to analyse the characteristics of the sector in relation to industrial production proper.[1] Later, in Chapter 6 ("The Costs of Circulation"), Marx refers more specifically, in the third section, to the "Costs of Transportation". In this section, Marx points out that, unlike all other costs of circulation "which arise only from changes in the forms of commodities [and] do not add to their value" (*Capital*, Volume II):

> [...] quantities of products are not increased by transportation. Nor, with a few exceptions, is the possible alteration of their natural qualities brought about by transportation, an intentional useful effect; it is rather an unavoidable evil. But the use-value of things is materialised only in their consumption, and their consumption may necessitate a change of location of these things, hence they may require an additional process of production, in the transport industry. The productive capital invested in this industry imparts value to the transported products, partly by transferring value from the means of transportation, partly by adding value through the labour performed in transport. This last-named increment of value consists, as it does in all capitalist production, of a replacement of wages and of surplus-value.
>
> (Ibid.)

In the *Grundrisse**, the difference between costs of transportation and other costs of circulation appears as follows:

> Only in connection with interest and particularly with credit can we speak of the costs of circulation arising from circulation as an economic act – as a relation of production, not as a direct moment of production, as was the case with the means of transport and communication [...] The more production comes to rest on exchange value, hence on exchange, the more important do the physical conditions of exchange – the means of communication and transport – become for the costs of circulation. Capital by its nature drives beyond

> every spatial barrier. Thus the creation of the physical conditions of exchange – of the means of communication and transport – the annihilation of space by time – becomes an extraordinary necessity for it.
>
> (*Grundrisse,* vol. 2)[2]

Marx continues:

> Only insofar as the direct product can be realised in distant markets in mass quantities in proportion to reductions in the transport costs, and only insofar as at the same time the means of communication and transport themselves can yield spheres of realisation for labour, driven by capital; only insofar as commercial traffic takes place in massive volume – in which more than necessary labour is replaced – only to that extent is the production of cheap means of communication and transport a condition for production based on capital, and promoted by it for that reason.
>
> (Ibid.)

However, "if an individual capital is to undertake this – that is, if it is to create the conditions of the production process which are not included in the production process directly – then the work must provide a profit" (ibid.). In this passage, Marx then uses the example of a road being constructed to discuss the general conditions of production, which refers more to the subject of the relations between capital and the state (see Bolaño, 2003 and 2003b) than to the question that is of particular interest to us at this point.

The conclusions to be drawn from all of this are as follows: (a) that taken together, the "means of communications and transport" are understood by Marx to be part of the general conditions of the reproduction of capital; (b) that they play a role in the establishment of consumer markets and the provision of raw materials and intermediate products required by industry; (c) that they form a specific sector of the economy with particular characteristics, which (d) is productive and creates value. There are certainly a number of different lines of approach that can be developed using these quotations from Marx as a starting point, which have special relevance for defining the technical sectors of communications (e.g. telecommunications) but which are also pertinent to other important discussions, such as that of the general conditions of capitalist accumulation or that of the productive or unproductive nature of the communications and advertising sectors.

Nonetheless, these quotes cannot serve as the basis for an adequate Marxist treatment of the subject of communications, much less of "culture under capitalism". No amount of reductionism will suffice to combine, in terms of the functions of production, a means of communication such as television with one such as railways. They are two different things, two different connotations of the term "means of communication". I do not deny that there are certain interesting interactions between them. Railways and other means of transportation certainly have a role to play in cultural integration, whether by drawing geographically separate groups of people into closer proximity, thereby modifying behaviour patterns or altering the forms of perceiving reality, or whether simply by the fact that, like satellites, they serve as a means for transporting information and cultural goods. The same channels that carry television programmes also deliver quantities of fictitious capital that can modify the financial situation of economic agents. It was certainly with these correspondences in mind that Marx always referred, in the passages cited, to a broad-brush "communications and transport" sector. It would appear today, however, that significant theoretical problems arise from lumping together even two means of communication as radically different as broadcast media and the telegraph or telephone.

The passages from Marx cited above are obviously insufficient for constructing a theoretical approach to the subject of mass communications under capitalism. The theoretical approach adopted here, on the contrary, takes as its starting point an inquiry into the *form of communication* appropriate to Marx's general definition of capital, and accompanies the logical trajectory of *Capital* in seeking to identify, at the highest level of abstraction, the basic category that accommodates all of the features and inherent contradictions of the capitalist form of communication. Our starting point thus shifts from the analysis of functions germane to constructions mounted upon the base/superstructure model, towards the so-called method of the derivation of forms (Bolaño, 2003). Although I cannot indulge in the comfort of direct support in the form of quotations from Marx, I believe it will be possible to defend my project in rigorously Marxist terms, following the method of Marx himself, beginning with the analysis of simple circulation through to exploring aspects which, if not relevant to Marx's needs, for my purposes will assume a fundamental role requiring detailed treatment.

On the other hand, I believe that it is better to make clear at the outset that I will not refer at any point to an ideal concept of communication or information. The aim of the present work is to construct a theoretical concept of information capable of being adapted to the most abstract general description of the capitalist mode of production. However, if other forms of communication and other types of information exist in concrete reality that fail to fit the precise definition proposed here, that does not invalidate my present effort. On the contrary, if these various forms of communication and types of information appear jumbled together in reality, nothing is more necessary than a rigorous analysis that might provide the tools to better distinguish them.

Simple circulation and information

Exchanging goods is a process of communication between private owners of goods that goes beyond the mere economic relationship on which it is based. The phantasmagorical appearance of a relationship between goods, to use Marx's picturesque turn of phrase, reduces this to an impersonal relationship in which the agents of the exchange are reduced to mere bearers (*Träger*), automatons programmed to operate the machinery of the circulation of goods. But this merely conceals a complex relationship between human beings who undertake the act of exchange in order to satisfy specific human needs that could not be met by the independent production of a single producer in isolation. This is the anthropological presupposition that underlies the basic contradiction of the commodity form of the products of human labour. Nor is this foundation altered even when one among the innumerable commodities becomes autonomous and assumes the function of a universal equivalent. On the contrary, when the use value of the commodity of money is elevated to represent the exchange value of all other commodities, it is clear that we are not dealing with an accidental exchange relationship, but rather with a social norm that, among other things, must be backed by an extra-economic coercive power. It is no coincidence that Marx's first reference to the state in *Capital* appears precisely in the chapter on money in Volume I.

The social norm to be extracted from the analysis of the commodity relation involves a particular form of the relation between human beings – an economic relationship of buying and selling goods – which involves a particular form of communication: different, for example, from the form of communication between sexual partners, co-workers or members of a religious group. It consists, in the case of commodity exchange, of verbal communication about objective information. The price of the commodity is itself a basic unit of information without which no exchange relationship is conceivable, and without which the buyer cannot exercise his capacity of autonomous decision-making. And the relationship between buyer and seller also involves other essential information concerning the use value of the commodity in question, its quality, the type of raw material used, the skill of the producer, production circumstances, the distance of the production facility from the place of exchange (which, by requiring the activities of the transport industry, alters the value of the merchandise itself, as Marx noted in the quotes above) and the unique characteristics of the product, in addition to the likelihood of the buyer having sufficient financial resources and, in the case of buying on credit, for example, the financing terms, schedule of payments, interest, etc. In short, information is a precondition for the existence of a market economy.

Commodity circulation represents the moment of equality that characterizes the capitalist economy, marked, however, by the fundamental inequality that still cannot be grasped at the level of appearances (*Erscheinung*), which concerns the analysis of simple circulation. Here, the social relation is a relationship of formal equality between individuals who share the character of private owners of commodities and arrive at the marketplace with the identical objective of buying and selling.

At this point we may reconsider the question of truth, one of the characteristics, according to Habermas, of normal, undistorted communicative action. While the information involved in the commodity relationship is objective, it is not necessarily true. There are certainly ways of confirming the truth of information of this type (such as inspecting a horse's teeth or checking the length of a piece of linen with the buyer's own rule), but it is always possible that the seller, for example, may lie about the quality of his or her goods, or that the buyer may lie about his or her financial resources (and here, as well, instruments exist for confirming the truth, such as requiring payment by certified cheque or guarantors). The existence of verification tools only demonstrates that there are indeed objective limits to the falsification of this type of information, owing to the very objectivity of communication that is characteristic of the commodity relationship in its pure state. More than lying, however, untruth (particularly as regards the manipulation of information by those who dispense it and have the power either to withhold and not report, or to unleash a stream of irrelevant information that impedes the autonomous decision-making of those who receive it) is always possible and is linked, on the one hand, to the very nature of money and the attraction it exerts on individuals, and on the other, to the fact that the commodity has a use value that corresponds to objective material needs, whether these be related to the stomach or the spirit.

This already demonstrates the implicit possibility of manipulating information through advertising, which may be successful in altering the relationship between the cost of production and the price of the commodity, thereby providing higher returns to the unscrupulous businessperson and, therefore, competitive advantage. But this must be left, at this level, as a mere possibility, since in the terms of commodity circulation all individuals are formally presumed equal: equally private owners of commodities, which presumes them equal before the law, and equally capable of having access to or withholding true or false information.[3]

The fact, regardless, is that the relationship established between two commodity owners facing one another in the marketplace constitutes a complete communicative act. This is the result, of course, of the existence of a community (or *Lebenswelt,* to use Habermas' term), which although not determined by Marx in his analysis of the commodity, exists as a fundamental anthropological presupposition of his entire derivation of the concept of capital. In the final analysis this fact also justifies the whole theoretical argument of this work, since our starting point is precisely the establishment of the theoretical element that was not explicit in Marx, but that can be considered an implicit presupposition in *Capital* if we reflect that behind the metaphor of the phantasmagorical character of commodity exchange are human beings who establish a social relation among themselves.[4]

Let us take the simplest case in which two commodity owners confront one another in the marketplace. Let us suppose, for example, an individual A, owner of a certain quantity of any commodity (say, wheat) and an individual B, owner of a certain quantity of money, who meet at the marketplace and perform an act of communication there, with the object of undertaking an operation of buying and selling. We may observe at the outset that the observations made by Habermas in his example of a group of workers who decide to meet for a beer at lunchtime (Habermas, 1981, Chapter VI, Section 1.1) are generally valid in this case. Thus, A and B perform a "co-operative process of interpretation", referring simultaneously to something belonging to the objective world, the social world and the subjective world, seeking an "understanding (*Verständigung*), [a term that means] that participants in communication reach an agreement (*Einigung*) concerning the validity of an utterance" (Habermas, 1981, vol. 2, p. 171).

The topic of the dialogue between A and B is wheat; the aim is the act of purchase; the normative framework is the fact that both are private commodity owners. A is a seller and B a buyer; the situation is defined by the two having met at the marketplace. The dialogue begins when B asks A about the price of his wheat. Suppose that the sum of money requested by A for a given amount of wheat does not initially meet the expectations of B. In this case, B will make a new utterance, responding (for example) that the price is quite high in view of his own knowledge of the market, to which A will eventually respond by referring, say, to the allegedly superior quality of his product, and so on. In all its aspects, the situation is adjusted to reflect the characteristics of a communicative action as described by Habermas.

In our example, the wheat belongs to the objective world; the environment, consisting of the market and by the status of buyer and seller of A and B respectively, defines the normative framework given by the social world; meanwhile, the subjective world of each of the participants in the communicative act in question is one that only they themselves are privileged to access, although it is reflected by means of "dramaturgical action" throughout the negotiation process. Thus, for example, B may assert that, despite the high quality of the product, he is not personally interested in acquiring it under those conditions, preferring other wheat of inferior quality at a lower price. Similarly, other elements of a normative order may intervene in this case; for example, an assertion that the seller does not accept payment by cheque.

Here we also have a series of elements comprising a situation (the market, the price of wheat, the quality, the financial position of B, etc.) and other circumstances that are not relevant (such as the fact that the transaction is taking place on a Saturday), but which, with successive redefinitions, may become so (thus, the fact that the transaction is occurring on a Saturday may assume importance when A states that he does not accept cheques as payment and B explains that, since banks are not open to the public on Saturdays, the transaction may be impossible, since he does not have enough cash on hand). The same could be said of the constant presence of the "lifeworld" of each of the participants, or of the inclusion of language or of underlying cultural patterns of interpretation. But it is not necessary here to extend this comparison further, as our interest is not specifically in developing a theory of communicative action.

The theory of the derivation of the state has already demonstrated that commodity circulation presupposes the existence of the legal form guaranteeing the rights of individual owners over their goods (and to dispose of them by sale) and ensures the honouring of contracts – which defines, already at this level of abstraction, one of the basic functions to be performed by the "extra-economic coercive power", which forms the starting point of the derivation performed by Blanke, Jürgens & Kastendiek (1977). With regard to communication, I hope to have made clear thus far that there is an information form specific to the commodity relationship, characterized by objectivity and by its verbal character, and which satisfies the necessary conditions for being considered a complete communicative action in Habermasian terms. Additionally, I have pointed out that already at this level of abstraction, the manipulation of information by advertising is possible, a possibility which nevertheless is not actualized because at this level information is still not considered to be a source of power, since individuals are taken as formally equal. Communication is still conceived as communication between equals. However, if this level already admits the possible existence of an extra-economic coercive power, one must consider that this power must also define a specific type of communication, in ultimate contradiction of the type we have defined based on our discussion of the commodity relationship. In other words, once this extra-economic power appears as a power alongside and above the relations of exchange, it already appears to be ultimately capable of monopolizing information (or at least one type of information), making it one-directional and thus in contradiction to the market.

In other words, from this point forward, the possibility is established of using information as a source of political power, as propaganda, in the same way that we have already established the possibility of distorting information through advertising. Once more, however, this possibility is merely formal, not only because we still do not have a completely derived state, but primarily because, in the realm of equality, information can only assume the form of "advertising" or "publicity" in the sense of "to make public". This is so both from the point of view of the market and from that of the extra-economic coercive power. Publicity is the form that information must acquire to accommodate the demands of commodity circulation. The ideological character of information, whether direct (propaganda) or indirect (commercial advertising, which creates a lifestyle, or advertising per se), is still not fully determined at this level of analysis, in which the moment of equality that characterizes the appearance of the system is prevalent. To rectify this error, it is necessary to abandon the sphere of exchange, that "very Eden of the innate rights of man", as Marx ironically described it (*Capital,* Volume I).

It is surprising that an author such as Lyotard remains, in the final analysis, essentially a prisoner of that semblance of equality. In his short but well-known work from 1979, Lyotard attempts to discuss the question of the legitimation of science in what he and others call postmodernity. He initially defines the difference between the modern scientific narrative, whose language is denotative, and the popular narrative, in which legitimation is found within the narrative itself, through the identification of the narrator with the story (Lyotard gives the example of the popular narrative among the Cashinahua Indians). Scientific discourse, in contrast, requires an external by means of "metanarratives", grand political (emancipatory) or philosophical (speculative) narratives, both teleological.[5] The postmodern condition is characterized precisely by the failure of these grand narratives that guaranteed the legitimacy of scientific discourse. The result is that science and understanding now can only be legitimized through power. For Lyotard, the reciprocal relationship between technology and wealth is established during the industrial revolution of the 18th century with the realization that "there is no technology without wealth, but no wealth without technology". The second aspect of this statement constitutes the novelty of the realization:

> A technological apparatus requires an investment; but since it optimises the efficiency of the task to which it is applied, it also optimises the surplus-value derived from this improved *performance*. All that is needed is for the surplus-value to be realised.... And the system can be sealed in the following way: a portion of the sale is recycled into a research fund dedicated to further *performance* improvement. It is at this precise moment that science becomes a force of production, in other words, a moment in the circulation of capital.
>
> (Lyotard, 1979, p. 81)

The result is that the "technology became important to contemporary knowledge only through the mediation of a generalised spirit of performance". Science is also subordinated to this capitalist logic. In fact, "the 'organic' connection between technology and profit preceded its union with science" (ibid., p. 82). Both the state and capital follow, in this regard, the rule of maximum performance. Thus, the production of proof in scientific labour passes through language games that are, in reality, power games. But it is precisely in these terms that domination is legitimized. Science then becomes instrumental in the accumulation of wealth, and therefore a key element in the struggle for power. What is at issue is no longer justice or truth, which have been displaced from their former, privileged position in discourses of the of knowledge, but power itself, since insofar as technological development allows better knowledge of reality, and thereby a closer approximation to "truth", it also allows the determination of the criteria of justice. Therefore, he who controls science legitimizes his own status by legitimizing those who have no such control, becoming lord of both truth and justice:

> [Power] legitimates science and the law on the basis of their efficiency, and legitimates this efficiency on the basis of science and law. It is self-legitimating, in the same way a system organised around performance maximisation seems to be. Now it is precisely this kind of context control that a generalised computerisation of society may bring. The performativity of an utterance, be it denotative or prescriptive, increases proportionally to the amount of information about its referent one has at one's disposal. Thus the growth of power, and its self-legitimation, is now taking the route of data storage and accessibility, and the operativity of information.
>
> (Lyotard, 1979, p. 84)

However, this situation can be perfectly explained without reference to narratives and metanarratives. Generalized computerization is absolutely not a consequence of the new form of legitimation of science, which has always been (at least since the 18th century, as Lyotard himself noted in the previous quotation) linked to economic and political power in capitalist society, if not bound up intimately with the very development and expansion of capitalist logic concerning information. *Performance* maximization is a requirement of a system characterized by competition, in which technical and scientific knowledge serves the needs of capitalist accumulation. Information thus acquires a crucial role, whether from the perspective of controlling the work process, of gaining access to technical and scientific knowledge that might yield competitive advantages to an enterprise, or from the point of view of the state, which as an ideal collective capitalist requires information and knowledge as a means of legitimizing control (each of these points will be discussed below). Be that as it may, the overarching logic is defined by capitalist expansion, which stimulates and requires the evolution of information.

For Lyotard, however, power games are restricted to the control of information and the control of the circulation of knowledge as a commodity. Under these conditions, a divergence will appear between the "pragmatics of science", to which performative criteria are largely irrelevant, and social pragmatics, resulting in a divergence between scientists and the decision-makers (technocrats) who control the means of scientific research funding (cf. Lyotard, op. cit., Chapters 13 and 14). In this context, the computerization of society (which excludes any possibility of knowledge which does not fit the "machine language") leads to the following alternative:

> It could become the "dream" instrument for controlling and regulating the market system, extended to include knowledge itself and governed exclusively by the performativity principle. In that case, it would inevitably involve the use of terror. But it could also aid groups discussing metaprescriptives by supplying them with the information they usually lack for making knowledgeable decisions. The line to follow for computerisation to take the second of these two paths is, in principle, quite simple: give the public free access to the memory and data banks. Language games would then be games of perfect information at any given moment.
>
> (Lyotard, 1979, p. 120)

This final solution proposed by Lyotard is remarkably illustrative of the internal contradictions of his discourse. The supposed difference between modern and postmodern science is that the former required legitimation in the form of a meta-account in the narrative mode – that is, non-scientific (non-denotative) – whereas the latter does not. Now, since postmodern science is legitimized by power (contrary, it would seem, to modern science), and insofar as this situation allegedly sharpens the contradiction noted earlier between scientific pragmatics and social pragmatics, an obvious humanist solution would be to search for another space of legitimation linked to narrative knowledge. But that would be a return to modernism, a route Lyotard explicitly rejects by way of dismissing Habermas' solution:

> Consensus has become an outmoded and suspect value. But justice as a value is neither outmoded nor suspect. We must thus arrive at an idea and practice of justice that is not linked to that of consensus. Recognition of the heteromorphous nature of language games is a first step in that direction . . . The second step is the principle that any consensus on the rules defining a game and the "moves" playable within it must be local, in other words, agreed on by its present players and subject to eventual cancellation. The orientation then favours a multiplicity of finite meta-arguments, by which I mean argumentation that concerns metaprescriptives and is limited in space and time.
>
> (Lyotard, 1979, p. 118 ff.)

His rejection of Habermas' solution thus leads Lyotard to embrace the second option, a form of liberalism applied to information, leaving aside all the objective determinations of power that had been to some degree acknowledged in the passages quoted earlier. To the first option of a monopoly of terror, he responds by advocating free competition made possible by free access to information, achieved by some unknown means. This solution is, frankly, idealistic. If power derives, according to Lyotard himself, from the existence of "incomplete information games" and if we recall that this is due, as he also points out, to the reciprocal relationship between wealth and knowledge, it is difficult to envisage a situation in which the wielders of economic and political power rescind such an important instrument of control. But Lyotard forgets that. Having exorcized the Marxist utopia (one more of so many failed metanarratives), he finally arrives at the idea of a society of free debate, in which free access to information would ensure justice – that is, he returns to the liberal utopia of free competition.[6]

Information and capitalist production

The type of communication that takes place in the capitalistic production process is hierarchical and bureaucratic, compatible with the structure of power in the factory. The worker, by selling his labour power, is obliged to submit to the capitalist's interests and the needs of the production process; he must relinquish any power to define not only production's aims, but the also the work methods, the allocation of his time and of all the resources involved in production. The factory is the capitalist's fief, in which the state itself may only intervene on a limited basis. Certainly, under specific conditions, the capitalist may grant the worker, or a special class of workers, certain degrees of power in decision-making. But this hardly changes the substance of the matter. The worker receives his orders from the capitalist himself or from management, which wields knowledge and power in the company on the capitalist's behalf.

What is evident here is the fundamental inequality of the system, masked by the apparent formal equality defined at the level of commodity circulation. Communication also ceases to be communication between peers and is transformed into class communication. The bureaucratic company management communicates with the worker by distributing information in the form of directives regarding working methods and the pace of work, the organisation of the workplace, the type of instruments and materials, etc. Information thus acquires its specifically capitalist form in reference to the work process. Beginning with Taylorism, "management science" has been based on this one-way information organized in accordance with the needs of capitalist accumulation, and regardless of subsequent advances incorporated from academic psychology and sociology, it cannot conceal its characteristics of power and domination.

If we consider that, in Habermasian terms, this is the way in which the economic system is anchored in and colonizes the lifeworld of workers, it should be clear that the "medium of control" is not money, as Habermas believes, but rather a form of power that is, in this case, beyond the reach of the capitalist state. Money, at this level, is merely a precondition. Once money has been advanced in the form of wages (or once the employment contract has been signed), the worker is subject to capital throughout the process of production, where communication is direct and unmediated, or mediated exclusively by the bureaucratic structure of the large company. What is thereby established is a relationship of power, submission and subjection. This is the essence of the capitalist social relationship: a relationship of power and domination.[7]

It is in the process of labour that the true face of the system is revealed, and the exploitative relationship shows itself to be also a power relationship. On this basis we can define the features specific to capitalist communication: hierarchical, objective and direct, unmediated. In this sense, one cannot speak of "means of communication" in relation to the specifically capitalist process of communication. The reports, written instructions, etc., cannot be understood as such. They are merely the supporting means for direct communication within the company, a requirement of bureaucratic, impersonal forms of control. The same may be said for company newspapers and other publications directed to employees (this obviously does not include union and associative publications), which merely reproduce this aspect of the labour process – a fact well known to journalists and other professionals working in the sector.[8]

Thus, the movement of rationalization and bureaucratization of the labour process can be understood as, among other things, a movement for constructing a communicative basis for capital in its process of producing surplus value. This movement, in turn, requires direct communication between the different elements involved in production, which determines, one the one hand, a form of the colonization of the *Lebenswelt* by the system (to refer once again to Habermas' term), but on the other hand causes determinations germane to the former to constantly penetrate the sphere of the latter. This means, in Marx's terms, that capital, in creating the collective worker, also creates the conditions for its own abolition as a form of the social relation, a relation for which the money advanced to pay the wages of the individual worker functions ultimately as a precondition or determinant.

Our discussion of capitalist information reaffirms and incorporates what Habermas himself considers the superiority of Marx's analysis in relation to all others made at the same level of abstraction: his ability to unify in a single principle the two forms of interaction (social and systemic) – to which Habermas refers in proposing his analysis of the relationship between system and lifeworld:

> Through his analysis of the double character of the commodity, Marx arrived at basic value-theoretical assumptions that enabled him both to describe the process of the development of capitalist society from the economic perspective of an observer as a crisis-ridden process of the self-realisation of capital and, at the same time, to represent it from the historical perspective of those involved (or of a virtual participant) as a conflict-ridden interaction between social classes.
>
> (Habermas, 1981, vol. 2, p. 472)

Or, further on:

> On the one hand, labour power is expended in concrete actions and cooperative relationships; on the other hand, it is absorbed as an abstract performance by a labour process that is formally organised for purposes of valorisation. In this respect, the labour power sold by producers is the site of an encounter between the imperatives of system integration and those of social integration: as an action is belongs to the lifeworld of the producers, as a performance to the functional nexus of the capitalist enterprise and of the economic system as a whole.
>
> (Habermas, 1981, vol. 2, p. 473)

Thus, the immanence of labour power in the subject, which distinguishes it from all other commodities, implies that "in wage labour the categories of action and functioning, of social and system integration are inextricably intertwined", in the words of Offe, cited by Habermas (ibid., p. 474).[9] For our purposes, this means that there is a contradiction in the form of communication in the labour process, which requires not only a hierarchical information process allowing those who hold power in the company to pass their decisions down to those who labour directly, but also a mode of horizontal, cooperative communication among these same individual workers who, as a whole, represent the collective worker – collective, not only in serving the needs of capital valorization, but also in the sense of a group of individuals of the same social class brought together under the dominant and exploitative power of capital. It is thus that, at the level of the labour process, information unmistakably acquires the form of *class information*.[10]

But if information in the labour process is characterized by a fundamental inequality in which the worker is the passive recipient of a communicative process whose presupposition is the wage relation, whose aim is to transmit the decisions of the bureaucracy of the capitalist enterprise, orientated towards capital accumulation, down into the heart of the production process, reinforcing the power relationship established under capitalism between capital and labour, this occurs only because there was historically a process of capitalist appropriation of the knowledge of skilled craftsmen and its reprocessing that formed the communicative basis of domination that I referred to earlier. That process, initially described by Adam Smith in the famous example of the pin factory, was carefully analysed by Marx in the historic chapters on the passage from simple cooperation to large-scale industry and from formal subsumption to real subsumption of labour under capital. That is the basis of Taylorism and all so-called management science.

I refer to that process as the *primitive accumulation of knowledge*, since it is also the basis for technological development promoted by capital. With the appropriation of the knowledge of skilled craftsmen, allied to the development of the physical and natural sciences, the objective foundations are laid for the permanent revolution of capitalist productive forces. But information here acquires a new characteristic, that of serving capitalist competition – becoming at times a commodity that can be exchanged in a specific marketplace, at times a secret, holding the key to competitive advantage for certain enterprises. But even as a secret, technological information possesses the features of the commodity – one of high monetary value which, if not available at a given time within the formal intercapitalist market, also has an informal market that is accessed by means of industrial espionage.

Interestingly, the process that begins with the primitive accumulation of knowledge eventually produces a bifurcation in which two basic types of information are generated: one linked directly to the process of commodity production and which is not itself a commodity, but rather direct, hierarchical, cooperative, objective and unmediated communication; and the other which is added as one more input into the production process and which, controlled by the technical and bureaucratic departments of the capitalist enterprise, is always, in fact or potentially, the *information-commodity.*

It is precisely the fetishization of this second form of capitalist information, fundamentally intertwined with the production process, that is behind the thesis now so much in vogue concerning the "information society".[11] It is apparent that one of the features of capitalist development is the increasing sophistication of the tools for storing, manipulating and disseminating information, culminating in the most recent developments of informatics and telematics. This scenario is not only related to the objective conditions of the production process, but also to other competitive needs such as knowledge of the economic situation of distant markets, of political and economic conditions that might have an influence on decision-making, of geographical and climatic conditions, etc. The expansion of global capitalism and the development of an integrated financial system require the parallel expansion of communications and transport systems, as Marx himself accurately described in the passages quoted above.

The historical process that culminated in the formation of so-called monopoly capitalism was accompanied by a series of technological changes in the field of communications that served to confirm and accelerate existing trends in the social organization of information following the logic of capitalist development. Moreover, the apparent demands of competition were able to shape the internal laws of that sector, as the expansion of large capitalist enterprises, financial capital and nation states in globalized capitalist competition produced demand for technologies commensurate with the system's enlarged scale and scope, leading to the perfection of the means of long-distance communication. The introduction of the telegraph in the mid-19th century was followed by the telephone at the turn of the 20th, allowing greater flow of information relevant to competition, and also later facilitating the international expansion of blocs of productive and financial capital.

Tauille (1989), citing Chandler, notes that the settlement of the western territories of the USA (made possible by the development of railways) led to a managerial revolution in American companies capable of operating over such an extensive domestic market, which now required administrative structures compatible with the new demands of gathering and processing information. This not only explains, as Tauille points out, the development of the telegraph and later the telephone, but it also shows the affinity between those technologies and the new series of administrative changes that would intensify the process of subsumption of labour under capital with the expansion of mass production and the introduction of the assembly line. As Tauille also notes, in this context modern accounting and macro-information systems were developed, necessary both for large industrial corporations, enmeshed in a proliferating web of information, and more generally for the capitalist ventures that were fostered by financial capital. Tauille describes the resulting changes in the labour process thus:

> Thus, the formal structure of the production process was eventually determined by various levels of administration and management, whilst its content, i.e. its technical conditions, was crystallised into fixed capital in the form of machinery and equipment, on the one hand trickling down more or less sparingly among direct labourers and, on the other, being concentrated among the emerging category of intellectual labourers.
>
> (Tauille, 1989, p. 97)

As a consequence, macro-information systems came to depend less and less on the information represented by the skilled labour of individual workers, while the outcome of these transformations was that technology production, as we noted earlier, became the production of a commodity – a special commodity, which over the course of the 19th century would become the main source of inequality among capitalist nations. The advent of radio and telecommunications systems would further accelerate this process, constituting what Tauille calls mega-information systems, capable of exponentially increasing information-processing and storage capacity while increasing transmission capacity. These, together with the emerging electronics and computer industry, would ultimately allow (as a consequence, I must stress once again, of the demands imposed by capitalist competition) new advances in the appropriation of workers' knowledge by capital and its crystallization into elements of fixed capital, transferring to the domain of capital information that formerly belonged to workers. "Only that now, all the information transferred is explicitly expressed in mental activities (intellectual work), whether creative (scientific work, engineering, etc.) or pre-programmed (accounting, desktop services, etc.)" (ibid., p. 103).

Despite being a preliminary work that, as its author acknowledges, only systematizes information that is already widely known, Tauille's book is of the greatest interest to our present discussion, since that systematization focused originally on explaining precisely the historical process that is relevant to our discussion of the question of information under capitalism. Tauille is thus able to describe, in a few pages, the intimate relationship between the development of communications technologies useful to competition and those relevant to the labour process, shedding light on the related changes in managerial structure and their consequences on the technical and social division of labour, while reaffirming the recurrent character of the expropriation of workers' knowledge by capital.

From our point of view, it is interesting to note that from the beginning of the process that I have called the primitive accumulation of knowledge, we can observe two different types of information: one tied to the labour process and the other to capitalist competition, whose evolution is nonetheless simultaneous and mutually reinforcing. Two great communications systems come into being during this process: the telegraph and satellites. But we must not forget that this development does not abolish, as some would have it, the inherent contradictions of the capitalist form of information. The error of all liberals and postmodernists when defining the present situation as a historical novelty (or, as they would put it, "post-historical") precisely on the basis of advances in mass communications technologies is that they ignore the essential contradiction of information under capitalism, bowing instead to a golden vision of a marketplace of information.

This is, strictly speaking, the basis of Lyotard's liberal utopia. His work ultimately has the ideological effect of merely restoring the moment of equality at the level of competition, while masking the essential inequality that operates at the heart of the capitalist production process, in which information acquires the unequivocal form of class information. By disguising that class character of capitalist information, information theorists (or, more generally, "bourgeois" communications theorists) confirm their own class identity and ideological function in the service of perpetuating the system. But in this they are not alone.

The mass media operate in the same way. By guaranteeing the apparent equality of free access to information in the public domain, they also mask the fundamental inequality expressed in the class character of information in the labour process, performing, to use the terms of Rui Fausto, the misappropriation that causes information to acquire a form that is, in this sense, distinctly ideological. Thus, by preserving the moment of equality of universal access to information, the mass media allow inequality to be exercised at the level of production.

This occurs when a specific sector of capital or of the state exercises a monopoly over information directed at a public so generic that it is defined, not by the class situation of its members, but by such a vague concept as that of "mass". Thus, *mass information* and mass communications mask the eminently class character of information and communications under capitalism. I will hereinafter refer to this directly ideological form of information as *propaganda*, as opposed to *advertising*, whose character is also ideological but different, indirect, related to the creation of a *lifestyle* that serves as the basis for constructing a specifically capitalist mass culture.

With the advent of the information-commodity in the sphere of competition as a consequence of the primitive accumulation of knowledge, there is, as we have just seen, a shift with regard to the essential determinations of the capitalist mode of production, so that information is elevated once more to an expression of the system's appearance. We have seen that both mainstream communications theory and the media itself play the role of blurring the contradiction thereby established between class information and mass information, by exclusively favouring the moment of equality. But the appearance manifested in this instance (*Scheim*) must not be confused with that which I spoke of in the earlier section (*Erscheinung*, phenomenon), referring to the laws of simple circulation. At that point, we were dealing with the appearance taken on by capitalist competition.[12] But it is precisely at this moment, with the emergence of the information-commodity and its autonomization, that the internal contradiction of the information form becomes evident and advertising and propaganda emerge as opposite functions to be carried out by a specific instance of the system.

Capital and state, advertising and propaganda

There is, therefore, a fundamental contradiction between the essence of class information and its appearance as mass information: the same contradiction that exists generally between equality and inequality, between contradictory and non-contradictory, and that distinguishes the bourgeois ideology of *Freedom of Information*. The greater the number of individual capitals or public institutions participating in the monopoly of information, and the greater the amount of information actually supplied to the public, the more the appearance of equality is reinforced. This is perfectly consistent with the qualitative logic that has characterized bourgeois culture from the beginning. But the qualitative difference that forms the basis of all domination does not disappear no matter how much information might be broadcast or published, since the public is always deprived of substantive information and always prevented from spreading its own messages through the media reserved for capital and the state. The bombardment of superfluous information that largely characterizes the present state of development of the mass media and capitalist culture by no means eliminates the gap between reserved information (i.e. information reserved to capitalist interests and the state) and information in the public domain, but only helps to disguise it.

The same contradiction appears in the separation between class information having to do with the capitalist labour process and other, apparently neutral information, which is incorporated as input into the productive process and acquires the form of a special commodity, of interest to individual capitals in competition. Neoliberal and postmodernist theorists and their followers, propagandists of an alleged "information society", today occupy themselves with masking that contradiction, upholding the second type of information in a fetishized manner and denying, explicitly or implicitly, the existence of the first. This ideological action is no different, in fact, from the one mentioned in the previous paragraph. The intellectual work of those theorists and their disseminators (academics, economists, journalists and others) validates and reinforces the work of concealment practiced by the mainstream media.

It can be argued that the present state of the mass media is an outcome of the process that Tauille has summarized in the passages cited above, since it was the possibilities offered by the development of macro- and mega-information systems, vital to the progress of capitalist expansion that gave rise to the electronic media. This is valid. Furthermore, I would argue that even the mainstream press could be described in this manner, since, as we will see later, it is in a certain sense merely a consequence of the advancement of the exchange of commercial information enabled by the development of printing techniques since Gutenberg. At this point, however, the explanation is not yet complete, since it accounts for only the possibility of the mass media's actual development and not its necessity. It is, rather, the above analysis of the movement of masking the essence of capitalist information (or the transformation of class information into mass information) that demonstrates the necessity of that development. From a logical perspective, the system of mass communications is completely determined theoretically at this stage, although nothing may be said at this point about its historically determined form, a subject we must address further on.

First, however, it is necessary to discuss a second element of contradiction that may be extracted from the foregoing analysis, one that has to do with a double determination that we find exerted over the mass media. If, from the point of view of social cohesion, information acquires the form of propaganda, monopolized by the state and those sectors of capitalism that control the mass media, from the point of view of capitalist accumulation it acquires the form of advertising, at the service of capitalist competition. Here we can observe the general contradiction we have noted since the first stage of this discussion: that between the propaganda and advertising forms of information.

In fact, the elemental form of advertising is already propaganda, inasmuch as it creates, through innumerable acts of buying and selling, a symbolic universe of undeniable ideological power. This may be seen as an indirect ideological function, sufficient for the propaganda needs of a system barely at the level of commodity circulation. But when we consider the full implications of the existence of capital and the capitalist state, it becomes clear that the rules of sociability defined at the level of commodity circulation are insufficient to maintain cohesion in a society founded on inequality. Such a society requires a state, and it requires that information assume a directly ideological character.

Certainly, at the empirical level, it is always difficult to precisely establish the difference between advertising and propaganda, since this indeterminacy has the function of adding a further element to the masking of the essential determinations of the system, which is reinforced by the distinctly verifiable tendency of professionals in propaganda and those in advertising to imitate the production techniques used in one another's fields. But that does not eliminate the importance of a clear distinction on the theoretical level with which we are now concerned; on the contrary, it increases it. This is because there is not always an obvious compatibility between the interests of the many competing capitals that employ advertising for purposes essentially related to the process of realization of individual capital and, on the other hand, the aims of the propagandists of the various political groupings and the state. Rather, the most suitable working hypothesis is to judge that this compatibility is only brought about, historically, by a complex set of alliances and strategies that cannot be defined a priori.[13]

The contradiction between advertising and propaganda must be juxtaposed, rather than conflated, with the contradiction of interests between the state and capital in relation to the mass media. In general, we can say that the state, as ideal collective capitalist, maintains the general interests of propaganda against individual interests, not only of advertising, but also of political groups and propagandists fighting to attain immediate strategic interests, even within the state apparatus itself.

At the confluence of these multiple dimensions of the problem of information under capitalism, it is evident that the lie, and above all, non-information, no longer remain mere possibilities but become a vital necessity for the system. Mass information is one-directional and may only take the form of advertising or propaganda, which obviously includes feedback but not exchange among equals. It also acquires technical measurements of efficiency (circulation, ratings and public opinion indicators). Thus, information is transformed into an instrument of power in the technical sense, employed not only by the state as ideal capitalist, but also by individual capitalists, both within the field of mass communications and in the communication and supervisory activities that the capitalist enterprise practices with respect to its employees. In the latter case, this is a restricted circuit to which the state has only limited access, a limit on its action consequent on its character as extra-economic coercive power.

The question of circuits is important because it is what defines the boundaries of action among the different communicative processes of capitalist society. State (or government) propaganda makes use of the widest circuits, intended to reach the broadest, most undifferentiated sectors of the public (which obviously does not prevent it from also functioning along more restricted circuits, addressing specific groups of opinion-makers), while advertising's circuits depend on the competitive strategies of each individual capital, which means that, for capital as a whole, it is necessary to maintain the greatest possible number of circuits of varying range so that each capital can make its strategic decision at any given time. There is an evident divergence of interests here between the state and individual capitals with regard, for example, to the expansion of the effective reach of the largest media. In the case of private television networks, for example, the state's interest in covering the entire national territory may conflict with that of the broadcast licence holders, for whom the investment required to extend their range to such an extent may not be matched by the potential gains in advertising revenue. Finally, confidential information uses the narrowest possible circuits in the service of competition and power.

Both in the case of confidential information and information meant for public consumption, there may exist a price, a market value, which constitutes a new facet of the contradiction between the state and capital – a consequence of the fact that control of the information media has become a source of profit, which does not always coincide with the interests of the ideal collective capitalist. An example of this is the historical debate between states versus market-orientated television systems.

But the question of circuits also brings us, for the first time, to the point of contact between *Information and Culture* whereby capital ensures that the evolution of the Culture Industry is determined by its own, expansionary logic. The space of culture is essential for a variety of reasons to the oligopolistic competition occurring worldwide within the industry, trade and finance sectors: because of its complex ideological function, of which the advertising of products is only an aspect, albeit a critical one; because it functions as a space of accumulation for certain blocs of capital; and because this space, being in fact a part of the space of communications, participates in the gamut of channels used for the circulation of the various flows that supply the global economy – flows of commodities, money, information and labour. One of the most important functions of nation states is precisely the creation and maintenance of the channels along which various forms of capital and information may flow. Moreover, the state itself and other groups require such channels to perform their functions with regard to the masses.

There are evidently more or less concentric circles. Information of interest to business, for example, is the most confidential information possible. We arrive at a moment in which information and money meet as utterly disembodied waves, commingling in satellites, to rematerialize in another place, instantly (at least as a general rule). This contributes to accelerating the cycles of capital and increases its efficiency. But the same channels by which capital circulates also carry cultural goods. The transportation of a roll of film or a shipment of newspapers, or the transportation of people (workers or tourists), letters, telephone calls and television programmes transmitted by satellite, are cultural movements conducted by the channels created to serve the state and capital. By all of these routes, land, air or sea, along cables or through the ether circulate cultural products and numberless quantities of information: from the necessary data of debit and credit transactions, reserved contracts, amorous contracts, the news, some of it also reserved (possibly even amorous), television programmes and so many messages for the consumption of the public; the masses. Thus capitalism transforms our vast world into a small village.

The contradictions of information also emerge. On the one hand, whether as a commodity or not, information serves the competition between individual capitals and circulates along more or less limited channels. On the other hand, the very development of channels to carry information relevant to business also permits the expansion of information delivered to the public, be it advertising (also determined by competition) or propaganda, whether public or private. The development of communications technologies to serve capital also allows the emergence of the Culture Industry. From these parallel processes emerge the industries of communications technology (networks and materials) and content (production and transmission).

Nor, on the other hand, can the Culture Industry come into being without a primitive accumulation of knowledge represented by the appropriation of popular culture, which becomes the raw material of that industry. In a process that has evolved from the dime novel to the soap opera (to consider just one of its aspects), popular culture and mass culture reciprocally influence one another in a perpetual movement. This circularity (which is the basis of the phenomenon of double appropriation of cultural labour, to which we will return more fully later) of the relationship between mass culture and popular culture (or more generally, between mass culture and cultures of resistance) is similar to the circularity existing in the development of information relevant to capitalist competition: in the process of production, the direct relationship between capital and labour requires that the innovations imposed by the needs of accumulation undergo trials, adaptations and redefinitions that are reflected back at the level of technology production. The adoption of such innovations, originally conceived in the spheres of administration and engineering, requires a communicative process in which elements of the lifeworld of direct workers are mobilized, demonstrating that the process of subsumption of labour under capital is incessant and accompanies the whole of capitalist development.

It will be useful now to summarize the ground covered thus far in our discussion of capitalist information. After initially discussing the information form as a presupposed category of commodity circulation, I described its internal contradictions from the moment that the capital relation comes into being, eventually requiring that movement of intervention when mass information recovers the moment of apparent equality expressed under the rubric of "freedom of information" in bourgeois ideology, masking the fundamental inequality present in class information, which constitutes the ultimate characteristic of information under capitalism. In this last section, we passed to the more concrete level of analysis in considering the two "functional forms" (advertising and propaganda) that will be taken up again later as a starting point for constructing an analytical framework for the study of the concrete historical process. I also explained the possibility and necessity of the emergence of the mass media, although we have not yet arrived at a precise definition of the historical form it assumes.

At the functional level we are discussing at present, the contradictions inherent in the capitalist form of information may be classed under the binomial "restricted information-mass information". From the point of view of capital, the first term comprehends all information directly related to the production process, such as information concerning the strategies of an individual business against other individual business in the sphere of technical knowledge and knowledge of the general cyclical conditions affecting capitalist production, including information-commodity exchange and all information regarding the acts of exchange between different industrial, commercial or financial enterprises. The second term of the binomial, also from the point of view of capital, is defined by the advertising form of information.

From the point of view of the state, the matter is substantially the same. Here, too, restricted circuits of information exist, useful both in terms of the competition between the various groups that control or seek to control portions of the state apparatus and in the competition between various nation states. The outcome of this competition among various state interests and the interests of specific private groups is determined by means of a complicated network of information exchanges in which the possibility of corruption is always present. But the state also creates information for mass consumption and, in this case, the information is essentially propaganda.

Of course, propaganda in general cannot be the exclusive monopoly of the state. On the contrary, all groups, capitalist or not, with explicitly or implicitly political interests vis-à-vis the masses will seek the support of propagandists and the media to present their messages to the public. Nonetheless, I will refrain from considering this problem in what follows, such niceties of political analysis being nonessential to our present discussion. I will therefore rest with the assumption, not accurate in all cases, that the basic aim of propaganda groups operating outside of the state apparatus is to act upon the state so as to conquer a greater share of power in accordance with their private interests, so that it is possible to consider all propaganda to be related to the state and all advertising to be related to capital (which is also not always true, e.g. it does not apply to advertising sponsored by state-owned enterprises and even by certain public institutions). Only in the framework of a strictly empirical analysis, however, may this simplification become problematic.

Thus, with regard to information directed at the masses, which is what interests us most particularly at present, we can initially reduce its functions to two basic and interrelated sets, one consisting of the advertising form and capital, and the other of the propaganda form and the state. In the former case, a microeconomic rationality with macro-social effects; in the latter, the determinations imposed by the ideal collective capitalist with the aim of ensuring social cohesion against the disruptive effects of the petty interests of competition. Our simplification allows us to precisely define the basic contradiction that governs (from the point of view of the "system") the Culture Industry and mass culture, and which may be completely derived from the foregoing analysis of information and its contradictions.

Although the contradiction between advertising and propaganda emerges only in the historical period known as "monopoly capitalism", it is clear that the more general features described above are valid for any type of capitalism, insofar as they refer to the immanent laws of capitalist production. Thus, from the point of view of apparent forms, one must seek the specific characteristics that distinguish classical capitalism (competitive, with a liberal state) from the form that the system acquires as from the end of the 19th century, conventionally referred to as monopoly capitalism. In this latter phase, the traditional concept of the bourgeois public sphere, which will concern us next, loses its validity, and the general characteristics of the capitalist form of information are manifested differently, so that we are able for the first time to speak of a specifically capitalist form of mass culture, characterized by the existence of a lifestyle in accordance with the needs of capital accumulation and cultural production as the prevailing mode of industry. This will be the subject of the next chapter. First, however, let us examine how the elements we have discussed up to this point are articulated to form the so-called bourgeois public sphere of competitive capitalism.

The bourgeois public sphere as embodiment of the contradictions of information in competitive capitalism

Our analysis of the concept of information now turns for empirical support to the historical genesis of the bourgeois public sphere, reconstructed by Habermas in his celebrated 1961 work, which provides irrefutable insights into the public sphere, a central category for understanding the relationship between capital, the state and information in the period of classical capitalism.

Habermas begins his discussion by observing the ambivalent character of financial and trade capitalism as it expanded in 18th-century Europe, serving on the one hand to stabilize the power structure of the estate system, while on the other hand introducing precisely those elements of the exchange system that would eventually dissolve that power structure; viz.: "the traffic in commodities and information created by early capitalist long-distance trade". Habermas considers the development of these two types of commerce as parallel movements in a complementary relationship. As commodity exchange spreads through long-distance trade, supported by instruments of financial capital (letters of credit and promissory notes), there emerges, on the one hand, "a far-reaching network of horizontal economic dependencies... that in principle could no longer be accommodated by the vertical relationships of dependence characterising the organization of domination in an estate system based on a self-contained household economy" and on the other hand, inasmuch as "with the expansion of trade, merchants' market-orientated calculations required more frequent and more exact information about distant events", regular communications are institutionalized with the emergence of the first postal services (organized by trade associations from the 14th century onward as a guild-based system of correspondence to replace the old exchange of business letters between merchants) and of the press (Habermas, 1961, p. 28 ff.) However,

> The merchants were satisfied with a system that limited information to insiders; the urban and court chanceries preferred one that served only the needs of administration. Neither had a stake in information that was public. What corresponded to their interests, rather, were "newsletters", consisting of private correspondences professionally organised by newsdealers. The new system of social communications, with its institutions for traffic in news, fitted in with the existing forms of communication without difficulty in the absence of that decisive element-publicity.
>
> (Habermas, 1961, p. 29 ff.)

That situation began to alter in the 16th century with the formation of national and territorial economies and the absolutist state, which proved a critical element for the expansion of commercial capitalism by providing the political and military means to ensure the expansion of its markets. With the emergence of this new state, organized around taxation and bureaucracy, there was a continuous state activity, embodied in a permanent administration and a standing army, to correspond to the continuity of contact among those trading in commodities and news. At this point, according to Habermas, the separation between the public and private spheres acquired the following configuration:

> Public authority was consolidated into a palpable object confronting those who were merely subject to it and who at first were only negatively defined by it. For they were the private people who, because they held no office, were excluded from any share in public authority. "Public" in this narrower sense was synonymous with "state-related". [...] The manorial lord's feudal authority was transformed into the authority to "police" the private people under it, as the addressees of public authority, formed the public.
>
> (Habermas, 1961, p. 31 ff.)

However, the expansion of capitalism under mercantilist policies brought about a revolution in the structure of production itself, with the interests of manufacturing capital prevailing over those of commercial capital, a situation nowhere more tellingly reflected than in the activities of the state. Thus,

> Administrative action was increasingly orientated to [imposing] the capitalist mode of production through administrative measures to break the privileges of trade guilds, whilst production was regulated "down to the last detail". Under these conditions "civil society came into existence as the corollary of... state authority". Thus, "activities and dependencies hitherto relegated to the framework of the household economy emerged from this confinement into the public sphere" (ibid., p. 32 ff.) so that while, as Schumpeter noted, "each family's individual economy had become the centre of its existence, [and] therewith a private sphere was born as a distinguishable entity on contrast to the public", (cited in Habermas, 1961, p. 33) this new private sphere took on new "public" relevance. The economic activity that had become private had to be orientated toward a commodity market that had expanded under public direction and supervision.
>
> (Habermas, 1961, p. 33)

Although Habermas does not frame the matter in such terms, as he describes the historical emergence of the various features noted in our earlier derivation of information, we can observe articulated to their fullest extent not only the basic contradiction of the capitalist mode of production analysed by Marx, but also the contradiction between capital and the state (which will eventually require the formation of the liberal state) and, more appropriate to our discussion, the internal contradictions of the specifically capitalist form of communications. The contradiction between information directed at the public and information whose circulation is restricted, for example, is clearly discernable.

> The first journals in the strict sense, ironically called "political journals", appeared weekly at first, and daily as early as the middle of the 17th century. In those days private correspondence contained detailed and current news about Imperial Diets, wars, harvests, taxes, transports of precious metals, and, of course, reports on foreign trade. Only a trickle of this stream of reports passed through the filter of these "newsletters" into printed journals. The recipients of private correspondence had no interest in their contents becoming public. On the one hand, therefore, the political journals responded to a need on the part of the merchants; on the other hand, the merchants themselves were indispensable to the journals.... It was essentially news from abroad, of the court, and of the less important commercial events that passed through the sieve of the merchant's unofficial information control and the state administrations' official censorship. Certain categories of traditional "news" items from the repertoire of the broadsheets were also perpetuated – the miracle cures and thunderstorms, the murders, pestilences, and burnings. Thus, the information that became public was constituted of residual elements of what was actually available.
>
> (Habermas, 1961, p. 34 ff.)

To explain why this sort of periodical existed, Habermas argues that the part of the answer is the fact that "the traffic in news developed not only in connection with the needs of commerce; the news itself became a commodity" (ibid., p. 35). But he accords more importance to the interests of state authorities, which began to use the press as an instrument for promulgating administrative decrees. "The addressees of the authorities' announcements genuinely became 'the public' in the proper sense." This is not, evidently, a public in the wider sense that it will acquire later on, but rather quite a specific stratum of the population:

> Along with the apparatus of the modern state, a new stratum of "bourgeois" people arose which occupied a central position within the "public". The officials of the rulers' administrations were its core – mostly jurists [...] Added to them were doctors, pastors, officers, professors, and "scholars", who were at the top of a hierarchy reaching down through schoolteachers and scribes to the "people". [Also,] the "capitalists", the merchants, bankers, entrepreneurs, and manufacturers (at least where, unlike in Hamburg, the towns could not maintain their independence from the territorial rulers) belonged to that group of the "bourgeois".... This stratum of "bourgeois" was the

> real carrier of the public, which from the outset was a reading public. Unlike the great urban merchants and officials who, in former days, could be assimilated by the cultivated nobility of the Italian Renaissance courts, they could no longer be integrated *in toto* into the noble culture at the close of the Baroque period. Their commanding status in the new sphere of civil society led instead to a tension between "town" and "court".
>
> (Habermas, 1961, p. 37 ff.)

This tension makes the newly established bourgeois public sphere a critical one. The emergence of scholarly periodicals, initially intended for an audience of educated laymen, in the last third of the 17th century, and the introduction of the essay, in the form of "learned articles" appearing in the daily press in the first half of the 18th century, introduce an element of the critical judgment into a public sphere that without question had counted as a sphere of public authority, but was now casting itself loose as a forum in which the private people, come together to form a public, readied themselves to compel public authority to legitimate itself before public opinion. The *publicum* developed into the public, the *subjectum* into the subject, the receiver of regulations from above into the ruling authorities' adversary (ibid., p. 40).

Habermas thus seeks to demonstrate the "unique explosive power" of the press and, consequently, its potential for undermining the social basis for the absolutist state. In various countries of Europe during the 18th century, the formerly literary bourgeois public sphere began to assume political functions, becoming the very organizational principle of the bourgeois constitutional states that had parliamentary forms of government. Thus,

> The public sphere as a functional element in the political realm was given the normative status of an organ for the self-articulation of civil society with a state authority corresponding to its needs. The social precondition for this "developed" bourgeois public sphere was a market that, tending to be liberalised, made affairs in the sphere of social reproduction as much as possible a matter of private people left to themselves and so finally completed the privatisation of civil society.
>
> (Habermas, 1961, p. 93)

Or, further on, "the constitutional state as a bourgeois state established the public sphere in the political realm as an organ of the state so as to ensure institutionally the connection between law and public opinion". (Habermas, 1961, p. 101). Here we have, to use the terms of Habermas' *The Theory of Communicative Action,* a case of a systemic dimension (parliament) constituted on the basis of an element of the *Lebenswelt* (public sphere) as an expression of the latter's need to establish its power at the heart of the bourgeois state that it helped to found. But this element of the public sphere functioning as a political organ of the state thereby embodies a contradiction that is expressed in the very concept of law which, as an expression of popular will, "included as an element the claim, successfully asserted through recourse to violence, to the exercise of domination", at the same time that "the concept of law as an expression of reason preserved other, older elements of its origin in public opinion, still traceable in the connection between parliament and public" (ibid., p. 101). Here we might observe, to use once more the terms of *The Theory of Communicative Action,* the contradiction between system and lifeworld situated within an instance of mediation between the two.

While the bourgeois public sphere might be governed by the principle of universal access, its two admissions criteria (education and property ownership) effectively excluded the immense majority. This contradiction was resolved in terms of the political ideology of liberalism by classical economists' presupposition that all persons have an equal chance to attain those criteria – thus, "Jeremy Bentham was unthinkable without Adam Smith" (ibid., p. 106). If, given such presumed equality of opportunity, any person might aspire to the status of bourgeois, it was perfectly fair that only the bourgeoisie might have access to the public sphere. Furthermore, "only property owners were in a position to form a public that could legislatively protect the foundations of the existing property order" (ibid., p. 107 ff.). Further on, Habermas approvingly recalls Marx's critique of this notion, summarized in the maxim *le bourgeois, c'est l'homme*:

> Marx denounced public opinion as false consciousness: it hid before itself its own true character as a mask of bourgeois class interest [...] The emancipation of civil society from authoritarian state regulation did not lead to the insulation of the transactions between private people from the intrusion of power. Instead, new relationships of power, especially between owners and wage earners, were created within the forms of civil freedom of contract. This critique demolished all fictions to which the idea of the public sphere of civil society

> appealed. In the first place, the social preconditions for the equality of opportunity were obviously lacking [...] Similarly, the equation of "property owners" with "human beings" was untenable; for their interest in maintaining the sphere of commodity exchange and of social labour as a private sphere was demoted, by virtue of being opposed to the class of wage earners, to the status of a particular interest that could only prevail by the exercise of power over others [...] The view on which the private people, assembled to form a public, reached agreement through discourse and counter-discourse must not therefore be confused with what was right and just: even the third and central identification of public opinion with reason became untenable [...] Consequently, the dissolution of feudal relations of domination in the medium of the public engaged in rational-critical debate did not amount to the purported dissolution of political domination in general but only to its perpetuation in different guise [...] The separation of the private from the public realm obstructed at this stage of capitalism what the idea of the bourgeois public sphere promised.
>
> (Habermas, 1961, p. 149 ff.)

All of the contradictions of information we noted in our earlier description now become apparent. We have already seen how so-called political journals were founded precisely on the distinction between that information which business reserved to itself and that which was ultimately disclosed to the "public", whether because information itself had become a marketable commodity, or, mainly, because the state had an interest in the creation of a public to which official information could be directed. Political journals had a critical role in the establishment and articulation of this public sphere, which would actively participate in the overthrow of the absolutist state and the establishment of the bourgeois liberal state, under which it would be promoted to the status of a constitutive element of the structure of the state itself. But the apparent equality suggested by the incorporation of the bourgeois public sphere into the state apparatus functions precisely to mask the fundamental inequality of civil society, evident when we analyse the sphere of production.

What Habermas neglects to say is that, if Marx thus unmasks the essential contradiction inherent in the configuration of the bourgeois public sphere, he also unmasks the bourgeois concept of freedom of information, since as we saw earlier, in the sphere of production information is necessarily hierarchical and controlled, an instrument of domination of the working class by the capitalist class. What Habermas does demonstrate, with the utmost clarity, is the contradiction proper to the bourgeois public sphere itself, between the public (which, as he noted, was a reading public) and the non-public, between the minority that participated in civil society and the immense majority who were excluded. But that contradiction, inherent in the very structure of the liberal state, was fatal to the bourgeois public sphere:

> By about the middle of the 19th century it was possible to foresee how, as a consequence of its inherent dialectic, this public sphere would come under the control of groups that, because they lacked control over property and therefore a basis of private autonomy, could have no interest in maintaining society as a private sphere [...] The enigma of a "political society" ... found its resolution [...] in the phrase of a socialisation of the means of production.
>
> (Habermas, 1961, p. 153)

Thus, in Marx, "the liberal idea of a political public sphere found its socialist formulation" (ibid., p. 154).[14] At this point, the "structural transformation of the public sphere" is imposed. Under late capitalism, the state assumes the role of satisfying those needs that cannot be satisfied by the market, while the mass media transforms the "culture-producing public" into a "culture-consuming public" and destroys the institutions that had formerly lent an eminently critical dimension to the nature of the bourgeois public sphere.

The maturation of the contradictions inherent in the bourgeois public sphere and the very transformations that capitalism underwent from the end of the 19th century led to a radical change in the structures that legitimated the system, within which appeared key elements of the new configuration of the state: principally, the establishment of the so-called welfare state and the emergence of the Culture Industry. Later on, we will see how these new conditions led to a distinct, but no less capitalist iteration of the general characteristics of information analysed earlier. In fact, what occurred throughout the course of the 20th century was precisely the expansion of the logic of capitalism to include all realms of human socialization, ultimately giving rise to a properly capitalist form of culture on a global scale, although it was consequently necessary, as Habermas notes, to bury the old bourgeois dream of a critical and independent public sphere. It is under these new conditions that it is finally possible for the ultimate contradiction of information described earlier to emerge: the contradiction between advertising and propaganda, which did not arise earlier because commercial advertising had not yet attained the reach and importance that it would acquire in the 20th century. Until then, advertising (publicity) was still essentially synonymous with "making public".

2
Monopoly Capitalism and the Culture Industry

Up to this point I have only dealt with the specific problems of the Culture Industry at a very superficial level. I previously tried to define the relations between capital, state and information for a given level of abstraction, and especially the contradictions of the capitalist form of information as it can be derived from capital and the capital–state relationship at the same theoretical level. In the previous section I presented what Habermas considers to be the problem in the creation and the contradictions of the bourgeois public sphere, understood as where the contradictions of the information in classical capitalism come about. If this is true, then information would primarily take on a role of articulating the public sphere, ideologically intended to serve capital. However, it is only with monopoly capitalism and especially with the emergence of the so-called Culture Industry that information acquires this special importance in the maintenance of the system, from the point of view of both its ideological reproduction and the accumulation of capital.

The new configuration of capital

The changes in capitalism that were taking place towards the end of the 19th century with the major crisis of 1873–1896 resulted in a crucial reinforcement of the trend towards the concentration and centralization of capital, as identified by Marx. This led to the emergence of joint-stock companies and a new link between bank and industrial capital which shaped the new financial capital, studied by Hilferding (1910) in his major work, the emergence of the large capital enterprise and the beginning of the imperialist phase of capitalism, seen as its superior phase by Lenin (1916). That period of unusual structural change would lead to a devastating period of imperialist struggles culminating in the two world wars, and was known in Marxist literature as the time of transition from what was called competitive capitalism to what Baran & Sweezy (1966) called monopoly capitalism, following the expression coined by Lenin.

Although the term is widely accepted by Marxists of different trends, from Boccara to Mandel, there are many differences when it comes to theoretically distinguishing the ultimate meaning of the above-mentioned transformations. For our purposes, however, it is not necessary to enter this debate. A general description of the problem is sufficient in order to find the most significant differences with regard to the dynamics of economic development, of state action and of the "structural change of the public sphere" between competitive capitalism and monopoly capitalism in order to define the Culture Industry and the issue of lifestyle. In the following, I depend especially on a well-known article by João Manuel Cardoso de Mello (1977).

His main idea lies in the transformations of the accumulation dynamics resulting from the concentration and centralization of capital, which also brings about a change in the forms of competition exercised between large blocks of capital with greater offensive potential and an enhanced capacity for diversification in relation to the articulation permitted by financial capital. If at first glance this points to increased capital mobility, what actually happens is something quite different. This is because in each specific sector the magnitude of the investment and capital assets required, concentrated in a small number of large companies, become investment decisions which once taken are irreversible and which together with the barriers to entry, depending on the degree of concentration and monopolistic power of the companies, tend to crystallise into a range of profit rates, thus limiting the movement of capital between sectors.

The effect of this is that the trend in the redistribution of profit rates shifts to the financial sector, which then determines all the action logic for large blocks of capital in such a way that it tends only to occur between blocks of capital, and not directly between the productive sectors. This can occur either through the predominance of bank capital, as in the German case which formed the basis for Hilferding's study, or a conglomerate-type organisation such as that which was dominant in the post-war period, in which the holding company defined a global diversification strategy. This has the effect of breaking the self-regulatory mechanism of competitive capitalism that through its cyclical dynamics allows a redistribution of capital into different sectors. On one hand this was based on a movement that alternated economic expansion with the tendency to equalise profit rates and differentiation of the production structure, and on the other, on a crisis of over-accumulation with the consequent capital burn together with the increase in the profit rate of the most resistant companies and of expected returns in new sectors. This opens the way for a new period of expansion at a higher state of concentration, where the redistribution trend is reset through a new spectrum of sectoral profit rates.

In short, competitive capitalism possesses a self-regulatory mechanism that dispenses with direct state action. This is also the case with regard to wages, which rise during periods of expansion and fall during crises (with no replacement flowing from the redistribution of profit margins in accordance with the generalized unemployment which occurs during the capital burn and concentration process). This differs from what takes place under monopoly capitalism, where differentiated wage rates correspond to the crystallization of the sectoral profit rates spectrum. Under these conditions the distributive conflict is aggravated and capitalist competition, which even during prolonged periods of calm includes tacit or explicit agreements for the division of markets between the large blocks of capital, explodes in other more virulent forms, making the crises potentially more violent and deep and requiring direct and firm state action.

The crisis of the 1930s represents a time of fundamental and definitive rupture with regard to the economic liberalism that had previously typified the action of national states in capitalist countries. This action was theoretically supported by the neoclassical concept that until then had continued unchallenged among economists in the academic world, in contrast to a Marxist economy which was restricted to revolutionary circles and the intelligentsia of the Left parties. The violence of the crisis, however, and the obvious need for state action to overcome it, eliminated any pretence of legitimizing an academic economy, which at the lowest point of the cycle still attempted to categorise the problems faced as deriving from a defect of reality that did not fit the elegant model drawn up in the offices of economics professors who, from the theoretical revolution of Marx, were determined to purify the political nature of the science founded by Adam Smith. However, from the New Deal to Nazism, the governments of the major capitalist countries[1] acted firmly on the economy through fiscal policy and the regulation of wages, prices and financial flows. In 1936, Keynes provided the *coup de grâce* to economic neoclassicism, although not to the purist academics who began to regroup along new lines practically the day after the *General Theory* was published (Bolaño, 1987b).

The crisis which led to the creation of monopoly capitalism at the turn of the century was also the crisis of exhaustion of a long cycle of capitalist development, with its large cluster of technological innovations (the stainless steel industry, electricity, the internal combustion engine, the caustic soda and chlorine industry), which was known as the "second industrial revolution" and the crisis of British hegemony. This unleashed a period of struggle between the major capitalist powers which had in the previous period been capable of contesting the hegemony economically, politically and militarily. All this, combined with the crisis of the previous regulatory system for which the final solution was only achieved with the end of the great crisis of the 1930s, marks an extremely troubled historical period marked by the two world wars, and which was only resolved in 1945 with the stabilization of international relations under US leadership.

This new international structure also marked defeat for the alternative proposed during the Second World War regarding the form which the capitalist state should take in developed countries once the phase of liberalism had been overcome. After the defeat of the fascist alternative and with the international leadership crisis resolved, the political conditions for an unusually long phase of expansion were finally in place. This was marked by the introduction of the so-called welfare state in the major capitalist countries, and by the eternal threat imposed by the existence of a growing antagonistic bloc under the domination of the other great military power that emerged during the Second World War, heir to the imperialist trends of old Russia already denounced by Lenin (1916), and which was also achieving far-reaching economic and social progress. The unity that exists in the development of monopoly capitalism, the welfare state and the Culture Industry can clearly be seen during this period of growth, led by the new communication medium that came into being at the start of the 1950s: television.

All these changes in the dynamics of accumulation became the basis underpinning the idea of a non-interventionist state, the guarantor of public order maintaining the external conditions of what was seen as a natural economy, naturally able to function at an optimal level of activity and quite separate from the state. The historical realization of that idea in pure terms is now in itself questionable. It no longer fits, even approximately, within certain limits of the competitive capitalism phase in which the dynamics of price and wage formation are economically guaranteed (in a manner where the state can confine itself to fulfilling its traditional role of defending civil contracts, law and order, protection of market mechanisms, etc.). Additionally, it in no way fits monopoly capitalism, whereby the economic struggle is not limited to economic processes through self-regulation of prices and wages by market mechanisms alone.

Transformations in the state sphere

There is thus a "nationalisation" process of the class struggle to the extent that "processes of concentration and crisis pulled the veil of an exchange of equivalents off the antagonistic structure of society" (Habermas, 1961, p. 144 ff.). To understand the logic of this process and in what sense it is possible to use the expression "unmasking" that Habermas uses in this passage, we must return to the question of the functions of the state. Altvater speaks of two sets of state functions related to the two aspects of its action, which are economic policy and social policy. In the first case, it is the action of the state on the activity of individual capitals, and in the second, on the relations between the capitalist class and the wage-earning class (through macro-social control policies) and the capital–labour relationship within the production process (through a series of regulations on working hours, sanitation, etc.). In both cases, state intervention clearly alters the conditions of the capital accumulation process. The question that arises here is: what is new in each area with respect to classical capitalism that allows us, in a sense, to speak of unmasking?

Rui Fausto (1987) distinguishes two issues in relation to state intervention in the competitive process. First, he states that increased interventionism, as occurs from the end of the 19th century compared to the preceding phase of the system, means that the role of the state goes beyond being an arbiter of contracts and interferes in their content, so that the imbalances created in the level of competition become regulated by the state ensuring "more rationality in the mode of production". According to Fausto this means that "the essence of the system manifests itself essentially as a way making its appearance economy... this is the total capital... that which is used as a universal truth at state level" (Fausto, 1987, p. 316). He goes on to conclude that it is at this level of analysis (of competition, considering the state as an ideal collective capitalist) that it is possible to "reasonably" talk of the state as a real abstraction.

On the other hand, however, in monopoly capitalism the state not only interferes in the content of the contracts, but it becomes part of such contracts as owner of companies, transformed in this case into a full individual capitalist rather than the ideal collective capitalist. It is clear that this state action is along the lines of "filling a gap", assuming something that individual private capital will not or cannot assume, but the fact that the state itself becomes a capitalist has very serious consequences:

> Ownership of the elements of capital, presupposition of capital as such, undergoes a mutation. It is no longer assumed by individual capitalists but by the State... It is the character of the presupposition that is modified as well as the nature of the owner of the elements of capital that changes. More precisely, it is here rather than in the case of stock companies (in which the owner remains the owner) where it is necessary to talk about expropriation of the capitalists within capitalism and the negation of capitalism within the capitalist mode of production. Indeed, more so than in the case of stock companies, there is a kind of repetition of the expected primitive accumulation, which is actually a primitive expropriation. The separation between owners of the means of production and some of these means, but within the system... here involves the expropriation of the expropriator within capitalism (i.e. in favour of a new kind of capitalism).
> (Fausto, 1987, p. 326 ff.♣)

Thus, the contradiction between capital and the state now takes on a new, more radical form, acting on the basis of private ownership because the state "resumes the movement separating the means of production and its owners, which characterises the historical origin of the system's presuppositions", but this time on another level, as "state capital" (Fausto, 1987, p. 328). In this sense, the movement described "follows the classic appearance" of the state. On the contrary, the first point to which I just referred refers to the question of "breaking the appearance" of the system, in this case the appearance of competition (*Schein*). According to Fausto, however, under monopoly capitalism there is also a rupture of the system's appearance (*Erscheinung*), which can be understood if we return to the problem of the capital–labour relationship and the transformations it undergoes at this stage of its historical development.

What happens is that the positive law itself, generated by the state, questions the appearance of equality constituted by a legal relationship that masked the spirit of the mode of production, so that "the contract between capitalists and workers appears as being no different from other contracts governed by civil law". Yet with the development of capitalism, the social right arises as a particular form of law

> precisely on which is based the idea that the relationship between capitalists and employees is of a type that can no longer be treated as a contractual relationship regulated by the old civil law. The law comes to recognise that the contract is not equal, but that it is a contract in which one party is recognised as being weaker than the other.
>
> (Fausto, 1987, p. 317)

The consequence of this is that

> The system itself demystifies its appearance, but only its appearance. In effect, it is not the reality of the class contradiction that will be revealed... In classical capitalism the identity (of the parties) masked the contradiction (between classes). *In contemporary capitalism it is no longer the identity but the difference which hides the contradiction.*
>
> (Habermas, 1961, p. 319)

Thus, this "progressive revelation of the falseness of the identity of the parties to the employment contract" which "mitigates" the contradiction through the position of the difference, revealing the appearance of the system but still in a mystified form, alters the atomistic representation of the society "in favour of a representation in which the differences can be seen". With that, the state now appears "not only as arbitrator between equals... but as also having the task of correcting the differences", which is the centre of the reformism and the type of state that would be created in the developed capitalist countries after the defeat of the fascist option at the end of the Second World War. There is, in the terms of Habermas, a "socialisation of the state" which occurs in parallel to a "nationalisation of society", which when taken together, destroy the separation between state and society which is the basis of the bourgeois public sphere. The position Habermas takes can be summed up in two quotes:

> The concentration of power in the private sphere of commodity exchange on the one hand, and in the public sphere with its institutionalised promise of universal accessibility on the other, strengthened the propensity of the economically weaker parties to use political means against those who were stronger by reason of their position in the market... The labour unions constituted an organised counterweight not only in the labour market; by means of the socialist parties they strove to influence legislation itself; the entrepreneurs... responded by immediately exchanging their private

> societal power for political power.... The interferences of the state in the private sphere from the end of the last century showed that the masses, now entitled to political participation, succeeded in translating economic antagonisms into political conflicts: in part these interferences favoured the interests of the economically weaker strata, in part they served to reject them... The state interventions... were guided by the interest of maintaining the equilibrium of the system which could no longer be secured by way of the free market.
>
> (Habermas, 1961, p. 145–146)

For this socialization of the state, there is, on the other hand, a nationalization of society:

> As interventionism had its source in such interconnections, the social areas protected by interventionism should be strictly distinguished from a private sphere that was merely state regulated – the private institutions themselves assumed to a considerable extent a semi-public character... from the midst of the publicly relevant sphere of civil society was formed a repoliticised social sphere in which state and societal institutions fused into a single functional complex that could no longer be differentiated.
>
> (Habermas, 1961, p. 148 ff.)

Twenty years later, Habermas raises the same question in different terms. In *The Theory of Communicative Action*, he sees the historical development of the capitalist state as accompanying a trend towards legalization that starts with what he calls the "bourgeois state", active in Western Europe in the period of absolutism where the state and economy were differentiated into different subsystems. This was followed by the "bourgeois constitutional state" which found a prototypical form in 19th century German constitutionalism, with the institutionalization of public subjective rights of private individuals who "are given actionable civil rights against a sovereign – though they do not yet democratically participate in forming the sovereign's will". Such participation would come later, with the "democratic constitutional state", which first emerged during the French Revolution. These latter two forms of state were driven by bourgeois emancipation movements. The increasing juridification moves towards guaranteeing freedom and curbing the power of the state over citizens.

A similar movement would lead to the welfare state. The difference this time is that a brake was put on the economic subsystem through state social policy (Habermas, 1981, vol. 2, p. 356–361). That action was, however, ambivalent from the start. Together with the guarantee of freedom, the process of juridification leads to a deprivation of liberty resulting from "the form of juridification itself", since, in the welfare state, social action to "correct the differences", using the terms of Fausto or, in the words of Habermas, "deal with the risks of existence" imposed by a production system based on wage labour, is carried out through a policy of "restructuring interventions in the lifeworlds of those who are so entitled", according to social legislation characterized by individualization, specification, classification and reward in the form of monetary compensation, allied to social services providing therapeutic assistance (ibid., p. 361 ff.).[2] The result of all this can be summarized in the following passage:

> The more the Welfare State goes beyond pacifying the class conflict lodged in the sphere of production and spreads a net of client relationships over private spheres of life, the stronger are the anticipated pathological effects of a jurisdiction that entails both a bureaucratisation and a monetarisation of core areas of the lifeworld. The dilemmatic structure of this type of jurisdiction consists in the fact that, while the Welfare State guarantees are intended to serve the goal of social integration, they nevertheless promote the disintegration of life-relations when these are separated, through legalised social intervention, from the consensual mechanisms that coordinate action and are transferred over to media such as power and money.
>
> (Habermas, 1981, vol. 2, p. 364)

The difference between this and the previous work is evident. The Marxist language in the book of 1961, the idea of unmasking and the criticism of the dissolution of boundaries between public sphere and the state, all give way to the vision of the development process based on the opposition between systemic integration and social integration in that the first overlaps the second, resulting in the emergence of "pathologies of communication". Thus, from the above quote there is a substitution of the forms of systemic integration with destructuring effects on the lifeworld, such that organic solidarity, characteristic of the lifeworld, gives way to a state-mediated mechanical solidarity. Another problem that should be added to this is the fact that

> the unequal distribution of social rewards reflects a structure of privilege that can no longer be traced back to class positions in any unqualified way. The old sources of inequality are, to be sure, not

> sealed off, but now there is interference with both welfare-state compensations and inequalities of another sort.
>
> (Habermas, 1981, vol. 2, p. 348)

On the one hand, therefore, the compensation system contributes to the pacification of class conflict, while modifying the "relations between system (economy and state) and lifeworld (private and public spheres), around which the roles of the employee and the consumer, the client of public bureaucracies and the citizen of the state, crystallise" (Habermas, 1981, vol. 2, p. 349.). In other words, the "humanisation" of working conditions and enhancement of the role of consumer under the legitimizing conditions of mass democracy reduce the explosive potential of distributive conflicts, while the neutralisation of the role of citizen is offset by the inclusion of individuals as clients of the welfare state bureaucracy. With this, new possibilities for conflict appear exactly in relation to the roles of consumer and client, "conflicts that do not appear primarily in class-specific forms and yet go back to a class structure that is displaced into systematically integrated domains of action" (Habermas, 1981, vol. 2, p. 350).

This point is critical because this is where it can be identified that the Habermasian vision of the reification problem, which according to him was explained by Marx, is based on the conditions of industrial labour active in the early practices of industrialization. According to Habermas, this is a redefinition of the *Lebenswelt* spheres, "in the first instance, private households that have been converted over to mass consumption, and client relations that are coordinated with bureaucratic provisions for life" (ibid., p. 351). However, this colonization process by the system of the *Lebenswelt* faces "stubborn and possibly successful resistance only when functions of symbolic reproduction are in question" (ibid., p. 351).[3]

In both the 1961 text and *The Theory of Communicative Action* (*TCA*), the constitution of social right and the institutionalization of the collective bargaining agreement express a fundamental change in the previous condition of the system. We should add that the social structure of liberal capitalism has been radically altered. Within this structure the industrial bourgeoisie achieved hegemony through an agreement with the other bourgeois factions (which included a numerically small middle class, indistinguishable from the ruling bourgeoisie from the point of view of their ethical and moral principles), and where the subordinate levels could be guaranteed by sheer physical or ideological coercion and the mechanisms of liberal democracy – parties, notable censitary representation – so that one could speak of a state subject to its own laws and a public that understands and accepts that determination.

The creation and growth of the proletariat in, to use the Gramscian term, an alternative historical bloc, is more than evident as early as the end of the 19th century, and even more so after the Russian Revolution of 1917. The middle class also increased in number and acquired characteristics different from those of the liberal period, with the expansion of the middle classes within the bureaucracy of big business and the state and its proletarianised sectors not directly linked to industrial production – in short, with the huge differentiation of social structure and the opening up of the income strata, even at the proletarian level. That is without mentioning the differentiation that exists within the bourgeois camp itself between oligopolistic and non-oligopolistic sectors, between national and international bourgeoisie, allied to an alteration of the previous link between industrial, commercial and banking capital, etc.

It is this new social structure that forms the basis for the transformations that Habermas and Fausto speak of in the above-mentioned sections. It is the creation of a mass that transforms public opinion into something radically different from the time when the bourgeois public sphere of liberal capitalism was prevalent. Thus, the articulating mechanism represented by a press directed towards a limited readership must be replaced by more powerful means of communication, aimed at the entire population of a country. This implies an expansion of the form of propaganda that requires the creation of mechanisms for general mediation between the state and organized political groups on one side and this created mass on the other. As we shall see, it is also the institution and expansion of the form of advertising that imposes its own determination on the development of mass media.

Structural change of the public sphere and the advertising–propaganda contradiction

In this context, the question of legitimizing domination takes on a new form with the transformation, to use the expression by Habermas (1961), of the "culture-debating public" into the "culture-consuming public", which in this case follows the thinking of Adorno and Horkheimer. According to Habermas this transformation begins in the mid-19th century with commercial stabilization of a new type of literary magazine "through successful publishing ventures such as *Westermanns Monatshefte* and the *Gartenlaube*" that nevertheless "presupposed the family as a sounding board for literature", culminating in the construction of the mass media, from the mainstream press to television, radio and cinema.

The characteristic of all these "bourgeois forms of sociability" is that they "have found substitutes that have one tendency in common despite their regional and national diversity: abstinence from literary and political debate", at the same time that their consumption "takes place within a social climate, and they do not require any further discussion", so that the trend towards public debate (now formally organized in religious seminars, policy forums, literary organisations, radio listening clubs, etc.) becomes managed and is also transformed into a business through the collection of revenue and the creation of rules for presentation, demonstrating that not only cultural property but also discussion takes the form of merchandise. The very creation of works of art and cultural property is adapted to the demands of the market and "to the need for relaxation and entertainment on the part of consumer strata with relatively little education" (Habermas, 1961, p. 163 ff.).

Through this, the public sphere assumes functions of propaganda (for spreading ideas or concepts). It partly loses its publicity nature ("making public") and cultural consumption moves on to serve the "economic and political propaganda" (or commercial advertising and what we would regard as propaganda). The dominance of advertising is made explicit by Habermas in his excellent analysis of the history of the press, in which he draws attention to the process of concentration that led to the creation of the mainstream press before the emergence of the "new media" (radio, talking cinema and television) and the debate over whether its organisation should be public or private. In relation to this it is also worth noting the following observation:

> Thus the original basis of the publicist institutions, at least in their most advanced sectors, became practically reversed. According to the liberal model of the public sphere, the institutions of the public engaged in rational-critical debate were protected from interference by public authority by virtue of their being in the hands of private people. To the extent that they were commercialised and underwent economic, technological, and organisational concentration, however, they have turned during the last hundred years into complexes of societal power, so that precisely their remaining in private hands in many ways threatened the critical functions of publicist institutions... The separation of public and private spheres implied that the competition between private interests was in principle left to the market as a regulating force and was kept outside the conflict of opinions.

> However, in the measure that the public sphere became a field for business advertising, private people as owners of private property had a direct effect on private people as the public.
>
> (Habermas, 1961, p. 188–189)

He then clarifies that "business advertising... attained a scope worthy of mention only in the processes of concentration that mark industrial capitalism in the second half of the 19th century" (ibid., p. 190).[4] The explanation for this phenomenon is the existence of "oligopolistic restriction of the market", "monopoly competition" or "indirect competition via the generation of markets with clienteles oriented to specific firms" which replaces the price competition that operated previously in the system.

For Habermas, "the programme of the mass media, even in their non-commercial portions, also stimulated consumption and channelled it into certain patterns". Additionally, economic advertising acquires a political aspect since "the publicist presentation of privileged private interests was fused from the very start with political interests" (Habermas, 1961, p. 191 ff.) which can be clearly seen only in the "practice of public relations".[5]

It is the rise of advertising and its confusion with propaganda because of public relations which radically transforms the old bourgeois public sphere, eliminating its critical character in favour of a form that legitimizes domination by appealing greatly to a false representation of power (in the theatrical sense of the term), typical of feudalism.

Indeed, advertising is not only confused with propaganda, but it superimposes it, forming an alternative through the "integrationist culture" of the mass media, a "functional equivalent for the formation of ideologies" in late-capitalist societies which value the idea of "pacification of class conflict".[6] This idea appears thus in the *TCA*:

> In place of the positive task of meeting a certain need for interpretation by ideological means, we have the negative requirement of preventing holistic interpretations from coming into existence. The task, to be fulfilled positively, of ideologically covering a need for interpretation is replaced in these societies by the negative need to avoid that the interpretation reaches the level of integration that characterises ideologies... The functional equivalent... might simply consist in that... *everyday consciousness* is robbed of its power to synthesise; it becomes *fragmented*... In place of "false consciousness" we today have a "fragmented consciousness" that blocks enlightenment by the

> mechanism of reification. It is only with this that the conditions for a *colonisation of the lifeworld* are met.
>
> (Habermas, 1981, vol. 2, p. 355)

That is why, according to Habermas, the theory of reification must abandon the aim of ideological critique and look at the explanation for "cultural impoverishment" and the "fragmentation of everyday consciousness".[7]

There is a criticism of the approach taken by Habermas in his analysis of the relationship between capital and the state in that the rationalization process leading to the formation of the two subsystems is seen only as a universal process in which those elements are displaced by determinations of the lifeworld itself, thus establishing a competition between forms of integration (social and systematic). This approach does not take into account the contradictions between the two subsystems in terms of the distinct challenges that each has in relation to the lifeworld.

This weakness in the approach taken by Habermas is reflected in the analysis of the mass media, in which he simply outlines some arguments for the resilience of the *Lebenswelt,* against the pessimism of Adorno in this regard. This is correct, but does not take into account what Benjamin and Brecht had already established decades ago about the emancipatory potential of the mass media, a question which was further developed by Enzensberger in a well-known text which I will examine later. The fact is that it would be quite difficult to understand the development of the mass media merely through the study of the bureaucratization and legalization process. In relation to the mass media, Enzensberger never refers to the problem of differences between the interests of state and capital arising from differences relative to the systemic imperatives (to use the terms of Habermas) that each sphere imposes on the lifeworld related to the internal contradictions of the capital–state relationship, themselves derived from the logic of articulation between these two spheres in an economic system marked by the need for an extra-economic coercive force imposed on individual capitals to ensure the conditions of capital reproducibility as a whole, systematically threatened by the production anarchy and by the contradictions inherent in the system (Bolaño, 1996a).

Furthermore, this limitation already appears in some form in the 1961 book, preventing a deeper analysis of the contradiction between advertising and propaganda. The relations between them are thus seen only from the point of view of the confusion between the two and the dominance of the first during late capitalism. If indeed there is such confusion, it would be appropriate for the theory to clarify the internal contradiction over which it presides.

If I may now jointly interpret the two main works of Habermas cited here with regard to the issues raised, I would say that the coexistence of two opposite and complementary movements relating to the establishment of the welfare state is obvious: one of fragmentation and another of integration by the mass media and its advertising culture. On the one hand, once the totalising capacity of the second-generation ideologies is neutralised, the system operates to prevent an alternative aggregation driven by the interpretive operations that occur at the *Lebenswelt* level. On the other hand, the "integrationist culture prepared and disseminated by the mass media" allows the ideology to be "fitted and supplemented" into the field of "consumer culture". This in turn integrates the determinations of advertising, propaganda and cultural production under a form of advertising that ultimately causes refeudalization of the bourgeois public sphere.[8]

Habermas perceives the overall function of mass media as being to promote integration of a disaggregated social body under the aegis of advertising that works, as well as an element that gives coherence to the new configuration of the public sphere, the consumers of the culture sphere. We must, however, add that this unity, contrary to what might be promoted by some kind of totalising ideology, in the words of Habermas, is not a designed unit. It is only defined as such according to the constitution of a way of living and consumption that underlie all publicity messages, whose form in advanced capitalism is also imported by propaganda and aesthetic creation itself. The action of the advertising, however, is directed precisely at the identification, segmentation and specification of the consumer, and is determined by the imperatives of individual capital that it disputes with other individual capital segments of the market.[9]

This demonstrates, on the one hand, the inadequacy of this kind of articulation that is contrary to the demands of propaganda, which is produced with an explicit articulation objective. The two forms of communication are complementary and are opposed not so much through a bureaucratic process, but more because of the expansion of capitalist logic to the broadest sectors of human sociability, which carries with it the expansion determinants of individual capital and total capital, whether by the form of its creation from individual capitals through the market (with regard to our discussion, this is reflected in the integrative role of the countless advertising appeals), or by the state as a collective capitalist ideal.

It is also clear that propaganda itself incorporates elements of competition between political groups in democratic countries, which also allows its "colonisation" through the language of advertising. If the result of all this at the concrete level is the confusion between advertising and propaganda, however, this does not eliminate the fact that the tension between these two general forms of information in capitalism is always present and always reappears, albeit disguised, for example in the dispute between capital and state for control of the mass media, whose most spectacular event was the struggle over the privatisation and deregulation of European TV that started, in reality, before the constitution of the state systems, but came to a head in the 1980s.

It should also be said that the unplanned nature of the unification promoted by advertising also demonstrates its strength inasmuch as its ideological function appears to be diluted and to also serve the creation of a capitalist culture in the broad sense of the term, a culture formed at the same time in individualization and massification, in the fragmentation and rearticulation of the social body and in compulsive individual consumption and mass production. Analysis of the "lifestyle" question should help clarify this issue.

Before this, however, and in order to conclude the point, it should be said that the transformation of the type of communication relevant to the phase of the old bourgeois public sphere in a communication structured on the mass media, which appears and is consolidated in the phase of monopoly capitalism, represents a phenomenon similar to the transformation of the liberal state into an interventionist state, as analysed by Fausto cited in the above sections.

For example, given the limited action of the bourgeois public sphere of classical capitalism, the emergence of the mass media is presented as an extension of the mechanisms of the public sphere to a public tending towards the entire population of a country. This trend would hypothetically lead to a democratization of information and its wide dissemination to ensure equal access, thereby allowing political participation of citizens in a situation where democratic mechanisms of the state is controlled by the masses replace the beginnings of liberal democracy. In other words, recognizing inequality and also the inequality of access to information and "culture", the mass media, just like the state, would eventually cover this inequality in order to reduce disparities and ensure access to the necessary information so that everyone can fully exercise their rights of citizenship.

But once again we are dealing with a system whose essentials are masked because the reason for the creation of the mass media is precisely determined, as we saw with Habermas, by the need to neutralise the critical potential of a public sphere that extended beyond its initial participation (ownership and culture), again becoming virtually explosive in character. Now the inequality appears, but still masked, as a difference to be filled by participation in a political process controlled by the mechanisms of the welfare state, and not as a class contradiction. The concept of the masses is used exactly for that. The masses are nothing but an abstraction that masks the real class contradiction.

This is, however, as should now be clear, a "real" abstraction built into the process of differentiation of social structure derived from the process of capital development and increasing social division of labour incorporated and developed exponentially in the framework of monopoly capitalism. The fact is that capital and state create a mass with which they communicate. While they create this mass in order to communicate with it, in general this is not done directly, but through the mediation of the Culture Industry. As this is a special type of work, it has the ability to create an audience composed of individuals whose conscience is that of the masses that capital and state try to mould according to their own interests. This conscience pushes back, however, and in turn the public also eventually imposes certain determinations on the production and distribution of culture under capitalism. However, this is a matter for discussion in the final chapter.

Capitalism and lifestyle

At this point I would like to resurrect a small book which can be considered a classic of French Marxist literature but is today systematically forgotten. This is a book from 1972 by André Granou, *Capitalisme et Mode de Vie,* in which the author puts forward ideas that were soon after taken up by the founders of the French school of regulation. In Chapter 1, he aims to show that the emergence of large capitalist enterprises in the 19th century occurs on the basis of an earlier movement that represents a much more important historic rupture, the emergence of manufacturing ("natural basis for the development of mechanisation and large industry"), not because of the creation of the technology base, but "mainly because production relations that it would rely on, and on the (social) basis of which large industry would grow had developed prior to this" (Granou, 1972, p. 27♣) which, however, was then "insufficient to meet the constantly growing local and colonial markets". Thus, if mechanization provides such a large boost to the industry, which expands worldwide supplanting artisanal manufacturing, it is because the capital invested in mechanization was able to produce a much more important surplus than that invested in artisanal manufacturing. This growth in surplus was "a result of the reduction in the value of labour force which translated into a fall in nominal wages and, to a more variable degree, real wages, particularly during the first half of the 19th century" (ibid., p. 29), as a result of the expropriation of the knowledge of the workers which went into the machines, allowing the addition of a huge number of unqualified workers in the production process, including women and children.

However, even this addition, combined with the extension of the working day and other ways of increasing exploitation, would not be enough to produce the surplus necessary to maintain the high rate of capital accumulation, since that same accumulation in the industry increases the organic composition, producing a falling trend in the rate of surplus value. The factor counteracting this trend, which enables the continuation of the accumulation process, is the increase in labour productivity, which increases the number of goods produced per unit of time, reducing the value of each one. This means that the most important factor for the growth of production in large-scale industry is the production of machinery and intermediate products whose development can increase productivity and work rate, consequently increasing the rate of exploitation and surplus value. To this is added the increase in the mass of surplus value produced by the expansion of production itself and of the working population that the industrial revolution leads to, which more than compensated the tendency to decrease the amount of labour per unit of capital, consequently increasing the employed human work force and therefore, the mass of surplus produced (Granou, 1972, p. 32 ff.).

Even so, capitalist development cannot occur without crisis. Thus, at the end of the ten years of prosperity that followed the great crisis of 1873–1890 the system was shaken again, to the point where at the end of the First World War everything seemed to confirm the imminent collapse of capitalism in the eyes of the labour movement. However, from the New Deal to Nazi-Fascism, the state, "after generating capitalist production relations, proved to be the best defence against any attempt to destroy the bourgeois 'order' " (ibid., p. 42). The state is not, however, able to permanently solve the problem since the production it can assume first restricts the accumulation in the "productive sectors", diverting part of the workforce that these sectors could mobilise, therefore reducing the mass of surplus value that could be produced. Second, in order to finance itself the state further reduces the mass of surplus value that could be accumulated in the following period. Thus, state intervention in order to "support the growth in production (of use value) and to allow further progress of capital accumulation" can only be effective in the short term and is not a durable solution (Granou, 1972, p. 21).

Therefore, if finally a new period of growth was established in the second half of the twentieth century, it was possible because

> Capitalist society had by no means exhausted all possibilities for extending the capitalist production relationships needed to ensure further development of the productive forces. Put another way, at that level of development, capitalist division of labour had not yet been imposed on the whole of society as the only governing principle of all human activity... In both manufacturing and mechanisation, the capitalist mode of production had only empowered the means of production... The reproduction of the labour force of the manual worker and, more generally the reproduction of the working class, did not refer to goods produced on the basis of capitalist production, apart from a few exceptions of negligible proportions.
>
> (Granou, 1972, p. 43♣)

The difficulties of expansion lay in the "poverty of the social base" (apart from the "insufficient consumption capacity of the working classes", according to the underconsumptionist thesis that Granou endorses on page 45) on which the surplus was produced and accumulated. The condition for overcoming these difficulties lay in the dissolution of the old lifestyle and its reconstruction "on the basis of capitalist relations", that is, in the imposition of the "realm of commodities". Until that happened the development of the urban system would collide with limits imposed by the remnants of feudalism. Thus,

> [...] the organisation of social life, family or, more prosaically, the use of tools and utensils remained largely dominated by social relations, values and, ultimately, the lifestyle inherited from the days when capitalism existed only in the state of future potential... The length of its reign actually depended on the possibilities of developing capitalist social relations outside the sphere through which the means of production are produced... Capitalism could not be definitively imposed on previous modes of production without the revolution born in the "mode of production" being transferred to the "lifestyle", in other words to the mode of reproduction of lifestyle.
>
> (Granou, 1972, p. 47♣)

For Granou, this "lifestyle revolution" starts in an imperfect and limited manner in some social groups[10] in the period between the two world wars. It is only after the Second World War that this "capitalist revolution" becomes the basis for the growth of the productive forces and the emergence "of what the bourgeois ideologists call the 'consumer society' ". Until then only the production of arms manages to avoid a recession, which as we have seen is a necessarily provisional solution in Granou's understanding.

But for capital to take over the reproduction of the labour force and to expand the realm of commodities to all classes, two conditions were necessary: (a) that part of the salary reserved for food be used in the purchase of industrial goods without reducing consumption (albeit low) of food for families; and (b) that the value of industrial goods was not so high as to exceed the salary committed to them and, also, that the wage should be sufficient to allow the purchase of a growing number of those goods so that production could expand. The first condition would be filled by the reorganisation of relations between agriculture and industry and through the increase in agricultural productivity, and the second through the development of consumer credit and the reduction in the unit value of industrial goods through large-scale production. Thus, criticising the "post-industrial society" idea, Granou states that "the starting point for the changes that exist should be sought in the development of the assembly line, mass production and the emergence of capital in the lifestyle, or to put it another way, in the extension of capitalist production relations throughout society that now, more than ever, can only be called capitalist" (Granou, 1972, p. 85). As we know, it is in the post-Second World War period that this model, called Fordist by regulationist authors (Bolaño, 1996a), is imposed, initiating an unprecedented period of capitalist expansion.

Here, however, it may be necessary to make some minor criticisms. In addition t his unnecessary adherence to underconsumptionism, Granou makes some historical errors, such as claiming that capitalism had not dealt with the reproduction of the labour force during the industrial revolution. On the contrary, the industrial revolution means precisely that capital finally manages to create conditions necessary and sufficient for the expanded reproduction of the labour force (through capitalist production of food and wage-goods) and not entirely of capital (with the production of machines by machines, which would only be achievable by permanently releasing major industries from the manufacturing output of goods in the second industrial revolution). The lifestyle revolution to which he refers is fundamentally linked to reaching a new phase of capitalist development and the institution of a new pattern of accumulation based on mass production of durable goods, with all the features of the Fordist period analysed by regulationist authors after Granou.

Furthermore, with the manner in which the issue is highlighted by Granou, it seems that the movement that occurred post-war was the conclusion of a process, with the imposition of the logic of capital throughout society "as a unique regulating principle". However, not only did non-capitalist institutions, such as churches and the family, remain and form new points of resistance, meaning that this imposition would never be definitive (Bolaño, 2003). It is also the case that for a sustained expansion of capitalism, it is necessary for lifestyle and consumption to undergo a reorganisation in order to create new social conditions without which a new development pattern cannot be adopted (and that is, indeed, the presupposition of regulationists when taking several ideas proposed by Granou in order to analyse Fordism and its crisis). Moreover, this rearticulation advances the commodification of life and expands the logic of capital that with the development of the Culture Industry and the so-called mass culture moves the symbolic centre of power in its favour. The question today is whether there is a new "lifestyle revolution", which is still not definitively explained by the regulationist concept of post-Fordism, and which fits the arguments of neoliberals, postmodernists or post-industrialists. To explain these new changes taking place just after the crisis of the pattern of post-war accumulation is one of the great challenges facing social scientists of our generation.

Returning to Granou, the most interesting aspect of the theory he proposed is his attempt to understand *lifestyle* "as a concrete totality [citing Kosik, 1963] produced and reproduced by the development of the mode of production", which requires "analysis of its transformations as a process destroying the old lifestyle, a destruction that is in itself the condition for the emergence of a new lifestyle that matches the new conditions of production" (Granou, 1972, p. 49 ff.♣).

Referring to the proliferation of consumer goods, Granou states that, from the point of view of the worker, "substituting direct social relations, merchandise... is above all a result of a lack of exchange between men, a lack of communication" (Granou, 1972, p. 53). At this point he cites Marcuse and then Baudrillard (1968, 1972) to assert that the "lack of communication" is due in large part to overproduction of symbols by the mass media, though with the caveat that "contrary to the central theme supported by Baudrillard in his work, this production of symbols does not at all improve the exchange value and consequently neither a new core of the capitalist economy" (ibid., p. 56). Thus,

> where the accumulation of capital corresponds to the abundance of use values, the symbols once again put everyone in their place: affluence, luxury and excess for the few; shortages, "standardisation", misery and dissatisfaction in meeting everyday needs for the masses. This universality of (access to) consumption that capital would impose on workers as new ideals of liberty, equality and fraternity, is but the veil of a new aristocracy of customs, of a "moral for the slaves". Thus, far from improving the exchange value, the symbols by their nature and their use, as much as in their very existence, are determined by the needs of capital and the conditions for their reproduction. A byproduct, but a necessary byproduct.
>
> (Granou, 1972, p. 57♣)

In addition,

> [...] capital cannot penetrate or confer traditional lifestyle unless it empowers the living conditions of individuals and, equally, the set of symbols that reveal the structure of the social order. Put another way, for this capitalist way of life, material production is not enough. It must also be produced "as an idea", on a new ritual and new morality level as well as in social order. It is definitely the ability of the capitalist mode of production to incessantly transform this ritual and moral so that at all times they match the requirements to reproduce production relations, on which depends its ability to materially alter the way of life and, therefore re-launch its own reproduction.
>
> (Granou, 1972, p. 57♣)

This is the core of Granou's contribution and must be clearly distinguished from the previously mentioned underconsumptionist error. If the reproduction schemes of Marx demonstrate the technical reproducibility of the system and those of Tugan Baranovsky also test the possibility of expanded reproduction of capital with constant consumption, they do so from a purely theoretical and strictly economic perspective. If through this they are capable of providing the basis for the refutation of underconsumptionists, they do not in any way endorse a position that underestimates the critical importance of consumption which is precisely the stability variable in the Keynesian model. On the contrary, consumption is the key variable that establishes the link between the economy and culture in capitalism. It establishes the social pact that cements the victory of this production system and played an important role in the collapse of socialism in Eastern Europe. In this regard, the suggestions by Granou in the two preceding paragraphs represent a more appropriate theoretical alternative than the "consumer society", formulated at more or less the same time. Granou has the crucial advantage of defining a notion (*lifestyle*) and noting another (*consumer mode*) that help make up a regulationist-style analytical table of undeniable effectiveness for proper capture of the concrete historical movement of capitalism.

For Granou, two elements were prominent in the constitution of the lifestyle established in the second half of the 20th century: urbanization and the introduction of the arts and techniques for designing consumer goods. He forgot something crucial: the Culture Industry, whose genesis is contemporary with the emergence of monopoly capitalism and which establishes "in theory" a cornerstone for the reproduction of the lifestyle. The Culture Industry is the means by which propaganda and publicity are developed and become widespread, ideologically structuring (especially advertising) the so-called "consumer society". Without considering the Culture Industry it is not possible to fully and adequately define concepts such as lifestyle, consumption mode, Fordism and post-Fordism. The Regulation school, heir of Granou, and unfortunately all Marxism, as we shall see in due course, have not been successful in dealing with this issue, leaving a clear field for liberals, postmodernists, pontiffs of communication and other theologians of capitalism, end-of-the world acolytes and all manner of snipers.

Dallas Smythe was right when he said that communications were the "black spot of Western Marxism". Granou, for example, in his brief mention of TV, supported Baudrillard's assertion that it produces "non-communication". In feudalism, all relationships (social or between individuals and objects) are always direct. With the development of capitalism, it is the opposite: "there can be no social relations or relations between man and livelihood that are not mediated by the acquisition of goods". This is just another of the many metaphors of this controversial French writer. If we return for a moment to the contradictions discussed above, we can see that TV, like any other mass media, does nothing other than allow a specifically capitalist communication, although, as we shall see later, certain concessions must be made by the system to ensure the attention of the public, who have little appetite for being the recipients either of publicity or propaganda. However, these concessions do not alter the characteristics of communication in its capitalist form, another instrument of power in the hands of the state and capital.

Far from creating "incommunicability", this media over-informs and over-communicates in an imperialist desire to dominate the whole of the communication processes that happen at the lifeworld level. That is why,

> in May 1968, when people wanted to communicate with each other... they did not resort to O.R.T.F. [*Office de Radiodiffusion Télévision Française*] [but] gathered in the factories, in the schools or on the streets which were transformed into forums. They wrote on the walls, copied their messages, edited their newspapers. They seized the words that had been taken from them and restored the direct relation between them which had been destroyed.
>
> (Granou, 1972, p. 55)

If we now consider that attractive, romantic concept of communication, which is indeed a rare form of communication, it is clear that this cannot be found through TV. Not only the Culture Industry, but the capitalist lifestyle itself has been responsible for embracing small groups of adolescents and the few heirs and survivors of the events of May 1968.

It is also clear that Granou, following Baudrillard, calls incommunicability a structural feature of the mass media. However, this is not because of any technical attribute (as per McLuhan, for example, whom Baudrillard venerates in his recent works), but mainly for the fact that they are media created by the state and capital, depending on the need for a particular type of communication with the aforementioned characteristics. The whole structure of the medium, its form of organisation (such as venture capitalist or state entity), its mode of action and its strategies obey that determination. There is no doubt that its transformation is in the realm of possibility, but this is not possible without profound changes in the social order itself. Technically, it is the contrary – everything is in place. The radio theories of Brecht (1932) are also valid for television. The choice of technology, however, is not neutral and the development of a specific possibility removes others, sometimes irreparably. A historical approach to the development of the Culture Industry can clarify this and other issues.

Observations on the Culture Industry

It is not possible to fully discuss this point within the limits of this study, as it would require in-depth historical studies to show how the development of the capitalist mode of production creates the material conditions for a specifically capitalist form of cultural production. The analysis of this history, whose roots must be sought in the Renaissance, traverses a series of events, among which I can initially mention the reproducibility of the work of art discussed by Benjamin in his classic work on the subject (1936),[11] the appropriation of the popular oral tradition by printing beginning in the 18th century, which would lead to the feuilleton press of the 19th century and, after this, the television drama of our time, as noted by, for example, Morin (1962); or the transformation of elite bourgeois culture itself into the culture of resistance, considering the founding work on the Culture Industry by Adorno & Horkheimer (1969).

On this last point it is worth considering that during the historical development of capitalism, while creating an appropriate cultural form, it brought with it from the beginning cultures of resistance characterized by fragmentation at different levels and which have different levels of association with the dominant culture. The same movement that took, for example, European cultures to America with the help of merchant capital and destroyed indigenous cultures (often physically), helped disseminate black culture on the new continent. It should also be considered that the capitalist or pre-capitalist forms engendered in this historic process are transformed into forms of resistance through the supplanting of an earlier phase of capitalist culture development.

This is the problem at the heart of the contradistinction between Adorno's pessimism and Benjamin's optimism. While pessimism is based on the depression of a conservative ideal, optimism is explained by faith in the possibility of universalization of a revolutionary culture of resistance, facilitated by the development of the mass media. Enzensberger, in his well-known essay *Constituents of a Theory of the Media* (1971), inspired by Brecht's *Theories of Radio* (1932) and especially by the 1936 work of Benjamin, seeks to emphasize the emancipatory potential of the mass media with the aim of founding a socialist strategy related to them. For Enzensberger, with the exception of these two authors, "Marxists have not understood the consciousness industry and have been aware only of its bourgeois-capitalist dark side and not of its socialist possibilities." He states "nor are the works of Horkheimer and Adorno free of a nostalgia which clings to early bourgeois media", but he especially directs his criticism at Lukács, whose "nostalgic backward glances" at the cultural landscape of the 19th century and at the unique work of art, "work as an end in itself", "are already the forerunners of socialist realism, which mercilessly galvanised and then buried those very 'cultural values', which Lukács rode out to rescue". However, the attempt to save those "reactionary ideals" would be condemned to failure because

> [...] the revolution in the conditions of production in the superstructure has made the traditional aesthetic theory unusable, completely unhinging its fundamental categories and destroying its "standards". The theory of knowledge on which it was based is outmoded. In the electronic media, a radically altered relationship between subject and object emerges with which the old critical concepts cannot deal.
> (Enzensberger, 1971, p. 30)

Under these conditions, the discussion about the death of the work of art is a vicious circle that operates using "criteria which no longer correspond to the state of the productive forces" (ibid., p. 28). With the possibility of technical reproduction, "what used to be called art, has now, in the strict Hegelian sense, been dialectically surpassed by and in the media. The quarrel about the end of art is otiose so long as this end is not understood dialectically" (ibid., p. 31). Enzensberger's idea is that just as classical physics survives as a marginal special case within the framework of modern physics, all traditional disciplines of art are subsumed and become special cases of a "general aesthetic of the media". Thus, current developments of these disciplines will be incomprehensible if seen "from their own prehistory" (ibid., p. 31).

From the point of view of the concerns of this paper, this issue of dialectical overcoming of the bourgeois concept of unique artwork should be interpreted in relation to the limits of real subsumption of cultural work by capital and the permanence of the concept of oneness within the Culture Industry itself, as a final determinative of all the specificities of the cultural commodity. I shall later carefully consider this subject in the discussion I will put forward on the French school of economics, communication and culture. It is worth at this point providing a brief introduction to the subject, emphasizing arguments of historical order that endorse the theoretical perspective that will be developed. Alain Herscovici searches the Renaissance for the genesis of characteristics of artistic work that determine the specifics of the cultural product:

> [...] the cultural activity, that is, the artistic work, is a "free" activity which is justified in itself... This relates to a modern conception of culture whose roots are in the Renaissance and is still valid today. A historical study of cultural production modes shows that during

> other eras, mainly in the Middle Ages, artistic work was not linked to a process of individualisation and personalisation; it was not sacred as such . . . ; artistic activities were part of crafts and the admission to those professions depended on "*savoir-faire*" . . . In the modern conception of culture, the artistic product is totally dependent on the personality of the artist and the specifics of their work.
>
> (Herscovici, 1991, p. 11♣)

Agreed, but we must add that there is another critical moment in the analysis of the historical development of capitalist cultural production that needs to be highlighted and represents a break in relation to the concept of the sacredness of the artwork, although the uniqueness of the cultural product remains. This is the moment of reproducibility, before which we cannot in any way speak of the Culture Industry. Reproducibility is what will allow partial subsumption of the artistic work, for which the figure of the editor is fundamental:

> [. . .] both historically and economically, the editor, as social agent, is the pivot of commercial cultural production and then, capitalist. It is through the agent that intellectual or artistic production becomes a commodity, in other words, when a product is both reproducible in large quantities and produced to be sold in the market.
>
> (Huet et al., 1978, p. 129♣)

This means two conditions are necessary for commodification: (a) certain technical conditions for registration, printing and reproduction of sound and image without which the action of the cultural work would be lost by its immediate consumption; and (b) reproductions have a usable value, that is, they can be socially validated as values linked to specific social needs. The first condition allows the emergence of the editor as "an intermediary between the design and manufacturing, which means [between] the cultural work and the industrial capital to be used for the technical reproducibility of the unique work executed by the designer" (Huet et al., 1978, p. 130).

If that position leads the editor to control and coordinate the separate operations of design, production, financing and distribution of the replicable cultural property, it also demands of them the security of its transformation into money (second condition). From being unique and random with regard to their chances of success, cultural goods must become multiples (through reproducibility) and of guaranteed marketability (through the action of the editor). I will return to the important issues of uniqueness and randomness of cultural production at a more appropriate moment. What matters here is that, to perform their functions, "the editor must intervene not only on a marketing level... but at the same time, at the conception level, where such intervention results in a profound restructuring of the labour process" (Huet et al., 1978, p. 130).

What the authors of this section do not make sufficiently explicit is that we are talking about a double expropriation of cultural work. On one hand, the transformation of the labour process noted above represents the beginning of the subsumption of this work by capital (the limits of which will be discussed later), and on the other, the first condition in itself means the elimination of the possibility for direct contact between the cultural worker and his or her public. In other words, the artist's work becomes subservient to capital (albeit indirectly) as both productive work (that produces use values that can be transformed into a commodity) and a work of social mediation.[12]

The same authors then refer to the current trend towards the establishment of a collective worker, using popular music[13] and publishing as examples of sectors in which there is a division of the work accompanied by the emergence of new organisational and command functions, an appropriation of the cultural worker's skills and the resulting depth of his subordination to capital and its agents (the artistic director, for example). According to the authors, this new type of work process organisation occurs especially in sectors where big business is more common (recording industry) or where it invested very quickly from the beginning (movies, TV). Its complete generalization in all cultural industries, however, is limited by the necessity to keep some trace of uniqueness linked to the use value of the cultural commodity (hence the importance of the *vedette*, artistic genius or the star system). It is further limited by the random nature of the transformation of that commodity into money, which requires a labour market structure featuring labour "nurseries" to which publishers necessarily have recourse for fresh form and content, and also by the fact that

> the emergence of capitalism in the cultural sphere does not necessarily translate... into a generalisation of salaried labour and the downward trend of the independent cultural worker [but], on the other hand, the system of copyright that governs the relationship between editor and cultural workers is becoming more widespread and complex.[14]
>
> (Huet et al., 1978, p. 136)

I will return to these issues in due course. For now, I must emphasize that, even without going into the minutiae of this complex discussion, Enzensberger seems to properly understand the issue when he uses the term "dialectically surpassed" in speaking of the unique work of art, as well making it clear that it is not possible to completely suppress the figure of the author or the traditional artist within the framework of capitalism, whose aim, however, should be to

> make himself redundant as a specialist in much the same way as a teacher of literacy only fulfils his task when he is no longer necessary. Like every learning process, this process too is reciprocal. The specialist will learn as much or more from the non-specialists as the other way round. Only then can he contrive to make himself dispensable... But strategically his role is clear. The author has to work as the agent of the masses. He can lose himself in them only when they themselves become authors, the authors of history.
>
> (Enzensberger, 1971, p. 36)

For this, the author must be capable of "using the liberating factors in the media and bringing them to fruition", which will involve it in "tactical contradictions" that "can neither be denied nor covered up". The process which for Enzensberger would allow that kind of action begins with the development of literacy (after "an incomparably longer time preceded it in which literature was oral") and especially the book, which "usurped the place of the more primitive but generally more accessible methods of production of the past".[15]

He recognizes, on the other hand, the partially progressive nature of literacy, citing the revolutionary nature of the press at the time of the rise of the bourgeoisie, as well as Marx's *Capital* and "its doctrines" which are the result of that culture. The book would thus be "a stand-in for future methods which make it possible for everyone to become a producer", a possibility that has, however, only become real with electronic media. The resulting high formalization of writing and high degree of social specialization, tending to transform professional writers into a caste, go hand in hand with the establishment of rules that constitute "normative power attributed for which there is no rational basis". Under these conditions, "learning to write forms an important part of authoritarian socialisation by the school". Moreover, "the printed book is a medium that operates as a monologue, isolating producer and reader", with the possibility of feedback and interaction being extremely limited (Enzensberger, 1971, p. 32–33).

With film, radio and television, such determination is altered. Although, as they are currently set up, those media "are burdened to excess with authoritarian characteristics, the characteristics of the monologue, which they have inherited from older methods of production", these "outworn elements" are demanded by social conditions and "do not follow from the structure of the media. On the contrary, they go against it, for the structure demands interaction" (ibid., p. 33). It is clear that the "structure" to which Enzensberger refers is the technical structure of the medium. It is necessary here to refine these conclusions a little, with a brief reference to two authors who follow the French sociological tradition of studies on the social uses of technological innovations.

Flichy analyses the historical development of the audiovisual sector (including film, television, radio and record publishing) and notes that although the technical innovations that gave rise to the record industry emerged during the last quarter of the 19th century, (sound reproduction in 1887 through Edison's phonograph, a year after Graham Bell's telephone and marketed before 1890, during the same period in which the gramophone and record were developed), it is only in the 20th century that this has taken shape. The same was to occur with the film industry, which only began significant commercial development after the first screenings of the Lumière brothers in the Grand Café in 1895. Flichy further notes that in 1863 (with the publication of *Le Petit Journal*), as well as the rise of mass media (Flichy, 1980, p. 18), and following Smythe (1977, p. 91 ff.) in the process, I might add, a "cyclical process of technical improvement" which translates to increased printing capacity, reducing unit costs and, consequently, price per copy, resulting in increased sales and earnings, enabling growth in the accumulation of capital and investment in new and more productive plants, a process which took place during the first three quarters of the 19th century.

But unlike the press, where the consumer is not "obliged to use a machine to gain access to the work", the audiovisual sector is characterized by the existence of a dual commodity-programme and a "dialectic" between industry and the market which makes the transformation of a technological innovation into a commodity complex, meaning that certain technical potentialities end up being discarded in favour of others, as happened, for example, with the telephone, originally used in France to broadcast sounds, "as a kind of cable radio", and which ended up as a two-way communication device, or as in the case of sound recording devices, the gramophone displacing Edison's phonograph, which allowed recording and listening simultaneously (Flichy, 1980, p. 19).

This is what explains the delay in the final adoption and stabilization of these commercial innovations that came about during the last quarter of the 19th century.

The study of what Flichy calls "founding systems" (records, film and radio) in the first twenty years of the 20th century shows a frustration of the "puritan bourgeoisie of the late 19th century [that] did not want a leisure use for these innovations. Such use was largely imposed by the evolution of capitalist production" whose new dynamic occurred between 1870 and 1890, precisely when all these innovations appeared and obliged "companies in state of the art technology sectors to enter the consumer goods market meaning these were no longer limited to the higher income classes" (Flichy, 1980, p. 32). This imposition in turn requires, first, a simplification of the equipment to suit the mass market and second, public awareness of the new media:

> Manufacturers of programme that were successful at that time were those who were able to draw on a number of elements from shows or particularly popular forms of entertainment (songs from opera or operetta for records, historical melodrama or illusionist theatre for cinema). These were reconstructed based on the characteristics of the media used and, finally, given a wider audience thanks to the potential of these duplication and mass diffusion technologies.
>
> (Flichy, 1980, p. 33)

He adds:

> If from an economic point of view it can be deemed that audiovisual proposed a substitute for live performance at a lower cost it must also immediately be said that the substitution changes leisure practices and rules for its creation.
>
> (Flichy, 1980 p. 34♣)

The need therefore exists for compatibility of interest, essential for the adoption of the innovations for mass consumption in both the software and hardware areas. Flichy makes it clear that the different groups involved in this "negotiation" have to give up something (both the bourgeoisie and the "masses" are frustrated and forced to change their leisure practices, and the "creators" their rules of creation) in favour of the interests of the culture and communication industries that end up forming powerful oligopolies in the sector at the end of the consolidation period when, on the other hand, the hard/soft interpenetration disappears with the retirement of electronics companies from the audiovisual sector, leaving only a few survivors such as RCA and Philips in the record publishing industry.

Flichy gives an example of this latter phenomenon based on data from S. W. Head on the origin of the capital invested in radio stations in 1923, with the largest share (39%) being from manufacturers and distributors of communications equipment, as opposed to only 12% from newspaper publishers and 5% from magazines. Fifty years later, he explains, the television industry is now 40% controlled by media companies and 28% by newspaper publishers. He also explains some recent capital movements (from the 1970s) from the commodities industries to radio and television, stating, however, that "such investment remains outside the norm and does not correspond to a change in trend... of the separation between hardware and software" (ibid., p. 184). The obvious question remains concerning the movements that occur from the end of the 1980s, within the framework of current technical changes, with regard to capital from the Japanese electronics industry to the American film industry.

Returning to the point in question, the choice of a particular technique over another depends not only on the compatibility between industrial interests with those of the consumer, but also on political interference and competition between different national industries. For example, the radio networks that emerged in the USA in the 1920s did not cover more than a limited zone around a big city. In France, by contrast, long wave was imposed for both political (centralized broadcast throughout national territory) and economic reasons. The *Société Française Radioélectrique*, for example, the country's first private radio station launched in 1922, opted for long wave transmission to market devices with different technical standards to those of the USA to avoid competition from producers of radio equipment there. In post-war Germany, the Allies only allowed the installation of medium-wave radios to avoid centralization, which also explains why it was the first country interested in frequency modulation (Grundig was the pioneer in commercialization of FM equipment). However, according to Flichy nothing compares with the great battles over the system for colour TV, which inevitably ended up dividing Europe (Flichy, 1980, p. 57 ff.).

Salaün takes up the point made by Flichy, pointing out that the relationship between technology and its social use is insufficient to explain the phenomenon of the end use of that technology. Thus, if radio and telephony can in principle offer the same signalling services, and if, at least in France, the radio, which was initially conceived as a bidirectional media, and the phone, designed as a means of dissemination, had their final usage curiously reversed, then according to Salaün that crucially relates to the funding model that each encountered.

> If the *flot* industries [radio and television broadcasters] were initially mass developed to use the airwaves for diffusion it is because they found users and partners interested in funding their programme, advertisers or governments, as well as the practical arrangements for their financing, sale of advertising space or charging... Once the charging scheme was regulated by the government, the network operators failed to imagine practical actions for organising a market, therefore today there is a structural link between the airwaves and *flot*.
>
> (Salaün, 1989, p. 24♣)

It is this structural link which makes television similar to radio in function and which prevents the emergence of pay TV until the arrival of cable and satellite connection.

> The telephone can also be developed in a similar manner because its promoters managed to charge for interpersonal communications transmitted by cable. From the moment when there was a tariff on dialogue, an industry producing programmes to justify the telephone network became useless.
>
> (Salaün, 1989, p. 24 ff.♣)

Thus, for Salaün the relationship between technology and media is abundantly clear: "it is not incorrect to say that technology drives the media, but it must be immediately added that this pressure is only determined when a configuration combines the technology and use through an economic link" (Salaün, 1987, p. 351). Once this configuration has been found, however, it acquires a significant inertia, and it should also be mentioned that this solution can evolve: "the telephone never completely abandoned the airwaves and has found a relay device for long distance using satellites; while television has only multiplied its channels by changing to cable" (Salaün, 1989, p. 29). Today we are in a curious situation that promises new investment resulting from the trend to pass audiovisual via underground cables and for telephone to occupy the airwaves with the development of mobile telephony (Salaün, 1990, p. 102).

The subject of technology will be resumed later. For now it is worth concluding that the structure of mass media is defined based on the range of possibilities available at the time of its launch and based on which the different agents will determine the organisation this media will adopt, including some technical options, a specific form of relationship with the public and a way of financing. Once defined, this structure acquires a very high level of inertia.

Such considerations should serve to reduce the excessive optimism of Enzensberger with regard to the development of the electronic media, though his position (which, we should recall, is the same as that of Brecht and Benjamin) essentially remains politically correct in my view, which is that the enormous development of communication technologies and the possibilities of interaction between them point to an unprecedented expansion of communication between people. "The general contradiction between productive forces and productive relationships emerges most sharply, however, when they are most advanced... Monopoly capitalism develops the consciousness-shaping industry more quickly and more extensively than other sectors of production; it must at the same time fetter it" (Enzensberger, 1971, p. 14).

Under these conditions, the goal of a "socialist theory" of the mass media is to make explicit the emancipatory potential of this "new productive force"; its "mobilising power" that "has been waiting, suppressed or crippled" represents the "decisive political factor" of the electronic media.[16] The idea is interesting and is valid today with the debate over interactivity restored by the development of optical fibres. Enzensberger's optimism does, however, seem at times exaggerated. At one point he states, for example, that "societies in the late industrial age rely on the free exchange of information; the 'objective pressures' to which their controllers constantly appeal are thus turned against them" (Enzensberger, 1971, p. 16).

The simplistic nature of the assertion is obvious. The analysis I made above should serve to demonstrate this. My aim was to make it clear that the capitalist system was able to identify different types of information that serve different functions and have different degrees of permeability, so that full freedom of information at the level of capitalist competition can coexist with the manipulation and censorship in mass communication and, especially, in the organisation of the work process. It is true that extending the possibilities of communication and interactivity redefine the objective conditions, making the contradictions in the system more acute. There is from that point of view, as Enzensberger insists, greater handling difficulty. But at the same time, these developments offer new control mechanisms.

The big problem with Enzensberger's work lies in its inability to fully perceive that while the process leading to the overcoming of the traditional bourgeois culture of the unique artwork etc. leads to undeniable potential towards the democratization of culture, it is essentially a process of creating a culture and a specifically capitalist form of cultural production, primarily representing the system's greatest victory: the extension of the logic of capital to the field of culture and to lifestyles in general.

3
The Culture Industry and Its Functions

In Chapter 1, I explained the derivation of capitalist information, highlighting its different manifestations and its immanent contradictions. This was in fact a purely formal explanation in an attempt to describe what we can term the "backbone of capitalist industrialized culture". However, at that point, it was not possible to provide a full designation of the Culture Industry. A number of key categories were missing that can only be understood on the basis of rigorous historical analysis. Derivation is a logical movement that only partially defines our objective and whose complete specification demands a subsequent shift in characterizing historic categories. Note that in the opening chapter I introduced the concept of the bourgeois public sphere, defining it as one manifestation of the contradictions of information in classic capitalism.

The Culture Industry, the specific focus of our interest, is the form in which the contradictions in monopoly capitalism are manifested. The whole of Chapter 2 was dedicated to this new definition where, together with other concepts linked to the transformation of the sphere of the state and capital, the structural changes in the public sphere and lifestyles were detailed. I also tried to shed light, in somewhat schematic terms, on those aspects of the historical development of the Culture Industry which are important for the theoretical characterization of the subject under study.

A full historical analysis of the development of the Culture Industry (and here it is necessary to speak of cultural industries), worldwide or in a specific country, calls for the construction of an analytical framework that cannot be deduced directly from the aforementioned theoretical proposal, but that should maintain with it a continuous, but not necessarily consistent, relationship. I will devote myself henceforth to the construction of this framework. In Chapter 1, the transition from the analysis of form to that of functions only approached the level of a general characterization of the two functions (advertising and propaganda) that the Culture Industry must fulfil in the historical context of monopoly capitalism. A more precise analysis of each of these functions was not conducted. More importantly, the question of their mutual compatibility and of the compatibility of both with the symbolic needs of the culture-consuming audience, as opposed to those of capital or the state, were not examined.

This last point is fundamental because it clearly shows the existence of limits to manipulation. The issue will be addressed later as a need that the Culture Industry has to respond to the demands of the audience itself. This, in turn, defines a third function (programme), on the basis of which the issue of mediation in terms of a dialectic between the system and the lifeworld, using Habermas' term, can be discussed.[1] This approach is of interest to our objectives given that it enables us to relate the product differentiation strategies of the consumer goods business sector to the distinction strategy of the consumer public, locating the mediation function precisely in the area of competition among the individual firms invested in the Culture Industry.

Let us, however, return at the outset to the problem concerning the shift of analysis from form to functions. We saw that two different conditions of functionality correspond to the advertising form and the propaganda form of information that the Culture Industry can replace in monopoly capitalism. It is now necessary to discuss in more detail each of these functionality conditions and the problem of their compatibility at a more concrete level of analysis.

In reality the majority of authors who have dedicated themselves in some way to the topic have based themselves on one of these two functions. Thus, we can speak of two traditional tendencies for approaching the Culture Industry in the field of Marxism, to which we need to add a third, known in French literature as "the economy of communication and culture". This third approach represents, as we shall see, a shift in the focus (from the debate over the functions of the Culture Industry to the valorization of the different cultural industries) in relation to the other two, neither of which it necessarily opposes. In this chapter and Chapter 4, I will summarize some of these authors'contributions and then attempt to formulate the bases of a theoretical alternative incorporating the most important concepts developed by them.

The Culture Industry and propaganda: Approaches based on the concept of ideological apparatuses

The Marxist tradition along these lines was constructed during the 1970s, based especially on Althusserian concepts of ideology and of the ideological apparatuses of the state. The literature is quite extensive, especially in the Latin American tradition of cultural dependence theories. I will examine these briefly, following a more important discussion of the work of G. Cesareo, a representative of a group of Italian authors who in my opinion developed the most interesting theoretical proposal along these lines. I will also look at the contributions of other authors such as Enzensberger.

As for cultural dependency theories, suffice to say that their political importance was very substantial indeed and a critical review of the vast literature on the subject would require a far greater effort of synthesis than I propose here. I will therefore confine myself to a very generic discussion, based principally on an interesting review paper by Ingrid Sarti.

The form of the mass media apparatus: Cesareo and the Italian school

Althusser himself has really nothing to say about the Culture Industry.[2] Poulantzas does not explicitly refer to the topic either.[3]

The Althusserian approach was partly reintroduced in the 1970s in Italy, by a group of authors such as Cesareo, Siliato and Mauro Wolf. This group, formed under the aegis of *Ikon* magazine, and revisiting the contributions of other key authors such as Brecht, Benjamin, Gramsci and Ensensberger, researched the form of the "mass media apparatus", seen as a particular way of organizing the processes of production, distribution and consumption of knowledge, information and culture in capitalism.[4] I will restrict myself to the article by Cesareo (1979), in which he seeks to summarize, in a single theoretical diagram, the set of cited contributions.

According to Cesareo, a contradiction exists between capital productivity and all social productivity, which generates "waste" even in the mass media field. Once television, for example, becomes an autonomous institution structured according to the capitalist enterprise model, it produces according to its own internal laws and not according to social process needs. In this way, the story presented by TV is, as a function of its "contemporaneity rupture" approach, different from the social story that we live on a daily basis, which "presupposes a significant waste, from the viewpoint of social needs, of the potential of TV for strengthening communication processes for social transformation, to the benefit of the dominated classes" (Cesareo, 1979, p. 34♣).

We can translate that into our own terms and affirm that television presents a fragmented and rearticulated reality to the target audience according to a specific logic based on its own needs (economic and political) and those of capital and the state. The representation of a re-elaborated reality by the Culture Industry occurs not only in terms of the temporary logic that presides over the historical process but rather in more general terms, by the articulation of different contents or different realities constituted outside of itself, given that this representation is no more than a social mediation element with power conferred upon it by the particular circumstances. Television autonomizes itself and proceeds to define the conditions of legitimacy of cultural productions as well as of all the different social agents that need it for communicating with the audiences. This obviously only occurs through the interaction between the different elements involved in the process, including viewers in the audience on whom it is incumbent to recognize themselves in some way in the reality that is built and portrayed by the media to ensure that the model works. This aspect will be addressed later.

For Cesareo, individual behaviour is determined in a dual way; on one hand by its own social practice (historical determination) and on the other by the media that produces behaviour guidelines. Individual expression only makes sense when it is seen as part of existing social relationships (of social experiences that, in turn, would be a useless abstraction unless linked to personal experiences). At the current stage of capitalist development the individual is finally separated from his/her experience and the apparatus of information, knowledge and culture production and distribution becomes an "extension of the human mind", in the same way that, for Marx, tools are the extension of the human body. In both cases, the object is separated from the subject and controlled by capital (or by the "dominant class", which amounts to the same).

Capitalist development gives rise to two conditions under which the mass media apparatus is created: a broad socialization of the labour process, from the stage of artisanal production to big business, and on the other hand a constant increase in the circulation of images and words as a result of the urbanization and concentration of human masses "which at the same time caused a rapid increase in the contradictions between city and countryside and a radical destabilization of traditional structures of socialization and control (especially of the family and religious institutions)" (Cesareo, 1979, p. 35♣).

Under these circumstances the "apparatus structure" conditions the production, structure and content of the cultural product, while at the same time transforming the organization of intellectual work, cultural production (conditioned and determined by a cultural market) and society as a whole. Furthermore, this structure has an impact on the audience's own lifestyle – a lifestyle which is in turn conditioned by the organization of material production.[5]

That historically determined form of mass media organization, the apparatus structure, calls for: (a) "the introduction of increasing quantities of information, at different levels, in the material production processes", with the purpose of increasing productivity, facilitating the control of enterprises that are increasingly more complex and "creating and channeling the market (consumer behaviours)"; and (b) the production of behaviour models that compensate for the decline in the discipline previously imposed by productive and repressive apparatuses. A need exists to produce behaviour models that implement or even substitute the norms that the educational apparatus (and family) is less capable of producing and transmitting to the younger generations. (Cesareo, 1979, p. 39♣)

Interpreting these two sets of functions based on our own theoretical framework, we find in the first of them the different forms of information used by the capitalist enterprise in the labour process, in its own bureaucratic organization or in production planning based on knowledge of the market. From the idea of "creating and channeling the market", or "consumer behaviours", the impact of advertising mechanisms in the creation of lifestyles fitting the needs of capital can also be inferred. Cesareo's concern at this point, however, is mainly with the information that the enterprise needs to extract from the market whenever the "mechanisms of 'perfect' competition no longer offer a valid form of information to the enterprises (price systems)" (ibid., p. 38). But it is the second set which most interests us. For Cesareo, the mass media systems would gradually substitute the education, family and religious apparatus in the production of behaviour models with the purpose of guaranteeing a discipline that cannot be adequately guaranteed by the simple action of the repressive apparatus or solely by the capitalist organization of the labour process.

It is clear that we could broaden the concept and speak also of the production of consumer guidelines to introduce the topic of advertising, according to the concept of lifestyle which undoubtedly (although not explicitly) underlies the author's analysis. Instead of that, I will be faithful to Cesareo's text and I address, in my own terms, a "propaganda function", defined by Cesareo as linked to the need to

> produce a social image ('fragmented' and 'balanced') able to obscure the origins of social conflicts and... to produce models of practical behaviour directed towards absorbing the impacts of contradiction and conflicts that inevitably emerge from the classist structure of capitalist society with the ultimate purpose of reproducing and reinforcing the existing texture of social relationships.
>
> (Cesareo, 1979, p. 39♣)

Observed together, these two groups of tasks to be fulfilled by mass media can "restrict and even contradict the profit motive", even when the action of the apparatus structure itself helps, in large measure, to create a new audiovisual market in Europe. Therefore, there seems to be, in the "dialectic interrelation between 'senses production' and 'goods production' that characterizes mass media processes", hegemony of the first. I should add, however, that with the development of the advertising form, parallel to the expansion of capitalist logic to all social relationships, this dialectic tends to resolve itself in favour of a mercantilization that is increasingly greater in cultural production and in the growing subsumption of cultural work in the business sphere, as we will have the opportunity to examine later. This dialectic does not obscure the fact that the Culture Industry is, above all, an institution of symbolic order of capitalist societies in its monopoly phase, thus making the "profit motive" necessarily subordinate to the "motives" of advertising and propaganda. Yet the idea of the existence of concurrent or complementary social logic is not part of Cesareo's categorical framework. He is essentially a prisoner of the Althusserian concept of the apparatus.

The capitalist model of industrial organization of information, knowledge and culture production and distribution adopted, according to Cesareo, the following characteristics: (a) there is an uneven development of different media that nevertheless come together to form a mass communication system according to a shared logic; (b) the business organization presupposes centralization of the decisions in a self-regulated and protected apparatus, in opposition to a fragmented audience with no chance to control or respond; (c) intellectual work is reduced to abstract work ("subject to the imperatives of a Taylorism-type organization") to fit "mass production, based on modular type prototypes and structures". For Cesareo, the type of complete organization of production seen in radio, cinema and television, and that tends to be generalized even to the publishing market, generates two effects: on one hand, the amount of fixed capital invested in each apparatus assumes increasing importance, implying "an enormous expansion of the structures and a growing degree of concentration of the decision-making processes" and consequently the need for long-term production planning and distribution, reinforcing even more the tendency to rupture contemporeanity (Cesareo, 1979, p. 41♣).

On the other hand, (d) the restrictions imposed by productivity lead to the progressive disappearance of "old style professionalism" and the creation of a new stock of intellectuals that tend to base their approach on an enterprise-type ethic. With this, censorship gives way to self-censorship and the contradiction between efficiency criteria and those of creativity arises – the traditional model of performance measurement, which is nothing more than the contradiction between abstract work and practical work in the sector. The "intellectual" emerging from this contradiction is a "quasi-intellectual", oscillating between nostalgia for the old working conditions and consciousness of the demands of capital and business. Finally, (e) distribution becomes a key element for the whole model, while planning dictates the end of the "author" figure (impersonal, total intellectual). Based on these reflections, Cesareo goes beyond the problematic of the propaganda form, expressing opinions on important issues developed by the political economy of communication and culture, as we shall see later.

For Cesareo, state action does not alter the essential aspects or the logic of the model but progresses to increasing public expenditure, and through it to the reorientation of consumption (or the creation of new demands) and to the "appropriation of the opportunities for social control provided by the apparatuses".[6] In this way the state "perfects and legitimizes the social function of the model, contributing to the tendency to confer upon these apparatuses the status of 'public service', a term that nevertheless ends up obscuring the real class needs that they serve" (Cesareo, 1979, p. 44♣).[7]

Cultural dependency theories

In order to conclude this point, I cannot omit citing what was the first great Latin American school of thought on the topic of the media and that, directly or via a Gramscian type derivation (e.g. Madrid, 1983, Lins da Silva, 1982), would continue as the predominant critical trend in our subcontinent until the consolidation of the theoretical line represented by, inter alia, the works of Jesús Martín-Barbero and Nelson Garcia Canclini[8]: the theory of cultural dependency or cultural imperialism, to which the most well-known intellectuals of the area of communications in Latin America contributed. I cite, among them, Herbert Schiller (1968, 1984), Armand Mattelart (1972, 1976), Luis Ramiro Beltrán & Elizabeth Fox Cardona (1980), Mattelart & Dorfman (1976), along with the contemporaries organized by Mattelart (1984), Fernando Reyes Matta (1980) and Jorge Werthein (1979) and Issue No. 9 of the Brazilian journal *Comunicação e Sociedade* (1983).[9]

It is not possible, within the confines of this study, to revisit all the contributions by this school, whose review and critical appraisal merit an entirely separate study. They were of key importance in the debate on international information flows, the denouncement of related forms of domination over them and, above all, in the historic struggle for the adoption of a New World Information Order that unfolded during the 1970s; this culminated in the US withdrawal from UNESCO in 1983, representing one of the key moments in the reassertion of American hegemony and coinciding with the rise of Ronald Reagan to power. The role of the above Latin American theorists was of central importance during this entire process.

From the theoretical point of view, however, we need to acknowledge that "dependency" or "cultural imperialism" theories are extremely limited. Lamentably, most of the second-rate literature influenced by them became a kind of widely disseminated ideology, contributing little to the advancement of scientific knowledge on such a weighty issue. I have referred to this problem previously (Bolaño, 1988, p. 17 ff., Note 8). I cited at the time a book by Carlos R. A. Ávila (1982) that sought to define the relationship between Brazilian television and "international imperialism" on the basis of the simple discovery that the Thompson Agency had been in our country for 50 years, that most big advertisers were foreign or, even worse, citing the three biggest advertising companies of US origin without even mentioning that the participation of Brazilian home-grown agencies increased during the 1970s, and that the three US firms were only three out of the ten largest operating here.

Brazil is a poor example of this type of ideological analysis because, as in Mexico, the development and international competitiveness of the Brazilian television industry has been faster than in most developed capitalist countries. At the beginning of the 1980s, the reduced

American influence in Brazilian TV was clearly evident (Straubhaar, 1983). In the early 1990s, Brazilian production from 6pm to midnight amounted to over 80% in the *Globo* and *Manchete* networks, and was significantly above 50% in the other networks (cf. *Anuario Brasileiro de Mídia,* 1991–1992). At prime viewing time this percentage was even higher, often as high as 100%. The simplistic analysis which I am bound to criticize here arises from an extremely limited view of monopoly capitalism and the evolution of the international division of labour in the post-war period.

It is clear that foreign participation in the Brazilian television industry is an important topic which should be analysed carefully; this is especially true of the programming aspect, including, more specifically, the children's programmes, which are almost entirely imported. However, unlike Ávila, we cannot come to rapid conclusions with the insufficient data available. The major participation of foreign advertisers, as well as of state-run outfits, simply reflects the general trend of the Brazilian economy, particularly during its most recent spurt of growth. The issue is more complex than it appears. An accurate analysis of the insertion of Brazil into the "transnational communications model" also demands knowledge of cultural market dynamics in the international arena as well as of the functions of the Culture Industry in each country. This includes knowing how these functions succeed in accumulating capital (from advertising), knowledge of a system's "ideological reproduction" (propaganda) and of the symbolic mechanisms that constitute "national culture". The latter is vital for maintaining the establishment's hegemony within a country's borders.

The effectiveness of the mechanisms of ideological domination through the Culture Industry depends on the industry's capacity to produce national programme content that can guarantee its broad acceptance by audiences. Moreover, international competitiveness vis-à-vis culture sector capital depends largely on constructing a production model containing the correct proportions of universality and a country's specific cultural reality. The success of Brazilian soap operas and Brazilian advertising internationally is proof of this. The predominant transnational companies in the different sectors of cultural production are fully conscious of that dialectic. The most obvious example is the record market. Thus, while a given trend may exist towards cultural homogenization globally, this is linked to a differentiated trend. This, in a globalized system of oligopolistic competition, tends towards the formation of a number of predominant "techno-aesthetic standards" (a concept which will be defined more precisely later), coexisting with a much larger number of other fairly important, sometimes experimental, ones that dispute different segments of the market both nationally and internationally. The most recent technological developments in the telecommunications sector, and the appearance of so-called TV market segmentation, point clearly towards the consolidation of this trend.

The complexity of the above situation cannot be fully understood from the two-tier viewpoint of cultural dependency theories, whose main problem, as I pointed out in my book mentioned above, is to confuse what is characteristic of any capitalist society with the particular place of that society in the international division of labour. This perspective blames all the evils of the system on the fact that a given country suffers under the yoke of imperialism, while omitting to mention that social domination involves mainly one social class presiding over another, unconnected to external circumstances, as if the economy of the peripheral states was confined to linking imperialism and national capitalism – a straightforward relationship between nationalist sectors of the national bourgeoisie and sectors linked to international money. The fact is that an analysis that starts from an ideological presupposition posing as radical thought is irrelevant when compared to the possession of objective knowledge of a genuine reality. Ironically, this serves as an ideological device for masking the real contradictions existing in any capitalist society and for simply transferring the entire debate elsewhere. This approach also impairs any understanding of the meaning of imperialist domination and the mechanisms through which it is exercised.[10]

The best appraisal of cultural dependency theories was made by Ingrid Sarti, based on the more general critique of dependency theories made by Weffort (1971). Initially recognizing the importance of the pioneering works of Shiller, Mattelart, Varis & Nordenstreng and others in demystifying the idea of the mass media being able to "ease the problem of underdevelopment", Sarti highlights among all the cultural dependency theories, "the undeniable merit (of the cultural dependency theories) in denouncing the process of domination, showing that these [forms of communication] do not exhaust themselves in purely repressive methods, but are rather insinuated through the tortuous paths of ideological support" (Sarti, 1979, p. 234♣).

The theoretical solution propounded by these authors is influenced by Althusser and the dependency theories in the following terms:

> within the Althusserian perspective, communication and dependency theorists seek to analyse the performance of the media, such

> as the ISA (Ideological State Apparatuses), and their specificity in the context of dependency. They initially postulate that the ISA in Latin America perform the ideological function of reinforcing the dependent character of the production relationships of Latin American capitalism.
>
> (Sarti, 1979, p. 235)

According to Sarti, the merit of that type of focus resides in "overcoming approaches of an evolutionist and functionalist kind, where 'backwardness', viewed in quantitative terms, corresponds to the 'backward' stage of development". Thus, "'development' as a solution to 'underdevelopment' is no longer proposed, [but rather]... the failures, the conditions of underdevelopment, are identified, as a result of the contradictions inherent in the means of production itself" (ibid., p. 235 ff.). For Latin American sociology this means "a step forward of undeniable historical value".

> In its version of communications theory, "cultural dependency" theory points to a process of ideological domination that is implemented as the "dependency" ties grow stronger. The task of the mass media, as an instrument of this process, is to propagate values and induce behaviours that are fundamentally defined by their externality in relation to the national context: they are values created in the hegemonic centers of capitalism....[11] Thus, the relationship of inequality that characterizes economic transactions of the capitalist world, as is pointed out in the "dependency theory"[12] is reproduced at a superstructural level. "Cultural dependency" is a criticism of the ruling ideology in Latin American countries, given that it is external to national interests, to the extent that it is imposed from the outside and for being antagonistic to the interests of the majority of the continent's populations given that it is capitalist, and as such, an expression of the interests of the establishment.
>
> (Sarti, 1979, p. 236 ff.♣)

Cultural dependency theories, in their "mechanicist approach" based on a "dichotomous vision of social reality", are unable to surpass the level of criticism of Latin America's social and communicational reality, explaining "very little or almost nothing" about the "dynamic of the ideological process". "The theoretical basis of 'cultural dependency' itself is responsible for invalidating the concept and transforming it into an ideology of radical nationalist type" (ibid., p. 240). For Sarti, "the fact that it is the concept of nation and not of class which prevails is determinant"[13] Therefore, she supports the conclusion that Renato Ortiz (1988) and I (Bolaño, 1988) draw in our aforementioned criticisms:

> [...] in their simplistic interpretation, the characteristic of dependency is highlighted to the extent that the essence of the problem is sidelined (i.e. its capitalist nature). Since dependency becomes the essence and not the complement, every aspect of a capitalist ideology is considered to be contrary to the interests of Latin America, so that "dependency" is reinforced and contradicts the "natural" course of Latin American development.
>
> (Sarti, 1979, p. 243)

The practical outcome of this theoretical position is the political option for "autonomous and democratic development" according to a developmental approach whose "objective continues to be the acceleration of capital accumulation in underdeveloped nations aimed at ensuring their participation in technological development" (ibid., p. 244). The advancement of education, technology, information and access to media are at the root of autonomous development. The problem is that "it is never specified who should control the process". Since all the contradictions are defined in the relationship between the "two poles" of global capitalism, class struggle in each internal context is not considered.

> In reality, it is never clear which is the type of change concretely proposed, nor which is the goal to achieve... the "programme of cultural dependency" implies an anti-imperialist but not necessarily anticapitalist struggle, given that class struggle is not even a constituitive element of the idea of imperialism.
>
> (Ibid.)

The ideology itself is seen as

> [...] an element external to the productive process from which it effectively emerges. The ideology is held as a model of values imposed from the outside by imperialist agents... Likewise, when internal elites and external agents of the domination process are distinguished from one another, the hegemonic center of capitalism (United States) is presented as the agent that produces and spreads the capitalist

> ideology that will be adopted and incorporated by the elites in charge of transmitting them to the "common people".
>
> (Sarti, 1979, p. 245♣)

According to Sarti, the difficulty of cultural dependency theories derives from their inspiration in the Althusserian concept of ideology and their "basic error" is that they do not consider ideology as "determined in the production process itself and involved in the fundamental contradiction of the capitalist mode of production", defining it as a "function to be performed by the state with the objective of ensuring domination". Thus,

> [...] just as happened with Althusser's notion of the AIE, the "cultural dependency" literature, aimed at highlighting the ideology-inspired phenomena, occupied the opposite extreme of the tendency that only considers the repressive nature of the capitalist state. It divided the process of domination into two closed compartments – one of repression and the other of ideology – omitting the first as if the state literally had "apparatuses" operating mechanically to achieve specific ends.
>
> (Sarti, 1979, p. 246)

Sarti concludes:

> Thus, what could be a merit, that of recognizing the need to study the process of ideological domination, ceases to be so insofar as the analyses of the communication media lose the notion of proportion and the role of powerful agents, almost autonomous in the process of production of capitalist relationships, is attributed to them.
>
> (Sarti, 1979, p. 246)

The Culture Industry and advertising

The analysis of the function of advertising in the process of capital accumulation follows two traditions among Marxist authors: first, a well-known one which happens to be outside the field of communication, represented by the classic work of P. Baran & P. Sweezy (1966), and second, by the both well-known and controversial article by the Canadian Dallas Smythe (1977). In addition to these two contributions, I will refer below to two recent theoretical propositions provided by two Latin American authors, one based on criticism of Baran & Sweezy and the other closer to Smythe's position.

Advertising and sales promotion in Baran & Sweezy

According to Baran & Sweezy, the difficulties developing advertising and sales promotion in monopoly capitalism are not due to the law of the gradual trend of declining profits. Rather they are to be found in the inability to absorb a growing surplus via "normal routes" (capitalist consumption, investment and other non-productive costs such as maintenance of the clergy, domestic servants and the mass of public employees), so that, without the presence of some countervailing factor, the system tends to stagnate. Advertising is seen, together with military expenditure, as being of this type and is defined as a "cost of circulation" in the Marxist sense, that adds no value to goods (Baran & Sweezy, 1966, p. 117).

For these authors, the substitution of price competition by other forms of competition in monopoly capitalism gives rise to a "qualitative transformation with far-reaching consequences", making advertising the main weapon in the competitive struggle between the big oligopolistic companies pursuing differentiation strategies. The outcome is a steep increase in advertising budgets that, in the USA, according to the authors, multiplied by a factor of seven between 1867 and 1890, and by a factor of ten between 1890 and 1920, at which point they reached US$3.426 billion. This amount was still significantly below the US$10.3 billion in 1957 or the over US$12 billion in 1962 which, added to the expenses incurred with market surveys, public relations exercises and related services, actually raised the total outlay by media businesses to US$20 billion in that year.

The authors can therefore confirm, based on a critical appraisal of welfare economics theoreticians, that "the economic importance of advertising does not lie primarily in effecting a redistribution of consumer spending among different goods, but rather in the effect of advertising on the size of global demand and therefore, on profit and employment levels" (ibid., p. 129♣). For Baran & Sweezy, the total advertising and other promotional costs are divided into two parts: on one hand, those which through the price increases paid by final consumers fall on productive workers, and on the other, those which are recouped by business leaders and non-productive workers. The first actually leads to a real reduction of the salaries in the same ratio as the increase in prices, which correspondingly boosts the surplus return (the difference between the total net production and the total real salaries of productive workers). The second "does not constitute an increase in the surplus, but leads to its redistribution" in favour of those who "obtain their income from salaries and earnings created by the sales "industry" itself (ibid., p. 130).

In both cases, the total (whether obtained from productive or non-productive workers or capitalist businessmen) is used to mount sales campaigns. This means that the sales part of the surplus is of a "self-absorbing" type: "contrary to the surplus that takes the form of net profits, the portion that takes the form of a sales expense does not demand compensation in capitalist consumption, nor investment dumping. It provides, so to speak, its own compensatory elements and distribution channels" (Baran & Sweezy, 1996, p. 130♣), with an impact on the income and production structure similar to public expenditure financed from tax collection. The exception would involve the consolidated earnings of advertising agencies and other companies that finance sales campaigns being traded off by capitalist consumption, investment or a combination of both.

Allied to strategies of planned obsolescence and frequent model modifications, sales campaigns help to push up the rate of demand for commodities replacement, thus constituting a "powerful antidote to the tendency of monopoly capitalism to sink into a state of chronic depression". Given the expanded role of advertising, this medium ceases being a "simple appendage of the production process", and becomes the cause of a "transfer of activity at the economic hub towards sales". In this way, sales campaigns "increasingly invade the factory floor and the workshop, dictating what must be produced according to criteria established by the sales department, and its consultants and advisors in the advertising industry" (Baran & Sweezy, 1996, p. 134 ff.♣).

A key question arises in these conditions:

> [...] a situation, in which sales and production combine in such a way that they become virtually inseparable, involves major change in what constitutes the socially necessary costs of production, and also in the nature of the social product itself.
>
> (Ibid., p. 136♣)

The authors go on to cite Veblen,[14] leading to a discussion about a method of distinguishing between production and sales costs. In the last item of their chapter, they seek to identify advertising with the resources earmarked to financial, insurance and real estate, arguing that they are all necessary costs of capitalist production, concluding that "what must be clear is that an economic system where these costs are socially necessary stopped being a socially necessary economic system some time ago". (Ibid., p. 145♣).

In her book about advertising in Brazil, Maria Arminda do Nascimiento Arruda (1985) offers an in-depth critical analysis of Baran & Sweezy's contribution. She argues that the inter- and intrasectoral displacements of capital, and the ongoing advancement of capital in relation to the variable and consistent increase in work productivity, are the "main mechanisms of intercapitalist competition", and not price competition mechanisms which are "secondary to the characterization of capitalism in any of its stages". Price competition, as an immediately empirical category, cannot be used as a nucleus to explain the general laws of production. In this respect there is a "great misunderstanding in the book by Baran & Sweezy regarding the confusion between the two levels of analysis " (Arruda, 1985, p. 33♣).

Furthermore, Arruda correctly criticizes the use of the concept of surplus, a derivative concept like that of savings, that fails to provide the basis for a theory. She also points out the ethical character of the authors' analysis of monopoly capitalism, seen by them as irrational (which would require the imposition of regulatory compensatory mechanisms external to the monopolistic structure). She states that this approach would appear to reflect disillusionment with the "American way of life", a characteristic of North American authors, whose sociological functionalist tradition was inherited by Baran & Sweezy. She also seeks an alternative interpretation for the idea of the system's irrationality and the need for rationally planned regulatory compensatory attitudes, aligning Baran & Sweezy's ideas with the traditional notion of economic rationalism expressed by Sombart, Weber and Schumpeter. Unlike the idea expressed by the last-named authors, the idea of "guided rational action" does not refer to personalized social agents (such as entrepreneurs), but rather to "corrective institutions", such as advertising or military expenditure. However, the result is virtually the same. According to Arruda, the attempt to associate the two authors with empiricist functionalism and Weberianism seems to be contradictory, and she asserts that "it is not by chance that the theory of action is strongly inspired by Weber". To support this stance, Arruda cites Verón, who argues that Weber is engaged in a constant struggle with the dilemma contained in his "attempt to build a sociology which is autonomous in relation to psychology and empiricist in terms of its methodological principles in the theoretical context of the idealist tradition" (cited by Arruda, 1985, p. 40 ff.♣).

Arruda herself confirms the thesis of increased rationality, concluding that at the current stage of development of the system, capitalist rationality invades sectors of society that were previously immune to its logic. This is corroborated by advertising (whose raw material, she argues, is ideology itself) and by the sophistication of the planning process which goes from production to final consumption, as well as by the new approach assumed by the state, which we discussed above in our own description of monopoly capitalism. Let us set Arruda's theoretical alternative to one side for the time being. We will return to it shortly.

Dallas Smythe's audience production

Written a decade after the publication of Baran & Sweezy's book, the celebrated article by Smythe is more concerned with the specific question of communication, that veritable "blackspot of western Marxism". Its basic thrust is to criticize explicitly all Marxist analyses that consider the political and economic importance of the mass media systems, regarded as "idealistic" and "pre-scientific", in terms of their "ability to produce ideology". Smythe's aim is to provide an historical materialist interpretation of the mass media phenomenon, questioning at the outset its economic function and raising doubts about the "commodity-form" generated by media systems.

According to Smythe, the idealist bourgeois vision "also adopted by the majority of western Marxists" (Lenin, Veblen, Marcus, Adorno, Baran & Sweezy) and by Marxist authors more directly linked to research on the media (he cites, among others, Nordenstreng, Hamelink, Schiller and himself in previous works), is one of the mass media commodity consisting of "message", "information", "image", "meaning", "entertainment", "orientation", "education" and "manipulation", all concepts which in Smythe's view are "subjective mental entities" or "superficial appearances" (Smythe, 1977, *Canadian Journal of Social and Political Theory,* vol. 1, No. 3, p. 2). Certain shortcomings can already be perceived in Smythe's formulation, which consists of a shallow, generic and reductive analysis drawing on a set of very disparate concepts, on various theoretical levels, conceived in very different situations and with highly heterogeneous analytical objectives. This can be seen by looking back at the preceding theoretical developments, which embrace the concept of information in all the superficial categories. I show that it is possible, on the contrary, to define a concept of information based on a high level of analysis such as the characterization by Marx of a simple market economy. I hope to have made clear that this definition will serve as a point of departure for the construction of a theory of communication under capitalism compatible with the Marxian method. Smythe fails to understand that it is necessary to incorporate each of the supposedly bourgeois categories into the analysis in order to specify their ideological character, as was discussed previously.

According to Smythe, the mass media commodity consists of the audience (or mass of readers) produced simultaneously by the media sector and the family. In the first case, he makes no reference to the work of artists, technicians and journalists in the media sector, as would normally be expected. He confines himself instead to attacking programmes as "bribes" aimed at guaranteeing audience loyalty.[15] By contrast, the concept of labour is placed by Smythe where it does not belong – in the audience, which is expected to render a "service" to the advertiser consisting of "learning to buy particular 'brands' of consumer goods". In short, "they work to create demand for the advertised goods". Further on the question is posited in the following terms: "the work of audience members is to learn certain codes that are used when the member of the audience makes his/her mental shopping list and spends his/her income" (ibid., p. 10). The result would be that the audience can be useful for the process of "managing demand via advertising" which Smythe sees, citing Baran & Sweezy, as a vital need of monopoly capitalism. To support this odd extrapolation of the concept of work, he cites another Canadian, Professor William Livant of the University of Regina. According to Livant, all time that is not devoted to sleep is worktime in which, increasingly since the middle of last century, practically all the time outside the factory or sleep serves to satisfy the needs of capital: travel between the workplace and home, workforce turnover, keeping abreast of the Culture Industry and media "commercial" spots.

This solution is ingenious, but it suffers from an obvious inconsistency: the relationship between the media and the audience is not a "work" relationship but one of communication. It is not just any communication either, but a specifically capitalist communication such as the one I mentioned above, with all its typical features: hierarchical, unidirectional, variously contradictory, etc. Furthermore, the gross generalization of the concept of work advanced by Livant is one of total reductionism. This concept goes no way towards addressing the substantial complexity of the issues involved in the analysis of the relationship between the logic of capitalist production and other social logics, whether conflicting or secondary, that can be observed in capitalist economic formations, or even in the relationships between work and leisure based on the expansion of the logic of capital beyond the limits of industrial production in the strictest sense.

The definition of audience commodity should show the specificities of the expansion of that capitalist logic in the sphere that interests us. Smythe's solution is, in that respect, clearly insufficient. Nevertheless, his contribution is not confined to making the existence of that commodity explicit. He also concerns himself with questioning its economic function and whether "its production and consumption" appeals to advertisers or not. In this regard Smythe makes an interesting observation, citing Mao Tse-tung at the beginning of his article, pointing out what he considers a "main contradiction" of the production process of audience commodity: "When the superstructure (politics, culture, etc.) obstructs the development of the economic base, political and cultural changes *become principal and decisive*" (ibid., p. 3).

Further on, Dallas Smythe criticizes the ambiguity of Baran & Sweezy's position that, as we have seen, refers at the outset to advertising costs as circulation costs that do not add value to goods, and later goes on to define them as necessary for capitalist production. He revisits the *Introduction to the Critique of Political Economy* to cite the well-known section about the dual relationship between production and consumption (Marx, 1859, p. 108–112), which he considers to be a good starting point for "a theory of advertising and of branded merchandise under monopoly capitalist conditions". In *Capital*, "Marx was concerned about the analysis of capitalist operation, under the then realistic conditions of [perfect] competition" without considering "the preeminence of branded goods nor the preponderant position of advertising". In contrast to that viewpoint in *Capital*, Smythe argues that the *Introduction* would aver that "The denial of the productivity of advertising is unnecessary and diversionary: a *cul de sac* derived from the pre-monopoly-capitalist stage of development, a dutiful but unsuccessful and inappropriate attempt at reconciliation with *Capital*" (ibid., p. 19).

Neither Smythe nor Baran & Sweezy perceive that the productive character of advertising and of the media sector in general can be drawn from *Capital* and the *Grundrisse*, in the passages cited here and at the beginning of my first chapter, when Marx refers to the transportation sector as a productive sector due to the fact that, for the value of goods to be obtained via consumption, "It may be necessary to move them [the goods], thus the additional production process of the transportation industry." Marx makes absolutely clear that the productive nature of transport "adds value to the transported goods", consisting of "the transfer of value of the means of transportation and by the additional value created by the transportation work" (*Capital,* Book 2). Also in the *Grundrisse,* as we saw, the question is posed in similar terms.

Now if we go back to Smythe's passage about the function of advertising in the production of an indispensable infrastructure in order for production to be undertaken under the historical conditions of monopoly capitalism, the possibility is clearly established for broadening Marx's position regarding the transportation sector to the whole of what he called the transportation and communications sector, even including advertising. This solves the ambiguity that Smythe detects in Baran & Sweezy: advertising evidently continues to be a circulation cost, but this is a special circulation cost needed for obtaining the merchandise, and it is therefore "productive".

Based on this, the "dual nature of advertising" highlighted by (Zallo, 1988, p. 40), which could be simultaneously an industry, just like any other cultural industry, and a "circulation capital" (although considered by Zallo a "false" or unproductive cost) can be asserted – a dual nature, incidentally extending to the entire Culture Industry, that must be viewed in different terms. Advertising is on one hand a cultural industry that produces a specific cultural product, and on the other an industry that, in common with the entire transportation and communications industry, is part of the social structure needed for obtaining and adding value to goods. However, the dual nature which, I must insist, is not limited to advertising, but is germane to all cultural industries, can only be correctly understood if we accept that these sectors are doubly productive precisely because they always produce not *one* but *two* goods, as we shall see in Chapter 5.

According to Smythe's article, the transition of early capitalism to monopoly capitalism is characterized by a large-scale rationalization of industrial organization so that (a) the preponderance of unbranded products in the consumer market comes to an end; (b) product distribution passes under the control of big business; and (c) advertising starts being used to manage demand. Under these new conditions, capital confronts individuals, both workers and consumers, in a new way: on the one hand, the scientific management of labour begins to evolve; and on the other, consumption is established as a planning variable of big firms. In the latter case, increased rationalization results from controlling demand, which is also approached in a new and qualitatively different way. Smythe therefore argues that there is no simple expansion of the network of door-to-door salespeople, commercial travellers, etc., as would have been possible in principle, but rather something radically different: the development of commercial advertising and the creation of a complex system of social communication whose functions, indispensable to the survival of monopoly capitalism, are summarized in the following:

> [...] the mass media institutions in monopoly capitalism developed the equipment, workers and organization to produce audiences for the purposes of the system between about 1875 and 1950. The prime purpose of the mass media complex is to produce people in audiences who work at learning the theory and practice of consumership for civilian goods and who support (with taxes and votes) the military demand management system. The second principal purpose is to produce audiences whose theory and practice confirms the ideology of monopoly capitalism (possessive individualism in an authoritarian political system). The third principal purpose is to produce public opinion supportive of the strategic and tactical policies of the state...the fourth purpose of the mass media complex is to operate itself so profitably as to ensure unrivalled respect for its economic importance in the system. It has been quite successful in achieving all four purposes.
>
> (Smythe, 1977, *Canadian Journal of Social and Political Theory*, vol. 1, No. 3, p. 24)

Let us leave to one side the evident drawbacks present in the above (again, these are: the question of the work needing to be done by the audience; Smythe's limited vision of the state; ignorance of the fact that the media are also a locus of political dispute; the failure to consider the phenomenon of competition in the consumer goods sector; and, finally, approaching the phenomenon solely from the aggregate standpoint.[16] Nevertheless, there is no doubt that Smythe has the merit of establishing here, although in a "preliminary" way, some of the general questions that must be posited when analysing the functions of the Culture Industry: functions germane to the capital accumulation process, those linked to advertising and those that are plainly ideological or linked to the needs of the state, and even to the "fourth purpose" detailed above – that of the media sector's own economy.

In the light of the above, and obviously of his definition of "audience commodity", Smythe's study must be considered a pioneer in the broad materialist historical approach to the phenomenon of mass media. The main deficiency in the study is that he fails to examine more than one product, totally rejecting the decisive importance of the programme with regard both to the dialectic established between the audience market and that of cultural goods, and to the function that these fulfil vis-à-vis the audience. Moreover, Smythe fails to account for the improvements made to previous Marxist interpretations by shifting the main topic of discussion from the function of propaganda to the media's advertising function, without perceiving the contradictory relationship existing between both reproduction demands of the system.

Advertising and consumer goods

In the theoretical chapter of her important study on the development of advertising in the USA and Mexico, Patricia Arriaga (1980) begins with an analysis based on the division of the economy into two large sectors (production goods and consumer goods), arguing on the one hand that "the increase in productivity or the development of productive forces in any sector leads to the creation of markets for the production goods sector, but not necessarily for the consumer goods sector" (Arriaga, 1980, p. 25♣). This argument, even admitting that the growth of production goods increases the demand for consumer products (owing to increased numbers of employees), "the creation of this additional market is surpassed by the market which opens for production goods, although it is not demand but capital that determines the limits of extension of social production" (ibid.). Following this, Arriaga criticizes the underconsumption theses based on three arguments: (a) that "the importance of the production goods sector in the capitalist dynamic is notoriously larger than in the commodities sector"; (b) that growth of consumption is the result and not the cause of expansion of the production process; and (c) that "businessmen or industrialists determine demand via investments in production goods and wages" (ibid., p. 26). The demand for capital goods is therefore more important in the creation of an internal market in capitalism, meaning that "internal market growth is subordinate to the pace of the accumulation process and the distribution that this imposes" (ibid., p. 27).

> Thus, apparently, society's capacity for consumption tends to expand due to the growing employment of workers and the increasing wealth of those in the business sector. This expansion however occurs in absolute terms, but not in relation to production, given that society's consuming capacity tends to reduce rather than expand. This is explained by the same process that substitutes variable for constant capital in capitalist dynamics (which imply unlimited expansion

> of production). But as relatively less and less capital is invested in salaries, society's consumption capacity will tend to decline.
>
> (Arriaga, 1980, p. 26♣)

From this analysis, Arriaga focuses on three elements key to the discussion on the function of advertising in capitalism. First, when the capital goods sector (which expands depending on the demands of the accumulation process and productive forces) develops faster than the consumer goods sector, demand in the latter has to be stimulated by advertising in order to avoid, using the expression of João Manuel Cardoso de Mello, a "crisis of dynamic profit-taking". This would prove, according to Arriaga, that "advertising originates in the capitalist production sphere and not the commodities circulation sphere as stated by many authors" (ibid., p. 28♣). Second, if the increase in the production of the capital goods production sector is absorbed by the expansion of the different branches of production itself, the same does not occur with the consumer goods sector, given that "society's consumption capacity tends to shrink", which could reduce profit and affect accumulation in this sector. The purpose of advertising and personal credit would be precisely to avoid this by stimulating demand in the sector. Finally, advertising would seek to boost consumption by high income sectors to compensate for the insufficient consumption by poorer people.

> It is worth clarifying that advertising is not able, on its own, to expand the internal market nor increase the number of consumers, given that both are subordinated to the accumulation and development of productive forces. However, it can increase consumption by certain groups or modify that of others, but the increase of any group is determined by the production process and its rate of growth.
>
> (Arriaga, 1980, p. 28 ff.♣)

Having established this, Arriaga focuses on a critique of authors such as Blair, Chamberlain and those who see advertising as a competition mechanism of monopoly capitalism, and others such as Bain and Stigler, who support the thesis that advertising is the cause, not the consequence, of the concentration and monopolization of capital. It is interesting that Baran & Sweezy are "curiously" also included in the first case. Arriaga's critique goes on to discount the idea that competition takes place within the sphere of prices which she views as, in reality, a mere "superficial manifestation of true competition, among capitalist enterprises, which obliges the capitalist to develop productive forces leading to cheaper consumer goods" (ibid., p. 30♣). She also argues that advertising cannot be considered as the main mechanism of competition in monopoly capitalism given that its importance is minimal in the capital goods sectors (precisely those sectors that tend more towards concentration). In this case, both of the above approaches suffer from applying the advertising phenomenon to the entire economic system in general, when in fact it is confined to the consumer goods sector. Hitherto Arriaga's critical approach seems fair. However, her main argument is that the cited authors are mistaken when

> [...] considering, as structural causes of advertising, superficial manifestations of a more complex and deeper phenomenon whose origin is in the area of capitalist production and not in the circulation of consumer goods. We refer *inter alia* to the error of attributing to advertising the capacity to affect aggregate effective demand, the level of income and employment.... We know that the market basically expands through the process of capital accumulation in such a way that barriers to market failure are broken down as the process moves forward. For that reason, advertising, as a manifestation of demand, cannot affect investment nor determine the production levels of diverse industrial branches because the production levels are those that ultimately determine demand. Finally, to attribute to advertising the wherewithal to create barriers to the entry of new capitalist enterprises [Bain's thesis] thus favouring concentration, is to forget... that such barriers consist principally in the increasing volume of capital and its organic composition, both required for establishing and maintaining competitiveness while securing an acceptable level of profit.
>
> (Arriaga, 1980, p. 3 ff.♣)

The last statement rings true: advertising is not a barrier to entering, but a consequence of the barriers to entering, so that only oligopolistic firms have general access to it. However, this only helps to reinforce the thesis that Arriaga seeks to criticize. In reality, the above excerpt contains a succession of errors among which this is a mere detail. The most revealing for us is her attempt to shift the phenomenon of advertising towards the production level. But her previous affirmation that "advertising originates from the production sphere itself" (which could be interpreted as a harmless reaffirmation of the primacy over circulation of the production sphere, and of the transformations it went through with the advent of monopoly capitalism), appears ultimately as a hazardous statement of principle. But let us leave that discussion for the moment. We will see in the next item the correct position of Arruda in this regard.

The phrase "in the final analysis" referring to production demand, on the other hand, allows us to see, in the above quotes, that support possibly exists for the highly discredited Say's law. Clearly one can argue that, on the contrary, it is precisely because supply does not automatically create its own demand that advertising becomes necessary. Adolfo Zinser, a disciple of Arriaga, puts this as follows:

> [...] advertising, while it manipulates demand, cannot affect investment levels or influence production levels. On the contrary, production levels themselves are those that in the final analysis determine demand, and advertising is the instrument through which this is manipulated.
>
> (Zinser, 1980, p. 97♣)

The true meaning of "manipulation" is not clear in either Arriaga or Zinser. The latter speaks of modifying the consumption pattern of the working classes and of transferring capitalists' profits from savings to consumption. These observations appear to accord with the last two elements proposed by Arriaga concerning the analysis of the function of advertising in the phrase cited above, where Zinser talks about consumption stimuli that appear to refer to a transfer of capital expenditure from investment to consumption. All the arguments raise extremely difficult questions, either because they probably support the principle of Say's law[17] through the adoption of a debatable concept of savings,[18] or through ignorance of the possibility of different patterns of development besides the pattern whereby the production goods department expands at the expense of the consumer goods division. Finally, the difficult issue remains of ignorance concerning how this pattern of development actually functions.[19]

Arriaga acknowledges that "advertising's immediate objective is to convince the individual that he/she must consume" and that "American society is characterized by a high rate of consumption of necessary as well as luxury goods." However, she does point out that "The function of consumption does not occupy a dominant place, nor is it a goal of all economic activity, and ultimately it is the business and industrial sectors, not consumers, who take basic economic decisions based on expected earnings." Similarly, while recognizing that "there is ideology reproduction in advertising transmitted by the mass media", she opines that this is "incidental and superficial and not the goal of advertising nor a determinant for maintaining the system". (Arriaga, 1980, p. 39♣)

Arriaga criticizes Mattelart and Schiller, as well as Althusser and all those who believe in mass media domination,[20] in the following terms:

> The principal error lies in that, by eliminating from the analysis the consumer goods sector, the mass media and consumers are divorced from every economic reality that makes them confront each other in different markets. When the media lose the market for their advertising services, a "new" product is sought (programme, ideology, etc.) for offering to a "new" mass market (receiving audience). As a result, consumers forego their status as consumer goods consumers and become consumers of programmes, ideology etc. More seriously, the consumers thus enter into a superstructural or idealist interpretation of social reality. As Livant argues (cited by Smythe, 1977) "the field of communications is a jungle of idealism".
>
> (Arriaga, 1980, p. 58 ff.♣)[21]

Following the same rationale, on the one hand Zinser makes a more balanced critique of that "Marxist idealism" that in mass media analysis would have the merit of denouncing functionalism (seen as a chain of doubtful scientific validity and intellectual honesty), although this would simply develop techniques to make ideological manipulation by the media more effective. On the other hand, Zinser criticizes the semiologic structuralism that, while purporting to study the ideological content of the messages, possesses no general categories capable of escaping the fragmentation of social reality. The "undeniable progress" obtained by "Marxist idealism" refers, according to Zinser, not so much to the content analyses which they conducted, based on semiology's own techniques, but especially to "valuable empirical studies that analyze the structure of the media itself, to establish the specific connections between specific economic groups, the media and its messages" (Zinser, 1980, p. 92♣).

However, the theoretical matrix which provides the basis for the development of such empirical studies is, according to the author, inadequate, given that it limits the media question to its ability to produce ideology, forgetting the "structural economic aspects". The critique is then focused essentially on two works by Javier Esteinou Madrid (1979, 1980) who insists that "[...] production, circulation and discursive inculcation that mass media practice must be studied in the field of ideology itself, that is, in the area of social cohesion through the creation and circulation of symbolic representations that are functional to the system and its corresponding process of social assimilation" (Esteinou Madrid, 1979, cited by Zinser, 1980, p. 90♣).

> The importance of the media arises from the fact that they constitute a fundamental apparatus for exercising hegemony, allowing for the construction of social consensus based on the ideological apparatus. They play an essential role in legitimizing, at lowest cost, the class that is regarded as dominant in the social conflict.
>
> (Zinser, 1980, p. 91♣)

On the other hand, given that the objective of the ruling class in capitalism is to accumulate capital, these studies do not fail to take into account the economic decisions of the mass media, acknowledging that these also contribute directly to the reproduction of capital. "Some accept that the structural determinants of mass media are, in the final analysis, of an economic nature. The main economic function is to accelerate the process of production, thus shortening the period between production and capital realisation. This is achieved via the fetischisation of goods" (ibid., p. 92♣). The emphasis, however, always continues to be on political analysis, obscuring what Zinser considers as fundamental: advertising, seen "only from the aspect of circulation of goods and services or as an activity for the investment of surpluses, with no consideration of its principal role is in the sphere of capital reproduction" (ibid., p. 93♣). In the light of these observations, which are generally correct if we discount the error (which reflects that of the other theorists criticized) of not giving due importance to political and ideological determinants which constitute the mass media, Zinser presents Arriaga's position as an alternative.

According to Arriaga, mass media originates from "the need for advertising to find appropriate channels that allow it to fulfill its function within capitalist dynamics"; she thus overestimates the role of advertising and underestimates the function of propaganda and the determinant needs of the state with regard to mass media systems. This indicates ignorance of the European case and displays an extremely erroneous, economicist view of the phenomenon of mass media under capitalism. By discounting the contribution made by political theorists of the mass media theorists, Zinser, in common with Arriaga, ends up making the opposite mistake of underestimating the political and ideological determinants of the Culture Industry, restricting his contribution to the function of the media in the accumulation process while neglecting the function linked to the ideological reproduction of the system of which they offer only a partial, limited explanation.

Advertising and obtaining added value

Following Baran & Sweezy's critiques that I recently summarized, I now turn to the work of Maria Arminda do Nascimento Arruda, who seeks to explain the relationship between monopoly capitalism and advertising. Like Smythe, she begins by citing the *Introduction to a Critique of Political Economy* (penultimate paragraph of item 2.c) in which Marx explains the reciprocity of action that takes place between moments of production, distribution, change and consumption, taken as "an organic whole" (Marx, 1859, p. 115 ff.). She subsequently cites another well-known passage from the *Introduction,* also cited by Smythe, in which Marx argues that "production does not only create an object for the subject, but also a subject for the object" (ibid., p. 110), and goes on to aver that

> Advertising operates visibly within the domain of consumption, although its presence is increasingly perceived in the creation of the actual products. As a component of sales sector planning, its importance increases the more complex the productive structure becomes and generates not only diversification but especially the existence of similar products. Thus, the role of advertising is to introduce a greater "certainty" of consumption
>
> (Arruda, 1985, p. 46♣)

The process of concentration and centralization of capital leads from early to monopoly capitalism while expanding the segment of workers not linked directly to the productive process, diversifying their wage scales and creating a broad consumer market. At the same time this process eliminates price competition, replacing it with product diversification and differentiation as means of engaging big business in competitive struggle. Advertising acts as a link between the differentiation and diversification of monopoly capital and the existence of that large "new middle class" whose desire to consume forms part of capitalist enterprises' business plans. While it is true on the other hand that "implicit determinants in the process of the creation of advertising intrinsically penetrate the productive structure", mainly reflected in product design, Arruda states clearly that she is not attributing to advertising "[...] responsibility for the generation of consumer needs", since "the 'possibilities' of consumption are present in the specific form assumed by production", and the "generating matrix of 'needs' that, are therefore historically situated" (ibid., p. 47).

> [...] But equally we cannot disagree with Galbraith who argues that needs only become susceptible to manipulation by advertising because their nature is not one of urgency. Advertising firms are planting in fertile ground, in which the sophisticated goods of modern society proliferate and where the basic elements for survival have long since been satisfied.
>
> (Ibid., p. 47)

The author's "core idea" is that, in monopoly capitalism,

> [...] advertising, together with the growth of consumer credit, helps to shorten the time of goods circulation, accelerates capital turnover and reinforces consumer needs. It becomes in this way the spokesperson for production, while the availability of credit facilitates the step from "need" to "satisfaction".
>
> (Ibid., p. 49)

Contrary to Arriaga's solution, the one presented by Arruda correctly defines the link between the moments of production and circulation, without underestimating that advertising must be understood within the added value realization context. Thus, in monopoly capitalism, the huge scale of production, by increasing the mass of values produced, naturally goes on to increase the mass of added value to be realized – which demands even higher circulation costs. At the same time, the rigidity of the organization of that expanded production and the strong links between different oligopolistic companies limit the possibility of changes in the production scheme, since all localized crises can spread to the entire system. Under these conditions, the productive structure must operate at high levels of productivity, with initiatives to support research and diversify production gaining importance in order to reduce the risks of being unable to produce the required goods. Arruda also points out, citing Marx, that even without creating value or added value, mercantile capital, by shortening circulation time, contributes to the added value produced by industrial capital.

> for production organized in the monopolistic mould, less circulation time of goods is fundamental, otherwise, the possibility increases

> of generating crises. More explicitly, if conditions are not created to reduce the period of circulation, it will be difficult to sustain a productive structure operating at "optimal" level. Since advertising focuses on maintaining demand via the dynamization of consumption, it can help shorten the moment of circulation; it abbreviates the reproduction process, enabling it to be restarted at another level.
>
> (Ibid., p. 62)

Thus, by contributing to increasing the number of rotations of all industrial capital, advertising contributes to increasing economic added value, the profit amount and, *ceteris paribus,* the rate of profit. Advertising is an indispensable element for capitalism in its monopoly phase.

Setting aside Arriaga's above-mentioned specific critiques of the advertising function, she is without doubt correct to note that advertising effectively brands itself in relation to the consumer goods sector. The question is not, however, as straightforward as it seems. Later in this study I will define an "expanded sector of differentiated consumer goods", which includes even industries producing serial capital goods, and inputs such as tractors and other agricultural implements that have been increasingly employing advertising, given that these are oligopolized sectors targeting a large number of producers.

We can argue in parallel that consumer goods-producing industries that are characterized by homogeneity (i.e. non-differentiated) are not part of that group of industries possessing an advertising action strategy. In a concise and well-executed analysis about the American advertising sector, Arriaga (ibid., p. 41–49) notes that the top advertisers are diversified businesses (with several product lines) that have expanded internationally. These are leaders in the consumer goods sector with an organic composition of capital greater than the average of the sector (ibid., p. 48). In other words, the large oligopolistic companies that adopt product differentiation strategies exercise price leadership in the fairly concentrated markets in which they operate, and are precisely the leading businesses in the sectors for which Baran & Sweezy's observations on the changes in the form of competition are valid.

4
The Political Economy of Communication and Culture

The second half of the 1970s saw the birth in Europe of a new critical economy of communications and culture. Richeri's 1983 publication is a collection of foundational literature on the subject. It brings together the work of Smythe and Cesareo (as previously discussed), a revised version of Garnham's classic article (1979a) and various other important texts. The question of the economy of the media is raised across Europe at this time, in reaction to the massive technological changes occurring in the audiovisual world – changes that were to completely transform the face of Western European television by the end of the 1980s.

I will limit my discussion here to the main works produced by a core group of economists who formed the research hub at Grenoble (France), or their close associates. Clearly, this is only a subset of the whole output of French research into the communications and culture economy.[1]

The French school (second generation)

The French school in this subject is centred around the GRESEC (Research Group on Communication Issues, Stendhal University, Grenoble). In 1978, this group published a research paper *Capitalisme et Industries Culturelles* (Capitalism and Cultural Industries). At the outset the authors define their contribution as being an alternative, not only to the views of the neoclassical economists (as represented by Thénevin) but also to state monopoly capitalism, which was supported by the PCF (French Communist Party), and to Baran & Sweezy's classic theories on advertising. They highlight the two common points of these three approaches: (a) no explanation is given for the "evolutionary process of cultural needs based on economic, political and ideological class relationships" (Huet et al., 1978, p. 19); and (b) all three come from "a market perspective: each is based on the assumption that there would be a 'spontaneous demand' for cultural products, which would impact the production systems. Cultural production would simply be naturally stimulated to meet the requirements of this demand", so that studying it would be no more than "banal sectoral research" (ibid.).

The authors believe that, on the contrary, "supply and demand are two complementary aspects of the process of capital valorisation within the field of cultural production" (ibid.). They place their research "within the framework of the analysis of production and reproduction of capital". In other words, contrary to Adorno and Benjamin, who the authors later criticize, they are of the opinion that a work of art has no value in itself; rather, its use value "is closely linked to the nature of social relations" (Huet et al., 1978, p. 20).

It is certain that this change in research orientation, away from the market and towards production, is of major importance. At the time it was produced, this work answered an urgent need for a more in-depth analysis of communications mass media and cultural production. But there are two major problems with the position that the authors take. On the one hand, they mistakenly identify market analysis with neoclassical analysis. For example, they state:

> An analysis in terms of the market does not seem relevant to us. To consider the Culture Industry only as the meeting point between supply and demand for cultural products cannot provide any insight into the conditions that lead to the birth and development of cultural production during social formation. This approach leads to the usual problems with neoclassical analysis. It reduces the study of the Culture Industry to a simple identification of the conditions to be fulfilled in order to provide maximum satisfaction to demanders and suppliers of goods that answer a predetermined need: the "cultural need".
>
> (Huet et al., 1978, p. 31)

The authors offer as an alternative an "analysis of the conditions of valorisation across a specific set of cultural products, whose social use cannot be defined independently of their conditions of production". This can only happen in the context of an industry considered to provide a specific production process for a given category of goods or services, which are unified by a shared work process (ibid.).

The authors' production analysis is, without any doubt, far more valid than the neoclassical approach, which they rightly condemn. They fail to realize, however, that it does not go beyond a sectoral perspective. It is unable to take into account the full spectrum of political, economic and social factors that are required in order to understand fully the role of the Culture Industry in the process of production and reproduction. This weakness, obvious throughout the book, is an aspect of a problem shared by the whole French school when trying to carry out a non-neoclassical analysis of this field. It is precisely from this angle that I approached my original criticism of the French school (Bolaño, 1993), and I will try and go into it more deeply in the next chapter.

It is only at the end of the book that the authors make another timid attempt to formulate a theoretical alternative to Marxist political analyses, affirming the need to direct research efforts towards the specific forms of economic determinism within the superstructure. They later add: "the interest of the study of the capitalist integration of cultural production does not, however, reside mainly in the operation of one particular field of production". The relationships and interactions found at this level are in fact involved in "a more fundamental process, which is that of the increased reproduction of capital". Here, the specifics of cultural production are relevant only to the extent that they relate to the "general laws that govern [the reproduction of capital]". In this way, they join a "more complex dialectic, that of the ideological reproduction of social relations, in which culture is not reduced simply to a means of capital valorisation" (Huet et al., 1978, p. 169 ff.).

The question is well enough formulated, but what it actually achieves is to highlight the limitations of the authors' own analysis throughout the whole book, which focuses on culture as a field of capital valorization. I will come back to this later. All I shall say for now is that it is only at this end point that the authors return to the theme of how the Culture Industry functions, within both the process of capital accumulation and the ideological reproduction of the system.

The authors basically see the former as a historical evolution. There is an initial stage, during which the increase in production allows new demands from the bourgeois class to be satisfied. This is followed by a second stage that allows increased consumption and the growth of cultural property to spread to other social layers and to the proletariat itself. This movement is based on the growing exploitation of labour and tends to strengthen capital's dominance over it, to the extent that "the scope of one's needs can only grow in line with the increase in one's level of consumption... Cultural goods are goods like any others, a new field for the extension of exchange value, for the extraction of surplus value" (Huet et al., 1978, p. 172). Goods and cultural services "participate in the expanded reproduction of capital, increasingly involved in the realisation of value" (ibid., p. 173). Note that not a word is said about the problem of advertising and its role in the process of capital accumulation. The authors' solution to the first issue remains far inferior to the contributions that we had occasion to appreciate in the last chapter.

Their comments on the "ideological reproduction of social relations" are limited to some observations on fairly specific issues, such as: the "demonstration effect" (correctly clarifying that a logic of exclusion is also in force here, since certain cultural goods and services have difficulty penetrating the lower classes); the ideology of the democratization of cultural consumption; the productivist theories of the PCF; how the dominant ideology controls the integration of cultural labour, through the application of pressure and filters in the cultural production industry; and how, on the other hand, the degree of freedom that the Culture Industry gives to the expression of anti-establishment ideas is dependent on the extent to which cultural investment is based on profit, or on non-commercial cultural action. Note that the latter, although ideologically opposed to industrialized culture, is also unable to stop serving it, both by acting as a "nursery" to a cultural labour force and by creating openings that will allow subsequent cultural market penetration of this labour force. However interesting some of these observations may be, they shed no light on the question of the relationship between the Culture Industry and the ideological reproduction of society (nor do the authors make any claim to the contrary).

But this level of analysis is not the most interesting part of the GRESEC's first book. What is interesting is their investigation of the processes used in the cultural field: both production and invested capital valorization processes. According to the authors, the existing notions of goods and services fail to provide a proper classification of cultural outputs. Being "defined on the basis of the material substance of the product", "they can only serve to 'designate' and 'classify' commercial products according to their external qualities". They should in fact start from the circulation of capital and the "requirements arising from its operation and reproduction".

The core concept then becomes that of value and, "more accurately, exchange value, which comes back to the fundamental distinction between productive[2] and unproductive[3] labour" (Huet et al., 1978, p. 23). In the former, labour is part of capitalist cultural production; in the latter, it is the inverse, being part of the non-capitalist production of cultural goods. The authors add to these a third type of labour, "indirectly productive". It does not contribute to production, but to the realization of value, which includes all the work effort spent on the integration of cultural products into the circulation of capital – *cultural labour*. The key feature of cultural labour is that the work process is not homogeneous, since production output is the fruit of two distinct processes: the creative design of the original work by one or more cultural workers; and the physical reproduction of that original work (a split that Zallo called the non-unity of the work process, 1988).[4]

> At the present stage of control that we have over artistic use value manufacturing processes, we cannot yet reduce the labour effort to abstract enough terms for the exchange of artistic products to be to subject the law of value (unlike certain other forms of conceptual work in the industrial or architectural domains). The artistic product, even when being physically reproduced, nevertheless remains atypical because its use value is in fact that of a *unique product*. So, we could say that a song performed by an unknown singer does not exist socially; but the same one sung by a *vedette* (pop star) is enjoyed and demanded by millions; that version is in effect "unique"... Methods may emerge [that enable] a rational creation process, constantly evolving to approach a true industrial mode, including wage labour. What remains important in the mass production of works of art, however, is to keep the illusion of singularity. There must be substitutes to compensate for the loss of this perceived and material uniqueness. The "star" is one of those substitutes.
>
> (Huet et al., 1978, p. 99)[5]

That is why the Culture Industry is a sector that, although it can be part of the creation and realization of value, does not lend itself well to the valorization of capital: in the eyes of the consumer, the cultural product is stamped with the personality of the workers who participated in its creation. This specificity in cultural production, this feature of uniqueness of cultural products, is a constituent part of its use value. This has three consequences:

The "unpredictability of valorisation" (Flichy, 1980); the "difficulties of valorisation" (Miège et al., 1986); and finally, the existence of "uncertain use values" (Huet et al., 1978).

This feature of cultural products is presented in all these works as an empirically observable reality, without any additional compelling theoretical explanation. In those terms, Flichy states the problem most clearly:

> there is no other category of consumer goods whose producers are so ignorant of the demand, to the point of being forced to do ten or

> fifteen trials to get a success. In the music industry, for example, for two similar products, sales may vary from one to a million. If cultural production seems like such a gamble, it is because each product is unique by definition.
>
> (Flichy, 1980, p. 38)

Flichy later points out that the *useful life* of the majority of cultural products is limited to a period of a few months to a year. A small number can greatly exceed this period; this depends on the strategy used, such us creating catalogues or distribution planning, as is done in the film industry, for example (ibid., p. 55).[6]

The GRESEC, as Zallo points out (1988, p. 4 ff.), deliberately confuses valorization (linked essentially to the characteristics of the labour process that develops from the moment capital begins to take an interest in cultural production), with realization of value. It is clear that demand affects subsequent requirements on production; it also influences the rate of profit, making it deviate from the rate of surplus value or provoking cross-sector capital transfer, etc. But none of this alters the fact that the characteristic unpredictability of cultural industries stems from a *randomness of production*. From that point of view, it is certainly more severe in cultural production than in other economic sectors.

That is why an ongoing need exists to find ways to control it. The authors of this first work from the GRESEC identify the following methods: (1) the creation of catalogues; (2) the creation of "artist nurseries" (or as I prefer to say, a Culture Industry reserve army). These additionally fulfil the requirement for constant creative renewal, which in turn is due to the characteristic of uniqueness that goods must have in this sector; (3) the control of distribution networks by monopoly capital. This gives capital control over, on the one hand, small independent producers; and on the other, the organization and rationalization of end-product distribution. This is not to say that distribution controls production, since "this trend corresponds to imperatives of profitability, which directly concern manufacturers, who in turn also invest in distribution" (Huet et al., 1978, p. 148). This pattern is obvious in France, as much so in books (Hachette) as in the cinema (Gaumont, Paramount France, UGC), or in the recording industry (Phonogram, Pathe-Marconi); (4) the use of sales promotional techniques; (5) the use of specialized distribution outlets for products targeted at the public with the highest purchasing power or higher levels of education (art books, classical recordings, modern literature); (6) the actions of the ideological apparatus of the state, which is both a direct customer of, and educator of the public for, the cultural market. It participates in launching and sustaining new markets (such as the introduction of audiovisual media in French schools) and even provides the venues and opportunities for commercial promotion of Culture Industry products (via the communications network, especially radio and public TV; libraries; cultural institutions); and (7) mail-order sales, which seek to leverage the distinctive effect that certain ostentatious goods acquire.

The "limits of reproducibility"

A characteristic of the Culture Industry is that the original prototype, which conforms to the principle of uniqueness, can have different levels of reproducibility. A work must have a distinguishing feature, making it unique. For example, within the art prints market, limited editions are a base element of the use value, which follows the "logic of numbering and 'authenticity' "; or, in the end, the logic of the mass production of cultural goods whose reproducibility also has limits. According to the authors, there are three types of limiting factor: financial (linked to the purchasing power of the different social layers); cultural (to the extent that certain products, to be consumed, require the consumer to have knowledge of a specific cultural code); and politico-economic (linked to the ability of producers from a "metropolis" to extend their influence to broader areas).[7]

The "diversity of the conditions of valorisation" (Miège et al., 1986) or the existence of "highly diversified economic structures" (Huet et al., 1978)

A characteristic of cultural production is the particular link that exists between the phases of the process of valorization and the specific role of distribution in the *circulation of capital*. The capital cycle is itself differentiated, in content industries, by two factors: first, the divide between design production and product reproduction (as we saw, product reproduction requires an editing process, "the specific change process through which, in the world of capitalist production, cultural labour is transformed into reproducible goods"); and second, the crucial importance of distribution, given the unpredictability of the creative side.

To this we can add the particular conditions of access to the labour force: capital is obliged to maintain relations with an artistic world that it often cannot simply bring to submission through wage labour. The demand for uniqueness and the difficulty that capital has in subsuming artistic work beyond a certain point, mean that *salaried employment* is only one facet of the relationship between capital and cultural producers. In parallel, artisanal production and piece-work continue, with the consequence that 90% of the professionals in the sector cannot live from their work, and are particularly prone to excessive exploitation. This in turn coexists with a star system, sometimes institutionalized through royalty payments, made up of millionaire stars and superstars. The bulk of the income from this sector, according to the authors, nevertheless remains in the editorial and distribution activities. Twenty per cent of the market remains in the hands of independent producers who self-publish.

In addition to that, the Culture Industry is characterized by the *coexistence of multiple distinct production relations.* Concentrated monopoly capital, multinational capital, small investors and artisanal production all live side by side. What is more, this coexistence cannot, according to the authors, be considered as a survival of archaic forms that will tend to disappear with the development of capitalism and the associated processes of concentration and centralization of capital. On the contrary, they are "constituent elements of the structure of valorisation of cultural products in monopolistic capitalism". In this way, "these supposedly 'archaic' structures simply occupy a particular place in the system of cultural production, as articulated and controlled by monopoly capital". This monopoly capital invests in certain branches of the industry, primarily distribution, leaving "the non-capitalist sector to carry out product design and creation and to take on the risk of the transformation of use value into exchange value" (Huet et al., 1978, p. 28).

Finally, cultural production lacks unified conditions of capital valorization: "the question of the value of a piece of unique artwork or of the activity of an artist is . . . a false problem, since there is no comparison possible with socially necessary work, and there are no average production conditions on which to base calculations" (ibid., p. 136). But the authors then take the recording industry as an example of the transformation of a cultural product into merchandisable goods; this industry is notable for its impressive standardization (or normalization) and collectivization of the work carried out in the creation of popular music. They conclude that

> Being increasingly collective, the process of production of cultural goods becomes a somewhat banalised production process, using relatively interchangeable work forces. This is so marked that one could hypothesise that this evolution will lead to the emergence of generalised production processes, in the sense that most of the

> types of work carried out can be reduced to a certain quantum of abstract labour.
>
> (Huet et al., 1978, p. 136)

Based on this, the *law of value* could be *partially applied* to cultural production. It would be characterized, on the one hand, by the possibility of valorization independently from production costs; and on the other, by the uncertainty of the transformation of concrete labour into abstract social labour.

> It would seem, then, that whilst cultural production is unable to escape the general laws of capitalist production (existence of general conditions governing production processes), it yet remains an important sector where the conditions of valorisation are very uncertain. Without doubt, this is what the development of speculative activity and the presence of small investors are due to.
>
> (Huet et al., 1978, p. 137)

Only two years after the appearance of the GRESEC's first book, Patrice Flichy published a new work (1980). Working independently from, but very closely with, the Grenoble school, he outlined for the first time the now widely accepted distinction between the *publishing industries* (literary, recording and audiovisual, including film), producers of cultural commodities, and what he called the "*culture de flot*", which is translated into English as "flow culture". The term "*flot*" is translated literally as "flow", given that its aim is to make it clear that it is not about a flux or stream, a distinction that is lost in English. Here, I will refer to "wave culture". Flichy (1980, p. 38) includes radio, television and the press in that definition, always using television as his paradigm.[8] Flichy identifies four features characterizing wave culture: the *continuity* of programming; very broad *coverage*; the instant *obsolescence* of the product;[9] and *state intervention* in the industry's organization (ibid., p. 55).

The state wishes to have control over this sector because it is an intersection point between culture and information, which makes it an ideological vehicle. Although Flichy does not go further into the subject, it is worth highlighting this brief comment as it is a penetrating insight into the relationship between culture and information, and the ideological role of the latter (characterized, as previously discussed, by a contradiction between the two generalized forms, advertising and propaganda). It emphasizes the wave culture's particularity: its central place in the Culture Industry as a whole on the one side, and, as Flichy says, its particular importance to the state on the other.

Further down the same page, Flichy clarifies the difference between cultural goods and the *culture de flot* by analysing the self-promotion that each does. In cultural product promotion what you see is the star, the singer, the actor, the filmmaker. Television, the paradigm of the *culture de flot,* uses unified programming to deliver "broadcasts that can include cultural goods"; its self-promotion aims at advertising the network or station (and only secondarily the "star"). This is obviously due to the particularity of wave culture, which forces the company to create and push a self-image in order to gain and retain audience loyalty. That is another insight Flichy has offered us, this time on the topic of competition; a subject that the French school I am discussing here mostly ignores, as we shall see later.

The GRESEC takes up and develops the distinction between the production of cultural commodities, the publishing industry and wave culture in their second major contribution, (Miège et al., 1986). This was written in the middle of the major restructuring process that the audiovisual sector was going through, especially the French television market. The end of this upheaval still looked a long way off and the outcome was mostly unpredictable. Within this context, the authors' methodology initially favours the analysis of what they call "social logics". They seek first to define a theoretical characterization of the different economic models around which cultural production is built; and second, to investigate the strategies being used by the key actors involved in this structural change. From this, the authors define five "social logics": cultural goods publishing/editing; the wave culture; written information; news and information production; and the broadcasting of live performances (including sporting events). The classification is based essentially on the production and labour processes specific to each sector, intentionally leaving to one side any other possible factors (Miège et al., 1986, p. 61).[10]

The authors retain Flichy's definition of *flot* (he in turn sticks to the definition of cultural goods given in the GRESEC's first volume), focusing on two elements that they consider to be essential: "the interface between the fields of culture and information" and "the need for programming continuity and constant product renewal and, therefore, the need to produce programmes with infallible regularity" (Miège et al., 1986, p. 68). On the first point, however, they confine themselves to commenting that wave culture products are mostly informational, with little interface to the field of culture (a claim that is, shall we say, at the very least questionable); and that the introduction of the so-called "new media" of mass communication should create increased market segmentation. There is no progress here compared with the ideas of Flichy (who, as I pointed out earlier, did not go further into this interesting point, either). The authors are more interested in the second question, which they consider is causing an increase in *rediffusion* (repeat broadcasts), in order to meet the problem of the supply shortage in the so-called "new media" (the authors specifically mention cable television and pay-to-view television).

Additionally, given the difficulties that local and regional stations have in delivering a full programme of their own productions,[11] there is a tendency towards concentration and centralization of production and distribution activities. A market structure of that kind, where there is such strong emphasis on production and distribution, and such a broad spectrum of customer types (local, national and regional terrestrial TVs; cable and satellite TV; film and video distributors; cinemas), obviously reinforces and encourages distribution planning and rationalization. That is precisely the strategy that the industry pioneers adopted to reduce the risks arising from production unpredictability and to maximize the commercial exploitation of each work, leading to the increase in repeats and multiple broadcasting. In other words: "the obsolescence of wave culture products will become less certain: strangely enough, everything will tend towards wave culture producing merchandisable wares, or at the very least, products that can be reused many times, such as a copy of a film" (Miège et al., 1986, p. 69).

I do not wish to deny the existence of this trend, but it is necessary to clarify its actual behaviour. As we shall see later, repeat broadcasting does not interest radio stations and networks with a large-scale mass-market strategy, other than in special cases (and always with restrictions), such as Canal Plus in Europe. Canal Plus shows the same film at different times, aiming to attract a larger audience, although each broadcast may have a relatively small number of viewers. Here, too, we can identify a strategy focusing on segmentation. Companies whose strategic target is prime time viewing, on the other hand, are only interested in repeats to fill in less important time slots in their daily programme schedules. Obviously, this does not change the fact that smaller companies are financially obliged to adopt segmentation strategies, including repeat broadcasting.

Whatever the case, the fact that it can be rebroadcast does not reduce the perishable nature of the *flot*; only that of the individual programme. That is nothing new. The global expansion of the major American studios always followed this pattern: generating stock footage for the large distributors, who created large catalogues and sold the screening rights to different markets. But it has never been possible to negotiate the rights on perishable goods. Multiple broadcasting is born out of the actual structure of the programme schedule, which I will analyse later. It generally follows the stock product pattern, the one important exception being the live performance, whose characteristics make it as perishable as wave culture. Sporting events are an extreme case: while one musical event can be based on the same editorial production practices as another, coverage of sports events is much more like a news programme, and only has very limited re-use value.

As previously stated, this does not refute the authors' assertion; it simply qualifies it. They are themselves aware of the problem: "Wave products and cultural goods are therefore tending to converge. This does not imply, however, that either one loses any of its specificity: together they make up the two possible [alternative] evolutionary paths of the new media" (Miège et al., 1986, p. 70). Or, further on, "One could say that the broadcasting industries provide an opportunity for the editorial and the wave models to meet and confront each other" (ibid., p. 79). This is why broadcasting is the paradigm for all cultural industries. Beyond this, GRESEC II identifies the press as a third paradigm. They contend that "Canal Plus and other future cable and satellite offerings (programme on demand, subscriptions, etc.) open the way for a third logic, which is similar to the logic of the press"[12] (ibid., p. 199). These three paradigms are therefore of major importance across all five previously identified "social logics". The authors' summarized feature list is given in the table below.

Salaun (1987) presents the historic make-up of each of these paradigms as a series of economic models (first editorial, then the press and finally wave culture) with a "dual dynamic", characterized on the one hand by an acceleration of economic activity in the sector of information and culture, and on the other by the distance between the user and the economic cycle (Salaun, 1987, p. 355). While recognizing that the GRESEC was not attempting a full categorization of all cultural industries, it has to be said that their vision seems to have been limited, certainly as regards television, to a purely French-centric viewpoint. Be that as it may, the importance of this first structured classification of the Culture Industry cannot be denied. It is from this one that more comprehensive taxonomies will be developed; Zallo's, for example, as previously referenced (Table 4.1).

Table 4.1 General trends of economic models in use in cultural and information production

	EDITORIAL (Book, album, video and cinema)	**WAVE (Radio and television)**	**PRESS (Newspaper and magazine)**
General characteristics	A set of cultural goods made up of individual works. Purchase drivers are personal pleasure (artistic, entertainment) or "branding", displaying membership of a cultural group (fashion trends, fads).	Continuous wave of daily transmissions, gain and maintain audience loyalty. Domestic and family audience, leisure-time planning. Wide variety of consumers in a mass market.	A range of products, regular and one-off purchases (big stories). Personal choice, linked to social, territorial, cultural or political relevance (lifestyle).
Leading role	PUBLISHER: selects works, selects design and creative teams; organizes production and reproduction.	PRODUCER: defines programming; manages internal production, external production and purchases.	EDITOR: chooses stories to run and page layout; organizes news coverage; is responsible for the content.
Economic chain	Production is sporadic, often by small companies without fixed capital. The teams are small and change with each new production. Jobs are temporary. Creative designers are paid through the royalties and copyright system. Infrastructure (studios, workshops, presses, printing) is shared.	The wave needs an almost industrial organization to feed it. Series have a key place in the shape of: [a] integrated production (live shows, news, documentary series, games, entertainment . . .); [in this case] jobs are regular, cross-product, planned and supplemented by temporary staff;	Importance of the design team to ensure regular news coverage. Low production costs but high creative, reproduction and broadcasting costs. Generally wage labour, supplemented by some piece-work (single articles). Affiliation to news agencies. Distribution through a collectively organized physical

Table 4.1 (Continued)

	EDITORIAL (Book, album, video and cinema)	**WAVE (Radio and television)**	**PRESS (Newspaper and magazine)**
	The financing of important productions is often complex (presales, participation levels, co-production). High-cost distribution networks of specialized shops and galleries. Distribution often has a strong influence on production.	materials and infrastructures often belong to the stations; [b] a subcontracted external production team for the more expensive series, whose organization is midway between the wave and the editorial models; or [c] broadcast rights purchased en bloc from catalogues, or permanent exchanges between channels. May have recourse to permanent direction teams to lead the design. Wage labour is the norm, but this is sometimes supplemented by the royalty/copyright system. Broadcasting costs are relatively low and its economic organization remains largely outside of the control of the programme industries.	network Nouvelles Messageries de la Presse (NMPP). Sales through often non-specialized distributors.
Design and creative roles	Actors, composers, film-makers, artists and performers. Specialized technicians. Wide variety of payment methods. Specialized performance employment agencies and agents. Very uncertain temporary employment ("nurseries" and small companies).	Authors, journalists, entertainers, performers, directors and specialized technicians. Long- and medium-term contracts (internal and external production).	Journalists and specialized technicians. Relies on interlinked networks of contacts (internal, correspondents, agencies, etc.).

Sales/revenue	Direct sales by individual product. Revenue proportionate to the public reached. The proportional system goes up the whole economic chain.	Indirect revenue (licence fees, advertising), global. Knowledge of audience ratings is very important. Licence and advertising revenue are managed by outside agencies, clearly separated from production.	Semi-direct revenue: retail and subscription sales, advertising.
Market characteristics	Segmented mass market. Individual purchase of an artistic work or rights of entry. "Hit or catalogue" dialectic compensates for the very random nature of commercial success.	Indirect and undifferentiated mass market. Hardware-linked (radio, television). Wave of instant obsolescence. Needs to retain and optimise the audience. Hence the importance of programme scheduling.	Segmented mass market. Personal reading experience. Loyalty. Dependence on news.

Source: Extract from Miège et al., 1986, p.80 ff.

The authors predict an increase of market segmentation and multicasting due to the emergence of the so-called new media. This will have a two-pronged effect on the film industry: on one hand, segmentation and the multiplication of media have a negative impact on cinemas (in the wake of television, cinema will have to face Canal Plus and its ilk, cable and satellite TV, and home recording, all major new competitors); on the other, the increased choice of media and growth of multicast strategies benefit film producers and the major distributors (Miège et al., 1986, p. 96 ff.). But the authors consider that rising demand will also have consequences: work processes will be impacted, given that the resources available to do the work will not increase in proportion to the demand. This issue will bring to the fore the question of *productivity*, leading to ever more "streamlined" production management, from the plot outline right through to broadcast. The authors consider that this trend was already visible at the time the book was written: in the preference for video over film in popular series production; the tendency to record in studios rather than external locations; and the use of *découpage* or other means to reduce shooting and post-production time (ibid., p. 110). In this book, though, the GRESEC do not yet develop the theme of the relationship between art and the economy in the cultural industries. That will soon be taken up by Salaun (1989), expanding on Flichy's insights, as we saw in the first chapter (see also Bolaño, 2004, Chapter 3).

Flichy additionally describes the main features of the *market structures* of the different communication sectors. Since the end of the 1950s, the electronics and photochemical industries had been going through a process of concentration, which transformed the originally broad market competition into an oligopoly dominated by a very small number of firms (Flichy, 1980, p. 139). Meanwhile, the record and film sectors had been highly concentrated from the outset, a few big companies dominating a large number of small ones, although these still occupied a non-negligible position (ibid., p. 140). By contrast, in literary publishing, market concentration started at the end of the 19th century and rose sharply in the 1960s (ibid., p. 150). The end result is, however, that both the *culture de flot* and telecommunications display a "strong monopolistic tendency which the state counters by setting merger limits or by nationalising the sector" (ibid., p. 140).

Flichy gives the example of film production in the USA, where market concentration has remained remarkably stable since 1925. On the eve of World War II, the market was dominated by eight "majors", (Paramount, 20th Century Fox, Metro Goldwyn Mayer, RKO and Warner Bros. in the top rank, followed by Columbia, Universal and United Artists). RKO ceased production in 1950 and Metro reduced their activities at the beginning of the 1960s, so that the number of large enterprises was reduced to six; meanwhile five new companies appeared on the market (Disney, MGM, Avco, Embassy, American International and Allied Artists). That was the situation as at the end of the 1970s: these 11 studios were responsible for 93% of sector activity in the USA The five largest had a 66% share of turnover in 1970, increasing to 68% in 1976.

It is a little different in the music industry, where the top five labels (which have not changed since the 1950s) share 59% of the market in France, 65% in Germany and 60% in the USA, according to studies carried out at end of the 1970s. In the UK, Decca and EMI dominated the market from 1930 to 1965. From that point, with the expansion of pop music, Decca gave way to CBS, Warner, Polydor and Phonogram. With that, the concentration ratio fell from 87% in 1967 to 58% in 1977. Flichy concludes that:

> Whilst the market concentration of the recording and film industries is old and very strong, it seems to have stabilized at a rate of around 60–70%. When it goes much above that level, as in England in the music industry, monopolies tend to lose their grip on innovation, which breaks away, leading to a reduction in concentration.
>
> (Flichy, 1980, p. 151)

The characteristic make-up of the market in these two industries, and also in literary publishing, is as follows: first, there are rarely more than five or six *major* business groups, generally multinational, vertically integrated across both production and distribution; in the latter, two of them may sometimes form an association. for example, in 1962 Phonogram (Philips) and Polydor (Siemens) created the joint venture, Polygram; similarly, Paramount and Universal created CIC (Cinema International Corporation) for distribution abroad. Second, there are a large number of *independents* (particularly in the music business, which require low investment, so that barriers to entry are small). They rise and fall rapidly, and are heavily dependent on the large labels, through whom they carry out most of their production work; generally, small labels only do the actual artistic activity in-house. Flichy points out that the large businesses also rely on the independents, which act as talent spotters and thereby fill the demand for constant renewal in the sector; so there is a certain balance, although it always works in favour of the major labels. You find the same balance in American cinema, between the majors and the independent studios.

> Parallel to their in-house production, the majors "sponsor" certain independent films. In these instances, they take charge of distribution and front part of the production costs. In return, the producer has final artistic control. This system allows them to discover and siphon off new talent at lower cost.
>
> (Flichy, 1980, p. 152)[13]

Finally, there are the *medium-sized* concerns, which have the potential to be part of the top group. They do not have an international distribution network, or only a limited one. If they do move into the top bracket, however, they become transnationals. Small businesses rarely grow to be medium-sized. It can happen in cases where a company is working in a specific niche market, such as Motown (black music) or K-tel (reissues). Some medium-sized companies will play an important innovative role, such as A & M in middle-of-the-road rock music. When they have no particular specialization, these medium businesses tend to be bought out by larger ones, as happened in 1979 when EMI bought United Artists' recording arm, and MCA bought the ABC TV network's music branch.

As far as *wave culture* is concerned, Flichy uses examples from US television broadcasting and the changes in Italy following the creation of local radio and TV stations, to show the strong tendency towards market concentration and the fierce competition in the sector. This leads to the double risk of uncontrolled use of radio frequencies and telecommunications networks, and the monopolization of information by a few private groups. In these circumstances, state intervention is required, either to regulate competition or to take over the broadcasting monopoly. But that state action, be it in radio, TV or telecoms, has the disadvantage of formalizing the status of a monopoly (Flichy, 1980, p. 159). Flichy also highlights the current trend towards "horizontal concentration" between the distinct industries of production and the wave, both to leverage certain synergies and as a financial capital agglomeration strategy (bank + industry, bank + bank or industry + industry). This phenomenon, of major importance, is best known today as *media concentration*.

Writing at the dawn of the huge transformation process that would lead to the end of state monopoly in European television markets, from the very first new launches Flichy sees a trend towards an *editorial model*: "the successive appearance, in recent years, of commercial radios, pirate radios and free radios, must also be understood as the creation of centres of innovation sitting outside of the monopoly, similar to the independent studios that we find in the film and recording industries" (ibid., p. 160). With the introduction of the new mass media and the proliferation of cable and satellite TV stations etc., it is pertinent to ask whether there is a tendency in this sector to move towards the market structure, similar to the tendency Flichy defines as characteristic of the editorial sectors. This seems to me to be at least a good working hypothesis.

To round off this critical rereading of the classics of the French school of the communications and culture economy, I cannot leave out the important article that Flichy published in 1984, in partnership with Paul Beaud & Monique Sauvage, "Television as a Cultural Industry" (Beaud et al., 1984). Picking up the distinction between cultural goods and *flot,* the authors draw attention to the importance of the role of programme scheduling. As an essential component of the television production process, its determining element is the "constitution of a continuous time-bound broadcast schedule, which imposes a clear type of programme and audience consumption, day by day, hour by hour" (Beaud et al., 1984, p. 189). On this basis, the relationship each individual programme has to the overall scheduling is more important than the programme itself. A station's schedule is the means by which it ensures continuity, offering several benefits. It helps the audience to stay loyal, avoiding changes to general parameters that affect audience choice, such as times, programme type and popular presenters. It helps the production teams, for whom "the schedule defines a number of product lines, aired at regular intervals, visualised as a number of boxes to be filled". In general terms, the schedule coordinates the range of supply, distributing content and genres across time. Its goal is to attract different audiences depending on the time of broadcast, by tailoring the offer based on audience availability and their expectations of genre and content, according to a "dialectic of audience loyalty/respect for consumer habits".

> This necessary conformity of programme style, bearing in mind the need to guarantee ratings, also makes it imperative to set rules of behaviour for sub-contracted companies, rules that certainly go beyond just production standards (duration, cost and media for each production stage), and that may include artistic or cultural standards (televisual handling of the participants in a debate, acceptable speech, behavioural guidelines, etc.).
>
> (Beaud et al., 1984, p. 190)[14]

For the authors, *innovation* in television occurs only within the limits of the overall planning structure; as well as being limited, as can be imagined, by the audience itself and its acquired audiovisual culture. The very quality (techno-aesthetic) standards themselves thus become a straitjacket when "planning for stability encourages repetitive product lines", to avoid the risks inherent in innovation.[15] Although they make no direct reference to Schumpeter, the authors' clearly Weberian argumentation is entirely compatible with the positive approach to competitivity that can be drawn mainly from the second part of *Capitalism, Socialism and Democracy*. So, given that the TV industry is always oligopolistic or monopolistic, as predicted planning and the economic rationality it implies progress, so the drive to innovate recedes. This does not mean that competition or innovation themselves have disappeared; nevertheless, this aspect of television management tends to be the rule for the whole Culture Industry, where both the production and distribution structures are increasingly centralized and systematised. This makes TV not just the dominant medium, but "the only true Culture Industry", the evolutionary model and paradigm for the entire cultural sector.

Citing a conference Adorno held in 1962 for the Universidad Radiofónica y Televisiva Internacional, Beaud, Flichy & Sauvage point out that, with the advent of television, the concept of *technology* in the Culture Industry changes status: it leaves the restricted field of distribution or mechanical reproduction techniques, as had been originally observed by the theorists of Frankfurt, to become an integral part of a global production process. The field moves from a state of pseudo-cohabitation between craftsmanship and industry, in which "the creator could still maintain an illusory sense of precedence (autonomy)", to an operation in which industrialization touches the entire production process.

Previously the "creatives" interacted with an industrial process essentially limited to production standardization or rationalization of distribution techniques; in the new world, the industry is dominated by a complex techno-economy, which precedes and predefines the production processes. Television itself went through a historic process in which, by means of structural or institutional reforms that introduced the notion of productivity, authority passed from the programme producer to the executive management layer. At least, that is what marks the move to industrial methods within the French and British TV sectors that the authors analysed. In their conclusion, quite frequently quoted, they compare TV to the "more archaic sector of cultural industries":

> Productivity and resource planning complete the process of transformation from craft to industry... [which] also implies a thorough integration of intellectual resources into the production machinery? In the "archaic" cultural industry sector, by contrast, the creator continues overall to sit outside the techno-institutional apparatus. Where the music industry only rarely puts its "communal creatives" on the payroll, television tends to make wage labour the rule... The creator moves from one double-legitimacy (public and micro-media) to another (public and institutional), which introduces a new benchmark into the cultural field.
>
> (Beaud et al., 1984, p. 193)

To use the more accurate Marxian terminology, what makes television the "paradigm of the cultural industry" is this *true subsumption* of what had to date been called "cultural labour", as the GRESEC defined it in their first book. But in terms of Beaud, Flichy & Sauvage, what are the limits to the expansion of the rule of wage labour in the TV industry? Audiovisual production covers a broad spectrum of types of work, whether at the conceptual stage (screenplays, scriptwriting, etc.) or in product build (technical trades, artists, etc.). This gives rise to a whole hierarchy of functions, each group of workers having a different relationship to capital. Technicians are most frequently salaried employees; actors rarely so. The general relationship between actors and capital is, according to the authors, a contract negotiation by product. For singers, the relationship is particularly complex, because in their case TV is principally a promotional vehicle. Other external workers (such as authors and scriptwriters) often appear to be independent, bringing them closer to the "normal situation in the rest of the Culture Industry; however, they are differentiated by having negotiated contracts per job, based on both internal norms and reputation; pay is not linked, as it is often the case elsewhere, to the commercial success of the production" (Beaud et al., 1984, p. 194).

The authors argue, then, that the rationalization of television production operations management is not necessarily based on a separation between salaried and non-salaried work. Instead, they propose the following hypothesis: "All those whose productivity can be measured and planned for are integrated into the institutional apparatus of production; the rest increasingly work on-demand... or are part of a more traditional 'nursery' available to the production company", which in this way seeks a maximum reduction of the risk created by unpredictability (ibid.). That helps to explain the birth and continuation of the super-rich superstar system, which the businesses are forced to maintain. It is precisely the success and notoriety of these artists, journalists and even con artists – in fact, the full range of "media people" – that greatly help to reduce that risk factor. Unfortunately the authors do not make explicit the link between the factors that limit subsumption of cultural labour, and the need for an empathic relationship between the cultural worker and the public to valorise capital. This need highlights the importance of the symbolic element to the sector's economic structure, a topic I will discuss in more detail in the next chapter.

Returning to the question of rationalization, the authors consider that in the European audiovisual sector, the "logic of industrialization" has led to the "political rationale" being replaced by an "economic rationale". Scheduling in the "political rationale" or "politico-culture" is state-policy driven, and staffing relies on the civil service. In the "economic rationale", scheduling is driven by the economy, and staffing needs are met through salaried employees or long-term contracts. This pattern is also present in other nationalized sectors of the economy when they are going through a process of privatization or deregulation. Until the 1960s, European television mainly fulfilled the political function of, to quote Louis Quéré, "daily reinforcement of the references by which individuals recognise themselves as members of society". It also met goals of cultural democratization by, to quote Thibeau, "re-stating facts in a way that conforms to official truths", "strengthening the social link" and "ensuring visibility of the governing power". To achieve this, over the years the state built a "formidable production apparatus" that reached the whole population, with the aim of ensuring uniformity in programme policy. From the 1970s, the need to control an ever-growing industrial setup and the introduction of advertising and competition between broadcasters led to the gradual dominance of the economic rationale, increasing market segmentation and programme diversity. From that point on, "industrial culture" prevails, as organizations seek to respond effectively to public demand and maximize audience.

And so it is that "behind the purely empirical distinction between public and private television, lie two different expressions of two rationales, one of an economic nature, the other political and cultural" (Beaud et al., 1984, p. 198 and s.). This observation clearly points to the need for the kind of theoretical development that I sought in the early chapters of this book. In these I discussed, among other things, the contradictions that exist between capital and the state in the Culture Industry; and different forms of advertising and information as "propaganda". It was this analysis that led us to the question of the workings of the Culture Industry, which I shall conclude later. But it is not only in this that the work of Beaud, Flichy & Sauvage supports the theoretical framework that I'm looking to develop here. The authors proceed to refer to the communications and culture economy, stating:

> By focussing essentially on production economy, they too often disregard the question, not so much of the social promulgation of Culture Industry products – that was not their subject – but more that of their dual nature: the same production process is both a meaning-maker and a creator of symbolic value that is not just a value-add, but is an integral part of the end-product's consumable potential.
>
> (Beaud et al., 1984, p. 201)

It was precisely these kinds of concerns that I sought to answer in my articles in 1993 and 1995(a), to which I shall return later. It is worth noting that as early as 1981 (when Beaud, Flichy & Sauvage carried out their project, as quoted by Miège et al., 1986) the foundations (albeit somewhat shaky) of a critical analysis of the communications and culture economy were already laid; and yet to date the French school has not made any attempt to reposition its findings. It is imperative for the school to be able to go beyond its fundamentally sector-based position. Unless it incorporates political, economic and social considerations, as the authors of the GRESEC's first paper sought to do, it will remain incapable of presenting itself as a credible alternative to the neoclassical school, the FCP's (French Communist Party) view or those of Baran & Sweezy. This issue is not addressed by the second generation of research that, in one way or another, follows the lines drawn by Grenoble, even if it undeniably makes significant progress, as we shall see.

French school (second generation)

Neither of the authors reviewed below is a member of the GRESEC. Alain Herscovici comes from another lineage: that of Baumol's French following, especially as influenced by the Parisian Dominique Leroy, responsible for the most authoritative study published on the performing arts in France (Leroy, 1980, 1990). Herscovici not only incorporates the progress made by the Grenoble school, but also seeks to place his own contribution within that theoretical framework. In his turn, Spaniard Ramon Zallo (cf.) carried out what is, in my view, still the most profound critique from inside the French school of communication and culture, thus greatly helping to refine their analytical toolset. Jean-Michel Salaun, the chief representative of the GRESEC, contributed to the 1986 publication. In Bolaño (2004, p. 85–93) I have already discussed what seems to me to be the most important aspects of this contribution, and I covered what interests us specifically here as the last topic in Chapter 1 of this book. At this point, it is only worthwhile mentioning that in his doctoral thesis (1987, published in 1989 with a few alterations), Salaun develops a reflection on television that extends and develops several points that had initially been raised by the Grenoble school. His affiliation to the GRESEC is evident not only as far as content is concerned, but also in the structure of his thesis: again, there is an underlying concern about evolutionary trends in the audiovisual sector in France and Europe; again, the study follows a dynamic perspective that links a theoretical structural analysis to an analysis of the participants' activities, although these two levels are not always clearly distinguished. As far as the more specifically theoretical issues are concerned, for Salaun, over and above audiovisual sector stakeholder strategies, there are two situational aspects that determine the sector's development: the evolution of personal choice, and technological progress. Salaun's main contribution concerns the latter (as discussed in my previously mentioned publications).[16]

Based on his criticism of the GRESEC (cf.), Zallo proposes his own alternative, starting from the definition of what he calls *creative work*. This is characterized by the worker retaining "a certain degree of autonomy"; this is a legacy of the "old system of unique works of art", and it allows the actors to exert some kind of "individual creativity". It is this special work-type that imparts uniqueness and hence use value to each cultural commodity. "The unique character of the use value is expressed in the repeated exchange value generated by industrial production of items that are identical and mass-produced, but that remain different from any other product line" (Zallo, 1988, p. 52). Zallo adds that *mass production* affects the *value* of cultural products. It accepts a level of devaluation, (without the original losing its advantage of uniqueness) in return for mass consumption.

There is no significant conflict of opinion, or progress, relative to the GRESEC. It is more of a theoretical refinement: the creative work-type becomes the starting point of the analysis. While it "creates a symbolic output that references the cultural codes, past and present, of a given society, contributing to its ideological and social reproduction" (Zallo, *Telos*, 10, p. 66), it remains clear that the uniqueness of the cultural commodity is due to the specificity of the work-type. "Creative work acts on cultural forms or content that, in every case, take the form of prototypes; they seek symbolic communication and social identification, appealing not only to members of rationalised cultures, but to humans of every type and society" (ibid.).

Zallo then moves on to discuss the "factors that erode uniqueness", which point to a growing substitutability between cultural goods. They are: salaried employees; continuity; and the methods of organizing work. With regard to the first of these, it is clear once again that uniqueness is the fruit of an archaic type of working relationship; this explains "the permanence and the renewal of the copyright system in industrialized culture", which ensures continuation of the system of intellectual property and related rights. Zallo returns to this subject, stating his position extremely clearly in the following quote taken from an article in the magazine *Telos*:

> Intellectual property signifies the persistence of an owner's moral and economic rights over intangible goods; they cede the right to exploit and reproduce the goods, through an agreement with a publisher or a distributor. We are therefore faced with social patterns that are particular variants either of the independent producer of goods – typical pre-capitalism[17] – or of independent, autonomous service providers.[18]
>
> (Zallo, *Telos*, 10, p. 68)

Wage labour, which implies the institution of a chain of command through the separation of labour and hierarchical management, destroys the individual creativity that characterizes cultural labour. Similarly, the trend in cultural industries is to design an organizational work structure that will reduce the degree of uncertainty present in works created outside of the industrial system. This is true of the incorporation of creative knowledge into machine systems, such as computerization in journalism or sound storage and processing systems in the recording industry. All of this leads to loss of autonomy for the individual producer and, therefore, to an "expropriation of creative knowledge". The best example of this is the new informational or cultural "telematic" services (the web, mobile phones, GPS, etc.). In these, standardization of information storage systems is taken to the extreme, and they become mere network feeding programme (Zallo, 1988, p. 53). This is real subsumption entering the field of cultural production:

> "Currently we are witnessing the introduction of Taylorism across the creative processes... combined with the partial introduction of automation..." This phenomenon, which classicists called the "real subjection of work", is a late but genuine phenomenon in cultural

> production and is accompanied by majority de-skilling and minority over-qualification. In any case, it announces the eruption of capital in the previously mysterious world of creation. "The preferred tool for such changes is new technology, not in itself, but as a mechanism for the organisation of work, in a Taylorist or neo-Fordist sense."[19]
>
> (Zallo, *Telos*, 10, p. 68)

Then there is *continuity*, a characteristic of the broadcasting industries and the press. They take in unique, differentiated works and absorb them into the programme scheduling or publication design. The unique item stops being an individual cultural commodity and becomes an enterprise, with a market identity displayed through its name, logo, cartoon versions and so on (despite the fact that "whatever form it takes, the principle of the unique character of the work – form and content – must at least appear to be respected") (Zallo, 1988, p. 52).

Zallo also develops the GRESEC's discussion on procedures for *reduction of the risk created by the unpredictability* (or uncertainty) of the marketing process. Some of these procedures (circulation cost increases; distribution networks; advertising; business concentration; market research; and specialization) are common both to cultural industries and to other economic sectors where unpredictability is not such a major issue. Others are more specific to cultural production: standardization; repetition of successes; specific state intervention, as we saw above; extension of broadcasting hours; oversupply followed by selection; grouping of goods of the same symbolic content (e.g. block programming); serialization; audience segmentation; publishing supplements; and so on (Zallo, 1988, p. 54). The battle against unpredictability is visible in the organization of capital in the cultural sector. There are multiple types of capital organization. Examples include: extreme specialization in the case of small capital; diversification within the same industry or media type, to leverage synergies in both production and distribution; and the planned release and distribution of a same product across different media and industries.

> But most important is that the global nature of capital management is impregnated by the need to reduce uncertainty... control of the distribution/publication methods is the preferred means of capital accumulation. Production can be decentralized via small publishers, following the tradition of specialized print editions... Areas that deliver experimental work using trial and error are not an important zone of capital accumulation; nor are the areas where they work on

> commission or through subcontracting. The important accumulation zone is in areas that rely on rights of exclusivity, reproduction and distribution.
>
> (Zallo, *Telos,* 10, p. 69)

In sectors characterized by continuity (radio, television and the press), the problem of unpredictability lies, according to Zallo, not so much in overall supply planning, as in its effect on specific scheduling time slots; the issue is judged less on the acceptability of specific content and more on audience loyalty. It can be eliminated, at least on the radio and on television, through surveys on programming and planning. The multiplication of channels and growth in competition has all the same reintroduced unpredictability, Zallo believes. Publishing presents us with a different picture: uncertainty is a feature of every individual work; the sector is essentially faced with what the French call the *dialectique du tube et du catalogue* (dialectic of the hit or the catalogue). Catalogues and libraries provide prestige and permanence, while sporadic successes guarantee profitability in the short term. Whatever the case, the presence of randomness is in inverse proportion to the formation of a capitalist production organization and the ability to forecast and plan for audience levels. In television, for example, the opposite frequently occurs: the market is guaranteed by controlling the growth of audience levels based on the existence of (public or private) monopolies or concentrated oligopolies (Zallo, 1988, p. 54 ff.).

A third feature specific to cultural goods is *renewal.* Zallo sees this, in the *Telos* article, as a necessary means to deal with randomness, together with "a certain minimum required quality". In his 1988 publication, renewal is stated to be "imposed by the very nature of symbolic-ideological goods as vehicles of legitimization of the dominant social relations, through both the mode of communication and the content", becoming "more necessary the more developed a society is, economically and culturally" (ibid., p. 53). Be that as it may, the need for constant renewal of product and content has important implications, both for the production process and for creation and sustainability of demand in cultural industries. On the one hand, as already raised in GRESEC I, renovation (so-called innovation) requires the creation and maintenance of "cultural nurseries", which form a veritable industrial reserve army. These are often supported by state-run cultural and educational activities; others are nurtured by the culture industries themselves, and yet others have only sporadic relationships with the industries, such as extras and other casual workers.

On the other hand, renewal is causing a "progressive shift from cultural creation towards information machines" (to use Ben Bagdikian's term), which maintain archives of material for possible future use. Although this apparently opens the door to "endless creative possibilities", it in fact causes standardization and reduces variety. That is just an extreme development of renovation, which, aiming to reduce the risks inherent in "real innovation", leads to: plots being variations on proven themes; an accumulation of amazing special effects and "high-tech moments"; new entries in prestige catalogues; a multiplication of similar offerings; and specialized offerings. Finally, Zallo takes up Flichy's argument, whereby the need for renewal makes the existence of small, independent companies mandatory. This means that, unlike other sectors, culture and communication are characterized by the coexistence of very varied production structures, "without endangering large company dominance". On this last point, it may be interesting to return to Schumpeter's concept of innovation. The distinction Zallo makes between *innovation* and *renovation* concerns the level of technical and aesthetic judgment applied within each artistic discipline. From the economic viewpoint, it comes back to the much broader question of techno-aesthetic employers, which I will discuss in the next chapter. For now, let us consider this: if a certain company, say, has a steady production pattern, which guarantees it a certain market position, then changes in the company's production can be handled in two different ways – either through renovation, without any significant alteration in the existing techno-aesthetic pattern, or through innovation, significantly altering its production methods or introducing an entirely original product form to the market.

It must be stressed that, to ensure innovation in the Schumpeterian sense, it is not necessary to have "real innovation" as defined by Zallo. The decisive element is the market impact that introducing a new production process or an original product may have; any effect on the history of art is irrelevant. Similarly, a "genuine innovation", let us say one created by an independent company, that will have no effect on its product lines, current production methods or market share, cannot be considered to be an innovation in the Schumpeterian sense of the word. In this instance it would be more correct to speak of an *invention* that fails to lead to innovation. Salaün (1989, p. 17) uses a distinction that approaches the Schumpeterian concept, referring more specifically to technological development in the sectors producing material linked to the audiovisual markets. In this instance he uses the term "innovation" to refer to something more than a mere technical invention. He also incorporates the stabilization of social use, in the sense that we have already discussed, using the term "popularization" to refer to the massification of the new product.

Salaün's proposal is interesting because it incorporates the important question, so dear to the French, of the social reception of innovation. Clearly, his considerations are confined to the consumer goods sector and to product – not process – innovation.

The distinction between invention, renovation and innovation clarifies, on the other hand, something that only Zallo and Flichy observed: the fact that the necessary presence of small independent businesses in the cultural sector does not, generally, eliminate large company domination of the sector. But for an independent-born invention to grow into an innovation, the said invention must manage to escape the boundaries of the cultural ghetto where it originated, and create its own market space in an industry characterized by oligopoly and mass consumption. To break these boundaries, the innovating company needs access to the distribution or broadcasting networks which are monopolized by a small group of extremely large capital enterprises. The independent producers have to form some kind of alliance with large capital if they wish to capitalise on their invention. An alternative route is unlikely, because it would lead to prohibitive distribution costs for independents, in addition to shouldering the risk of the unpredictability of cultural product production; a risk that the large capital organizational structure is, as we have seen, well placed to handle.

But let us return to Zallo's book. In Item 4 of Chapter 4, he proposes a hypothesis concerning "The components of *value* in creative production", taking four of the five value-components proposed by Molles as they apply to independent creative work (value of materials, design time, build time and "excessive complexity"). Molles subsequently concluded that Marxist analysis cannot be used to determine value in this field; it must be determined by demand. Zallo disagrees, affirming that these elements do indeed determine the value of cultural products, although this may not be reflected in market value. He then performs an analysis to determine average working hours for social media activities, taking as an example the freelance writer (item 4.5.1). I will not go any further into this here.

I would like to propose an alternative hypothesis: we should not seek the value of cultural goods in supposedly "objective" elements, such as those defined by Molles. We should look at the determining, singular property of cultural production (capitalist or not): it produces *symbolic goods*. This is what unifies the Culture Industry and differentiates it from all other capitalist industries. The economic value of a cultural commodity is above all the result of conversion of a symbolic value. Pierre Bourdieu will be of the greatest value in seeking the solution to that equation.

Zallo himself recognizes, as we saw, that creative work, by operating on "cultural forms or content", appeals to "rationalised cultures" and "to humans of every type and society", thus generating a "symbolic output" ("symbolic-ideological goods") that contributes to the "ideological and social reproduction" of society etc. His very definition of the Culture Industry[20] refers to the theme of ideology and the production of symbolic goods.

It is here that one must look for the very substance of cultural commodity value. Herscovici shows himself to be aware of this, but his conception of work seems a little problematic to me. He starts, for so-called operational reasons, from a "voluntarily restricted" definition of culture; he uses the broad concept of "fine-arts", including all movements "recognized as artistic". The *cultural field* is therefore defined by reference to "a set of products and services that contains in its manufacturing process a certain element of *artistic work*". Or again, "a working activity becomes artistic from the moment it is publicly recognized as such; when the creator's handiwork is individually recognised and revered, and it becomes a generator of symbolic value" (Herscovici, sd, p. 2).

This concept of work is, in my opinion, not only too vague, but also too restrictive. It excludes other types of "creative workers", such as journalists, for example: it is rare that their "handiwork is individually recognised and revered", but they still generate a symbolic value capable of being converted into an economic value, to use terms dear to Bourdieu and Herscovici. In another article (1989), the latter will speak of "artistic or intellectual work" so as to incorporate information workers within the same group as artists. But even this extended concept, closer to Zallo's view of *creative work*, remains inadequate. It still excludes the work done by TV presenters and others who, while they cannot be classified as artistic or creative, nevertheless create symbolic value through their special relationship with the public. This can be capitalized in economic and political terms. Be that as it may, in all of the pieces under review here, Herscovici is clearly circumscribed by the initial definition of artistic production (limited reproducibility, restricted markets) being used to cover the full range of cultural industries.

The advantage of Herscovici's definition lies in its consideration of *symbolic value* as a constituent element of the value or, more precisely, the *use value*, of cultural commodities. In this respect, his starting point is the concept of a "field of production", understood as "a socioeconomic space that produces, simultaneously, both the products and the need for them". The cultural field is therefore both the space where artistic production occurs, and the space "where the artistic gesture is revered, where the artist's reputation is built, where symbolic capital is created" (Herscovici, 1990, p. 113). Herscovici's entire analysis is based on Bourdieu, especially his important article of 1977.[21] Bourdieu originally formulated this definition in an analysis of the art trade, which "belongs to the class of practices where the logic of the pre-capitalist economy survives"; but even in Bourdieu's work, we can already see the problems that will be created by applying it to the whole cultural field, including the different cultural industries:

> Next to the search for "economic" profit... there is room for the accumulation of symbolic capital; a rejected, unknown and unrecognised form of legitimate and creditable economic or political capital, capable, under certain conditions and in the long term, of delivering "economic" gains. Creators and vendors of cultural goods who "go commercial" sign their own death warrant, and not just from an ethical or aesthetic point of view: they deprive themselves of the opportunities offered to those who, able to recognise the specific needs of this universe... give themselves the means to enjoy the proceeds of disinterest.
>
> (Bourdieu, 1977, p. 4)

That is to say, it is the "anti-economy" or "financially disinterested" attitude that, given that the specific modus operandi of the "field" enables the accumulation of symbolic capital, then creates the conditions for its later conversion into economic capital.[22] In other words, the capital invested in this field can only acquire economic value after having acquired symbolic value. The way this cultural field works is similar to the religious field, with its priests, prophets and lay people, which Bourdieu has analysed in some classic works. Within the cultural field, well summarized by Herscovici, there is a temporal dynamic between classic, modern and avant-garde art, which cannot be discussed at this point. What should be noted, though, is that it is a specialist field, with its own access codes and keys to interpretation. It is by nature separate from industrialized culture. To extrapolate these concepts and apply them to the whole of the Culture Industry, as Herscovici does, requires an additional theoretical effort which, at least in the texts cited here, he does not make.

But if we take the mode of operation of the Culture Industry today, what we see is that not only does "commercialism" prevail over "disinterest" where investment decisions are concerned, but that commercial success has increasingly become a factor in "recognition" of the product by a certain cultural elite. That was the case in Brazil, for example, where the "concert" given by the country duo Chitãozinho & Xororó, at the prestigious auditorium of the Maksoud Plaza Hotel, is a historical landmark; or in Latin America, where Madonna is assuming the legitimacy that, not many years ago, was held by Violeta Parra. This is an inversion of the "pre-capitalist" sector of cultural production identified by Bourdieu. It is, in fact, the logic of industrialization and massification of culture, and the progress of (economic) capital in the cultural field. For neo-liberalism, legitimacy can only be conferred by the market.

These findings do not, of course, deny that symbolic value is an essential part of the use value of cultural goods; much less do they deny the importance of Bourdieu in the explanation of this phenomenon. They do, though, rebut the extrapolation of specific attributes of the art market to the Culture Industry as such; an extrapolation already evident in Herscovici's definition of work, which he used to characterize the communications and culture economy. It is clear that an artist's signature or logo is an important element in the constitution of use value, mainly in certain specific sectors of cultural production. This is not, however, the pivotal element that defines the specificity of cultural products. The key is their ability to meet certain ideological, psychological and psychosocial *needs*,[23] often replacing other institutions that, in the process of the development of capitalism, lost their legitimacy to provide symbolic values.

From use value to *exchange value*, Herscovici takes up the Gresecian thesis that cultural labour can only partially be transformed into abstract labour, adding:

> It may also be noted also that the use value, at least in the case of the cultural product, it is not independent of the exchange value. It is not dependent on the physical or technical product characteristics: by nature, artistic appreciation is subjective and determined by social structure. This is dependent on the exchange value, to the extent that the methods of delivery of artistic products and the massification of that distribution, together with technological innovations, partially determine the social use and aesthetic characteristics of that product.
>
> (Herscovici, 1990, p. 116)

Herscovici suggests a second consequence of this idea, in addition to the fact that the standardization of cultural products is limited: he endorses the idea that the unpredictability of cultural production is felt at the level of valorization and not (as had been correctly proposed by Ramón Zallo) of realization. Hence, "valorisation of the cultural product is unpredictable. The use value cannot be defined on the basis of the product's technical characteristics, because it is subjective, and cannot be forecast" (ibid.). At this point, a distinction is clear between symbolic goods, with a subjective use value, and material goods, whose use value could be objective, or may be dependent on the "physical or technical characteristics" of the product, and predictable. It will be noted that this implies duplication in the defining criteria of what is subjective or objective. As far as the material goods are concerned, the objective aspect is based on technical and physical attributes; in other words, it is considered from the point of view of the production process. The subjective aspect of the goods' symbolic nature is based on the consumer's point of view.

We have known for a considerable time – at the very least since the appearance of the published works of Baran & Swezy, or those of the theoreticians on consumer society – that in monopoly capitalism, or in the cycle that governs the Culture Industry, consumer goods have a symbolic value that is a determining factor in an individual's purchasing decisions. As is well known, product differentiation is the principal competitive strategy model in the consumer goods sector, within monopolistic capitalism. It is essentially based on layout, packaging and other items not related to the technical or physical characteristics of the product, leading to a "general beautification" of capitalist production. It is not only symbolic goods that function according to the logic of distinction and *habitus* – to use a term coined by Bourdieu and dear to Herscovici. That is to say, material goods also have a symbolic value, also circulate as signals, as Baudrillard would say, and are also subject to the consumer's subjective judgment. Similarly, and increasingly since the birth of the Culture Industry, the production of symbolic goods comes about through the intermediary of economic capital, using more or less material means according to their specific mode of production. In the final analysis, this is where the entire communications and culture economy springs from, as do Herscovici's concepts themselves.[24]

The problem that the communications and culture economy faces arises from the fact that artistic work produces a symbolic value that cannot be quantified as socially necessary labour, but that is nonetheless part of the use value of cultural objects. This unquantifiable element becomes even more complex when any attempt is made to apply these values to the costs of production. But it is not exactly a question of randomness. On the contrary, the ingredients of symbolic valorization, including the "brand image" or "artist's signature", are known at any given time. The problem of unpredictability, as Zallo showed so well, is at the level of realization. There is no difference in the level of realization, when compared to any other commodity; just as there is no difference due to the mere existence of symbolic value, as I have just pointed out.

There is, though, a fundamental quantitative difference, as we saw with Flichy (ten releases for one hit in the recording industry), that the communications and culture economy has not yet been able to explain. Herscovici has the merit of bringing to light the subjective element of symbolic value as the qualitative determinant of this difference. The same basic problem faces monopolistic capital goods. There, manufacturers compete through differentiation and advertising, the first focusing primarily on packaging and other symbolic elements. The fundamental problem is realization of the symbolic value. Specific physical product differences are very often conceived more for strategic reasons, to exploit the target audience's desire for distinctiveness, than for actual usefulness. In the case of physical goods, the decisive factor influencing the consumer's pre-purchase product assessment lies in its "technical and physical characteristics". In the case of symbolic goods, the decisive influencing factor is the symbolic value of the product. This being the case, the subjective element is much more influential in the case of symbolic goods than that of physical goods and, therefore, the level of unpredictability is higher.

Herscovici makes the mistake, arising from the French school of thought in this area, of trying to define this subjectivity on the level of the creation of value, when it is clearly a problem of realization (or receipt, if you prefer). His position nevertheless, at least as I interpret it here, represents progress in defining the specificity of the use value of cultural goods, by incorporating the link between the symbolic element and its main function, that of "meaning-maker"; that is, a producer of meaning. It is this primordial ideological function that finally enables the symbolic field to transform itself into an area of interest to economic capital.

Herscovici also refers to another specific feature of cultural production, the one he calls "dual logic of differentiation" or "dual logic of distinctiveness" (1990). On the one hand, competition among cultural producers generates three types of differentiation: aesthetic differentiation between products; technological differentiation (e.g. distribution of a same product on different media such as cassette, CD or vinyl, in the recording industry); and media coverage differentiation, linked to "mediatic legitimacy" (the mass media's ability to manipulate the audience). "In this way, the cultural system will give priority to technological or media coverage differentiation, and this will permit a much greater aesthetic standardization" (Herscovici, 1990, p. 118). Note that here we again meet Zallo's idea of "genuine innovation", as discussed above.

On the other hand, there is differentiation on the demand side. Herscovici mentions this, using Bourdieu's concept of *habitus*, according to which "culture cannot be considered only as a factor of societal homogenization. A society with class antagonism generates a strong hierarchical structure, with pronounced cultural differentiation" (ibid., p. 119). For Herscovici, there was indeed a "dialectic of standardisation and differentiation", which he expressed as follows: "in the context of restricted markets, cultural consumption is explained based on a logic of distinctiveness; but intensified commercial exploitation of cultural goods and the development of mass culture are characterized by a homogenisation and a uniformity in the offer and the demand" (ibid.). This presents a threat to Bourdieu's idea, in which social groups auto-classify themselves based on identities built in opposition to other groups, as is the case with a class structure based on economic status, the main, but not the only determinant of this "logic of distinction":

> Mass industry creates the offer based on an audience viewed as a homogenous whole: the corresponding consumption is characterized by ideological neutrality. Since the product must be symbolically accessible to the greatest number of people, it will not generate any distinctive effect: the products offered are "decomplexified", aesthetically and ideologically, so that they can reach the widest audience. This is how a culture that eliminates class differences develops. But it would seem that, as a differentiating response, specialised markets endure, providing strong distinguishing markers.
>
> (Herscovici, 1990, p. 119)[25]

Homogenization is an obvious requirement for the mass production of cultural goods; however, it cannot ever be all-embracing, since differentiation is the lynchpin of competition in monopolistic capitalism, which governs the Cultural Industry. That being so, from the supply side the tensions between homogenization and differentiation are permanent and uncontrollable. Herscovici failed to identify a third and decisive differentiation, needed to have a complete understanding of the problem: the differentiation sought by the competing capital investors in the sector that I will call "expanded-differentiation consumer goods". This is crucial for a proper appreciation of the advertising function in the Cultural Industry, which to a large extent determines how the industry is set up. I shall come back to this later.[26] Neither Herscovici nor Zallo confer upon advertising this role of central articulation point for the whole system. Although questionably stated, the concept was present, for example, in Smythe. Without completely denying the general function of advertising, Zallo tends to see it essentially as one more branch of cultural production (which, it must be said, is not wrong from the point of view of a microeconomic and sectoral analysis); while Herscovici tries to account for it under the label of "*market intermediary*", following a theoretical perspective that is essentially based on Baumol. Let us examine this.

The conventional communications and culture economy provides us with two completely different directions from which to analyse the problem of cultural production costs. One follows the path of Samuelson (1964), while the other starts from Baumol's seminal work on the economics of the live performing arts (1968), which had great impact in France among authors who cannot, in principle, be considered neoclassical. "It is well known, indeed, that for Baumol, high production costs for this sort of event are an unrelenting feature, while receipts show, at best, only weak growth and artistic labour productivity is almost a constant: there are inevitable and increasing deficits" (Miège et al., 1986, p. 75 ff.).[27] Regardless of any detail-level disagreement with or criticism of Baumol, which we can't go into within the confines of this book, Herscovici adopts the idea that, given the "Baumolian deficit", funding of cultural production depends on external sources, public or private, whose contribution must constantly increase.

To explain the deficit, and based on an analysis of some recent trends in the audiovisual sector, Herscovici replaces Baumol's thesis on the generalization of wage increases in the productive sectors of the economy, by a view of labour in the arts sector, where productivity levels would stagnate.[28] In this way, the increase in the number of stations and the average broadcasting time will raise demand for programmes; but meanwhile, supply will remain comparatively tight, which will lead to higher costs, particularly for major stars and broadcasting rights for sporting events and movies. TV, being the dominant medium, imposes its grandiose aesthetic on live performances, demands videos from the recording industry (doubling their initial cost) and increases the importance of the star system. The subsequent cost increases spread to the entire system and this in turn leads to the development of "market intermediaries". In this category Herscovici includes advertising in all its forms,[29] "markets linked to secondary uses" (which basically covers the phenomenon of repeats or multiple broadcasting), and public grants and other state actions of a similar nature (Herscovici, 1988). That theoretical solution to the question of advertising shows that there have been some issues when trying to accommodate this element, so crucial to the very structure of the Culture Industry. The same can be said of the state's involvement, considered only from the point of view of its actions to protect the market.

On this, Herscovici correctly explains: "the state finances certain cultural goods, generally aiming at cultural democratization; lowering the price to the end consumer should increase consumption. But in reality, all the surveys carried out on cultural institution users show that only higher-income bracket social classes take advantage of this financing" (Herscovici, 1988, p. 129). Once cultural consumption based on *habitus* was in place, the state could do nothing but finance cultural products that "have a certain legitimacy in the hierarchy of cultural practices, that is, products representative of the 'privileged' groups, both culturally and economically" (ibid.). These findings are in addition to the profound research Herscovici provides into the question of *local or national identity*, criticizing in particular the argument that mass culture is a democratizing factor. "Culture, firstly, can only be regarded as a unifying element within a social class, group or subgroup", so that "in the framework of a national or local community, the issue of unification, or unity, can be nothing more than bewildering, since unity is an ideological construct that denies social contradictions" (ibid., p. 120).

So, both the Culture Industry and state action are moving towards the creation of a semblance of local, regional or national community unity; this also serves to improve the "media image" of these communities in the world economy:

> within the structure of the world economy..., spaces need to differentiate themselves to attract international capital...To support this, the government will fund infrastructure at a regional or national level, to provide the right conditions for the accumulation of international capital...Culture, as a producer of meaning, is an important element of differentiation.
>
> (Ibid., p. 130)

Clearly, with regard to local policies that seek to build a picture of the community, this differentiation of geographic space through cultural policy also serves to win public funding. From a more global perspective, this issue is of particular importance in Europe today, where the unification process leads to robust competition between different cities and regions; these are forced to mobilize all their resources, which include building the right media image, to be able to enjoy the fruits of the broadened common market.

5
From Production to Competition: Towards the Reconstruction of the Communication and Culture Economy

In his book published in 1990, Pierre Kopp attempts to use the instruments of the neoclassical school to prove that, applied to the study of television, they are not able to confirm liberal theses concerning deregulation, but rather reinforce the arguments of those who defend the existence of a public monopoly, regarding this as a particular example of a "natural monopoly". In doing so, he presents an argument germane to the neoclassical outlook which overall is of little interest to our objectives. But Kopp's book does make for interesting reading, because two important lessons can be extracted from it: first, that neoclassical formalism is incapable of furthering our knowledge with respect to television, whatever may be the case with other subjects; second, that it is unreasonable to leave the important issue of competition in the various sectors of the Culture Industry outside of the central topics of discourse in the unorthodox analysis of the communication and culture economy. Pierre Kopp's contribution lies, as I see it, in the choice of subject matter to be analysed, and in the challenge he presents to all who oppose the adoption of the neoclassical framework for the communication and culture economy, which acts as an implicit criticism of those approaches that frequently forget anything that is not directly concerned with the central theme of production.

Apart from the importance of studying the specificities of cultural production, remaining prisoner to this level of analysis means refusing to understand the fundamental role of mediation in the Culture Industry, an element that belongs, above all, to the symbolic order of 20th century societies. After all, it is the function of mediation itself that justifies a microeconomic analysis of the Culture Industry: on one hand, the interest of capital in the cultural sector is explained by the importance of mediation and the consequent convertibility, in the tradition of Bourdieu, of symbolic capital into economic capital, and on the other hand, it is the specificity of the so-called "cultural labour", "creative labour", "artistic labour" or whatever one wishes to call it, which defines the distinct characteristics of labour and valorization processes in the culture industries and which is due precisely to the need to anchor them in the lifeworld.

If it does justify (and demand) an economic analysis of communication and culture, the very existence of this function of mediation (which is what distinguishes the capitalist production of culture from all other types of capitalist production) makes its limitations, on the other hand, very clear, given that the emphasis on production makes it easy to forget aspects fundamental to the Culture Industry. There is no need, however, for the communication and culture economy to remain prisoner almost exclusively to the analysis of production. The field of competition, hitherto generally left to the neo-classicists, should be considered in depth. This brings us once again to publicity, the role of the state and of propaganda, power struggles in the sector, the question of the autonomy of mediation institutions, etc.

The hierarchies, the organizations and the performance of the actors that define the concrete dynamic of the Culture Industry (advertisers, private and public enterprises in the culture market, the state, the public, workers – including the star system (referred to earlier in this book) and what Cesareo called "partial intellectuals" – other actors and interrelated sectors (the electronics, telecommunications and banking industries, advertising agencies, research institutes, etc.) could all be considered from a general, static point of view. However, in my opinion it would be better to adopt a more focused economic analysis centred on competition. It is this transition from an analysis centred on production to an analysis centred on competition that allows us to re-examine the subject of mediation and to revisit production, to avoid confining it to the study of the particulars of the labour and valorization processes within the cultural industries, but rather to regard it as a fundamental element for structuring the capitalism of our time.

First of all, based on a critical reading of Kopp's work cited above, an unorthodox microeconomic analysis will be proposed, taking the concept of barriers to entry and market strategy-structure organization as the most important elements of an analysis, the suitability of which as an analytical tool I have already had the opportunity to test in my studies on the Brazilian television industry (Bolaño, 2004). The analysis will then shift to a more abstract level: the aim of the second section is basically to define the function of mediation in the Culture Industry. This will be founded on a discussion about the dual nature of the products of the Culture Industry, especially what I will refer to as the "audience product", which attract the interests of capital and the state: of institutions that are both economic and political in nature. It is the production of this particular good that forms the basis of the Culture Industry and awards it an important role in the organization of the body of the current capitalist system. With that discourse as a foundation, we can re-examine the subject of competition in order to define the concept of "techno-aesthetic standards", which will bring us back once again to production according to the terms proposed in the above paragraph. Finally, I will revisit the subject of regulation and propose an analytical framework for the culture industries.

The key microeconomic question derived from the discourse in the second section of this chapter is that of the mechanisms that enable audience-building and audience "loyalty". These mechanisms are intimately linked to the competition rooted at the heart of the Culture Industry among the various capital enterprises which regard it expectantly as a source of valorization. If the Culture Industry is an element of mediation between capital, the state and other economic or political institutions on one hand and the masses of voters or consumers on the other, this mediation is not taken forward in terms of major structures on the lines of the preponderant dynamic that can be derived from the base and superstructure model, but rather on the basis of the conflicting relationships between the different actors which, in the different interrelated sectors, participate in the particular flexible dynamic that responds (at all times and always problematically) to the needs of capital accumulation and the ideological reproduction of a system characterized by anarchy and contradiction.

Reflections on television and competition

Kopp distinguishes two types of television markets: the primary market, in which the networks demand products from their various providers, and the secondary, in which they offer their programmes to the public. His main interest relates to the secondary market. The question he postulates is the conventional one of the optimization of the utility of this market for the consumer. In this respect, he bases his ideas on those of Koford (1984), who proves, in a rather ingenious démarche, that in perfect competition, free television, mixing two inputs (the programmes acquired in the primary market and the advertising space sold by the networks for their marginal cost) leads to a state of equilibrium (achieved by the increase in the advertising segment by broadcasters until the marginal cost is equal to the purchase price of the programmes). Kopp defines this equilibrium as advantageous for the consumer who does not pay for access.

Kopp's critique of Koford concerns the unrealistic assumption of perfect competition among networks. Kopp attempts to prove that, on the contrary, as television is a collective good (both systems in which public service is predominant and in commercial systems financed by advertising) for which it is impossible to define a rule of exclusion as price does for private goods ("invisibility of demand"), it therefore constitutes a special case of a good whose production is characterized by the existence, as is not the case generally, of increasing income. Since "increased consumption by an individual does not lead to a reduction in the amount available for other consumers", the total cost remains constant over the long term, and the average cost therefore goes down as the number of users increases (Kopp, 1990, p. 19). Based on this assumption, Kopp seeks to demonstrate the characteristic of natural monopoly in the television sector;[1] I will not repeat his arguments here (see Kopp, 1990, p. 63 ff.).

It should be made clear that this démarche arises from an assumption that the increase in the number of viewers demands no effort on the part of the network, which is far from evident. On the contrary, this condition seems to be extremely restrictive if we think, for example, of the brutal struggle that the networks vying over the Brazilian market face when trying to compete with Globo. Thus, winning a point in the ratings demands so much effort and investment (the return on which is highly variable) that until the end of the 1980s no significant or even small modification with regard to the distribution of the advertising budget and ratings in the Brazilian television market could be detected. Today, a decade later, within a framework that has undergone significant change, these perspectives have changed very little (Bolaño, 2004).

Kopp's assumption is only valid in three situations: in an emerging television market in which increasing the number of viewers is fundamentally a function of effort – not on the part of the networks, but rather of the entities responsible for the transmission infrastructure – which would not yet have reached the body of potential consumers – and of the growth of TV set ownership; in perfect competition or in a monopoly. Now, if we eliminate the first case, which refers to a situation already resolved historically, as well as the second (which Kopp rejects because he rightly considers it unrealistic) we naturally come to the conclusion, as unrealistic as the previous one, that the television market always tends to organize itself into a monopoly.

In reality, the general form that commercial television systems take is one of "concentrated oligopoly'. Given this evidence, and after testing the thesis of the natural monopoly, Kopp goes on to use, when speaking of the actual markets, the term "oligopoly" in the less-than-precise sense of a "near-monopoly". This lack of rigour is due to the choice of the neoclassical paradigm itself, according to which all actual markets can be considered as an imperfect case of the "perfect" models: either competition or monopoly. The result is well-known: very elegant theoretical models whose importance in the analysis of specific markets is negligible. The entire chapter on "private TV stations", in which Kopp offers an interesting overview of the neoclassical contributions to the subject, is a clear example of this.

It is not possible to present within the limits of this work the set of theoretical alternatives on which my own perspective on the microeconomic analysis of television markets is based (Bolaño, 2004). It is important, however, to summarize some of its central themes. First, the concept of oligopoly – which is no longer defined in relation to the concept of perfect competition or of monopoly – assumes the status of the organizational form that markets generally take in contemporary capitalism. Oligopoly is thus defined as a species of market structure characterized by the existence of significant barriers to entry.[2] The concept of barriers to entry plays a central role here, since it is the key determinant (apart from other co-determinants, including, importantly, the restrictions faced by financial enterprises) of profit margins, for which it sets an upper limit. It is precisely that which brings together the structural determinations upon which business strategies must be based.

Kopp refers to the neoclassical approach to the concept of barriers, showing that, in the view of authors such as Ferguson or Stigler, its field of application is limited in relation to Bain's original version (p. 51).[3] In our view, the opposite is the case: the field of application of the concept is amplified to the point of considering not just the potential competition, but also the actual competition. In this way the difficulties facing Globo's competitors can be understood, including the problems experienced by competitors who have surpassed the "regulatory barrier" imposed by the concession/licence and who are already in the market, as a result of the powerful barriers to entry that Globo has imposed and that impede others from penetrating their audiences. But it is precisely the permanent struggle to impose or break down these barriers that defines business strategy in the oligopoly. On the other hand, it is the consideration of the business marketing/strategy-structure relationship that makes a dynamic analysis of the competition possible.[4]

The Brazilian case, which I analysed in detail in my 1988 book,[5] is exemplary: in a highly competitive market (that is, a market in which the barriers to entry did not play a predominant role, so that the leadership positions were extremely precarious and changing), which arose in 1950, Globo entered the market in 1965 with the political support of the new military regime and the financial and technical aid of the US group Time-Life. In two years it dominated all of its competitors and became, during the 1970s, the first and largest television network in Brazil, which would go on to become one of the most important communications groups in the world. Throughout this period, Globo dominion over the Brazilian market grew consistently, even after two major competitors entered the market in the 1980s. But these new competitors were faced with a market that had been completely modified by Globo's own strategy, in place since 1969, the year that Time-Life withdrew and the network began to be built. After destroying all of the weaker barriers imposed by their older competitors, Globo went on to build its own solid barriers. This involved, among other things, defining its own production methods capable of recruiting a loyal audience and an unbeatable, programming structure, especially at prime viewing time.

In this situation, in which the leader historically controls over 65% of the audience and the advertising receipts, the strategy of new competitors is limited by the required funds, industrial organization, knowledge base, etc., for productions that are probably not very different from those which the public has watched for over 20 years. The resounding success of the Manchete network in 1990, which I had occasion to refer to elsewhere (Bolaño, 2004, Chapter 10), was, for example, the fruit of eight years of investment and a basically correct segmentation strategy throughout. Even so, its success was largely unexpected and, worse still, ephemeral, largely due to the company's own strategic errors following the success of the telenovela/soap opera *Pantanal*. The directors of this soap opera seemed to have discovered the key to victory: creating a product very similar but necessarily different from that of the leader. It was not simply a question of dialectic homogenization/differentiation, which Kopp understands well. It was necessary to construct an alternative techno-aesthetic standard (see below), similar to yet different from the predominant one. This calls for serious investment and a high level of risk.

The randomness of the performance of cultural products is reaffirmed throughout the communication and culture economy. This is a central characteristic of all cultural industries, and television is no exception, although, because of its high level of industrialization, it is able to minimize this randomness. What is worse, when the communication and culture economy speaks of the reduction of randomness in the performance of culture products, it refers to a theoretical situation in which the dynamic of competition is not considered. In the particular situation at hand, however, randomness is total for companies seeking an offensive strategy aimed at penetrating the space already captured by the leader, and it is minimal for the latter, which enjoys the enormous advantage of precedence. It is clear that in a time of more robust competition, as was the case in 1990, the successful launch of a challenger partially upsets this balance. But since it was a victory limited to a specific time slot and product it was to be expected that once *Pantanal* ended the audience it had captured would return to Globo, as was in fact the case, given the absence of competitive loyalty strategy by Manchete. The fact is that the highly concentrated structure of television markets forces less powerful competitors into a segmentation strategy with the objective of capturing a more or less comfortable position which allows them, in the medium or long term, to make a more direct assault on the leader based on an occasional success,[6] as was the case with *Pantanal.*

This example shows that a number of complex questions exist, linked to both the structural determinations and the strategies of the various actors (economic, political, networks), which must be considered in the concrete analysis of television markets. It is not just a matter of questions of strategy and market structure. A plethora of other questions must be considered, such as those related to the macroeconomic and macrosocial situation and structure, international competition in the diverse related sectors (events at global level in the telecommunications industry have significant impact on the TV markets), the destabilising (and restabilising) force of the introduction of new technologies, etc.

An alternative theoretical approach: The dual nature of products in the Culture Industry

In the Culture Industry labour has a dual value. The proven efforts of artists, journalists and technicians create two products at once: the object or cultural service (the programme, the information, the book) and the audience.[7] Today, the capacity of "cultural labour" to create this second product, under given social and technical conditions, is evident. But all social and global geographical relationships had to be transformed by capital in order to reach the situation in which cultural labour has the capacity to transform human masses into an audience to sustain the publicity machine, the central element of the economic dynamic since the beginning of the 20th century, and to maintain the general conditions for the legitimization of the contemporary state.

Dallas Smythe (1977) was not successful in defining this product, as we saw in Chapter 3. I only return here to Graham's critique, with which I agree completely, to elucidate my own position on the question. In Graham's opinion, Smythe is guilty of extreme theoretical reductionism in defending the idea that "any political mass media economy must be based on its product form and, for him, the specific product form of mass media is the audience". Graham considers it important to recognize the production of the audience product, as "an instance in the complex circuit of capital that structures the operation of the mass communications media from the economic perspective".[8]

> However, Smythe's theory does not understand the function of the product form as an abstraction within Marxist economic theory and, therefore, underestimates the relationships between specific product forms, in this case the audience, and the product form in general. As a result, his theory lacks any sense of contradiction in failing to recognise the role of the state, failing to sufficiently elaborate the function for capital of publicity itself and, perhaps most crucial of all, failing to relate the audience production process by mass media with class determinants and class struggle.
>
> (Garnham, 1979b, p. 29)

But none of this should lead us to deny the existence of this product, as Zallo does (1988, p. 41). The observation that television produces a specific product (the programme), being, at the same time, an "instrument of the process of merchandise circulation", whenever it constitutes part of the "end practice of the circulation process of merchandise produced by the advertisers", does not alter the fact that the audience itself is a product negotiated in an intra-capitalist market (an intermediary good, therefore, and one of the most important ones today). All the elements involved in the advertising market and the entire neoclassical economy of television know this. If we want to critique the latter, commencing with the denial of evidence will not help our case. On the contrary, what should be done, if we are determined, like Zallo, to remain faithful to the tradition of Marx, is to return to Smythe's question, and seek the right answer.

The labour of the artist, technician or journalist is specific labour that produces a concrete product to fulfil a concrete social need (a need that may be, as for any product, "imposed" in some way).[9] But in order to create this product (the programme, the newspaper, the film), these professionals spend energy, muscle power and imagination. In short, they spend abstract human labour.[10] The subordination of concrete labour to the needs of capital valorization transforms it into abstract labour. But cultural labour is different[11] because it creates not one, but two products.

Let us examine, for example, the case of television: it is the attention of the individuals that will be negotiated in the market by the station or network bureaucrat. Attention can be measured in time (exposure of individuals to the programming and not the contrary), a perfectly homogenous unit of measurement, well-suited to neoclassical economists, but which must always refer to quantities (households or audiences) and the qualities (socioeconomic variables) of the audience, which indicates that the audience must have a use value for the advertiser. As for the broadcaster, its main interest lies in the exchange value of the audience.

It is not the concrete individual, with his/her conscience and desires, that is sold to the advertisers, but a quantity, determined in audience measurements, of men and women – of potential consumers whose individual characteristics can only be defined in averages. It is to an average individual, an abstract human being, that all "audience average ratings" refer. Yet it is the concrete human being that advertising and propaganda seek to reach. It is what all the communication efforts of advertisers, governments and politicians are directed towards. There is, therefore, an inevitable divergence between these and the networks, manifested in any discussion on segmentation, over the ideal audience measurement: in short, over all the elements placed on the negotiating table occupied by the buyers and sellers of the audience product (See e.g. Bolaño 1987, 1988, 1994).

The buyers of audiences themselves are of course the sellers of goods and services. These are the authorities, politicians and anyone who needs to communicate with the public. The programme fulfils its social function when it is consumed by the public, at which point it ceases to be a product and becomes pure use value. It is useful to the consumer because it offers emotions, fun, relaxation. But it is also useful to the audience buyers because it allows them to communicate with individual consumers.[12]

We can conclude that the subject (the worker) becomes, within the Culture Industry, an object: it is not just his/her labour power that is reduced to a product, but his/her very conscience and wishes are appropriated for facilitating the accumulation of capital. These subjects are, however, owners of their consciences just as they are of their labour power: once they have decided to "sell" it to capital (in this case not for a salary, but rather for fun, information, emotion), this power effectively becomes an instrument of the latter. The sovereignty of the worker in the world of work (to sell or withhold his labour power – and, in this case, to assume the consequences of this decision – to one capitalist or another) is similar to that which he possesses in the home environment (e.g. to switch or not switch TV channels). Thus, the subordination of the worker surpasses the world of work and enters the realm of the leisure world.[13] A perfectly Frankfurtian conclusion, still requiring a number of major modifications.

The symbolic space

We can approach this question by employing some fairly well-known concepts from Habermas: let us say that the previous conclusion is partial because the Culture Industry, the instance of intermediation between capital (and the state should be included) and the masses, was defined only in terms of the determinations imposed by the "system". But for even these determinations to be effective, it must also respond to certain internal needs of the *Lebenswelt*, namely the need for its symbolic reproduction. To put it another way, the Culture Industry will only be able to "colonise" the lifeworld for capital and the state, substituting its internal mechanisms of symbolic reproduction.

But assuring this mediation is the specific function of all the institutions that represent symbolic power. What characterizes capitalism is that this specific function of symbolic order is articulated over two different needs of the system, as a result of the separation between economic power and political power. It is because of this that two functions can be defined: advertising and propaganda. And what characterizes monopolistic capitalism is that these two functions tend to be fulfilled by a single institution, which is itself the fruit of capitalist expansion: the Culture Industry, which disputes the hegemony of the symbolic order with other older and not specifically capitalist institutions.

The Culture Industry represents, therefore, capital's most resounding victory and crowning achievement: the constitution of not just an economic system, but a whole universal culture (in the anthropological sense of the term), characterized by the bringing together of lifestyles and individual behaviours of entire populations and the impositions of the specific historical movement towards the accumulation of capital (and not just social reproduction in general). The Culture Industry is only a part of this, but this part is of crucial importance, as it means that capital has become culture itself, the intermediary uniting the holy trinity of production and power together with the lifeworld of men and women. But there is no mystery here. Everything can be fully explained if we understand the mediating character of the Culture Industry.

Let us take, for example, the case of a commercial television system in which the networks purchase programmes from independent producers (the "primary market" in Kopp's phrase) and distribute them freely to the public. The networks' profit is generated from the sale of the audience in the advertising market. In the primary market, as Kopp correctly perceived, it is not the product itself that is negotiated, but rather the broadcasting rights. And I would add that this means the utilization rights of the programme product to create the audience product. I will return to the question (of right) later.

For now it should be emphasized that there has been a dual expropriation from the independent cultural producer, separate, on the one hand, from the means of production and subjugated, on the other hand, to an entire intermediation machine that was imposed upon it, without which it would no longer have any means of accessing the public.[14] The communication and culture economy has been able hitherto to analyse the first form of expropriation, applying the classical instruments of Marxist theory. But the second can only be properly understood through knowledge of "dual nature" products in the Culture Industry. This theme is particularly evident in television because there is a kind of externalization (at least in the general case in point) of this duality: each of the two products is produced by a different capital, the programme by the so-called independent producer, responsible for the recruitment of the individual workers and for collective work action, and the audience by television, which simply transforms a set of these products, together with other types of broadcast, into a daily programming schedule which the French refer to as a *flot*. The amount of labour added by this operation is negligible.

It is the audience product, however, that is most "valued" by the market. Now, if we suppose a conventional relationship between value and price on the primary market, the valorization of the capital applied in the *flot* industry (obviously without considering in-house production by television enterprises, which would not change the issue in any way) cannot be explained without the idea of the conversion of symbolic capital into economic capital. There is no relationship possible between economic value and price in the television industry. All value added depends on the capacity of the programme to attract the attention of the audience and, therefore, its symbolic value.[15] The communication and culture economy was never able to draw this conclusion, which, nevertheless, is directly linked to the issue that it frequently discusses of the random character of performance in cultural industries.

The second expropriation of the artist allows capital to appropriate his capacity to create a sort of understanding with the audience, which agrees to give him attention etc. It is clear that in these circumstances it is possible to substitute the artist's labour for that of the athlete or the host (reflecting the grade of subsumption of cultural labour, which becomes progressively more redundant and disposable), but it is always a special type of labour whose product possesses the general capacity to draw the attention of the audience. It is this symbolic power that capital appropriates.

It should be made clear that the audience product is very special compared to other products, given that the process of its creation cannot be conceived simply as the action of a subject on an object. It is special even compared to immaterial products such as information. In a sense, it can best be compared to labour power: a power, a force or an energy that exists in subjects (or, in this case, in the relationship between the subject and the cultural producer) that can be appropriated by capital under certain social and technical conditions.

Capital can only appropriate this energy by expropriating from the cultural producer all forms of access to the public, which has become possible with the development of communications technologies and their imposition as a hegemonic form of the broadcasting of cultural products. What capital does is, first, use the symbolic power of cultural labour to create the empathetic effect that transforms subjects into an audience, and therefore into an object, and second, produce segmentations, classifications and specifications that will allow it to offer a differentiated product in an intercapitalist market.

In this process, it must take the actual works of specific artists, which will produce different empathetic effects on different segments of the audience. Each individual capital within the Culture Industry will have its own action strategy, defined as a function of its position in a given market structure and the opportunities and limitations that the situation imposes upon it. On this point it is possible to return to the question of competition to frame it in a broader perspective than that to which we limited ourselves at the beginning of this chapter. But it is precisely this return to competition that will bring us back to production. What follows proposes not a return to competition or production *tout court*, but rather a global analysis integrating determinations of the production, broadcasting and consumption of cultural products; of the programming, *flot* and audience production industries; of the advertisers' and broadcasters' need for differentiation and audience distinction.

Techno-aesthetic standards

In a book published in Italy in 1990, Antonio Pilati discusses, at one point (Chapter 2), the relationship between consumer and brand, affirming that when a symbolic aspect is introduced into the product, it serves to create a distinction that will differentiate it from all other products, making it possible to reduce uncertainty in its performance and giving economic and strategic advantages to the individual capital, which will therefore increase its regulatory and planning potential. According to Pilati, the generalization of branding strategies by enterprises in the consumer goods sector is linked to the transformations that, since the post-war era, operate on the organization of everyday life in capitalist nations. First, in the current period since the end of the 1960s, the sector has been demonstrating the conflict between the food industry (traditional, mass-scale) and the automotive and electric appliances industries (which already incorporate the symbolic dimension in individual capital strategies), which Pilati calls "time compressors". From the end of the 1960s, when the consumption of these latter products had already extended to the majority of the population of first-world countries, an entire new category of consumer goods was added, also linked to "domestic technology", which would quickly reach the masses: that of "experience amplifiers" (the prototype of which is television), at the same time that the food industry sector began to incorporate differentiation and branding strategies.

From the viewpoint of an analysis of competition in the consumer goods sector, these observations are not far from everything that has already been pointed out by numerous studies on the function of publicity, from at least Baran & Sweezy onward. Pilati's contribution is the connection he makes between the idea of differentiation and the transformations of "everyday life" (I would say "ways of life", adopting the regulationist terminology of André Granou – 1974) by the increased demand for symbols (caused by an increase in family standards and a spread of consumer society starting in the 1950s).

But the most interesting conclusion is that we clearly find ourselves here in the logic of the distinction and the *habitus* of which Bourdieu speaks. That is, at least, what can be deduced in the reading of Pilati: distinction and differentiation are found in the competitive strategies of enterprises within the consumer goods sector.[16] Now, what mass communications media do, with the help of research institutes linked to the advertising sector, is precisely the audience segmentation work that, under the audience product model, could be used by different individual capitals in their mass communications strategies. It is the Culture Industry (and television especially) that makes the connection between the differentiation strategies of the oligopolistic firms within the consumer goods sector and audience distinction strategies. And this work is done by the communications media themselves according to a competitive logic. Truly, this system of creation of a differentiated audience product is extremely complex, involving disputes and collisions of all kinds among the agents participating in this field of production, to use Bourdieu's expression.[17]

We have seen that the relationship between the audience and the artist has a symbolic power appropriated by capital investing in the *flot* industry. Television, appropriating this energy, can transform part of the population into an audience. The functionality of this joint framework depends on the capacity television (or the Culture Industry, in more general terms) has to ensure the attention of the audience. But it is not a relationship of simple functionality between, let us say, the needs of capital and those of the state in terms of communication with the public and the work of mediation that television does. On the contrary, the contradictions are many and varied, and even capital and the state are generally not in agreement over the function of the system of television. There is, consequently, always the need for some type of institutionalized compromise. In the case of market regulation, there exists a system of permanent excitement of the audience that is a result of competition among broadcasters. The solution of compromise is not in any way the work of an omnifunctional structure. On the contrary, it always happens because of strategic relationships, sometimes quite stable, among the individual actors. On this point, it is worth returning to competition to define the concept of techno-aesthetic standard, which will bring us back once again to the production sphere, closing the circle of our unorthodox critique of the communication and culture economy.

Originally called the "standard of quality", referring to the "Globo Standard of Quality", a term used by the broadcaster to promote itself, the concept was defined empirically (Bolaño, 2004, originally published in 1988), out of an immediate need to classify the two existing types of television in Brazil up to the beginning of the 1980s, characterized by two different television languages, associated with two types of programming and two specific competitive strategies, as a function of the existing conflict between two capital structures, of enterprise organization, two methods of management, two different levels of availability of technological resources, financial power, etc. The important fact was that the "Globo Standard" translated into demands on investment, technical capacity, organization, which prevented other companies from gaining access to the audience segments loyalized by the leader in the field.

This is just the type of notion that can serve as an interface between the concept of "barriers to entry" and the idea of symbolic power. It is not simply a matter of economic power: Manchete, despite massive investment since entering the Brazilian television market, had to wait almost a decade before it succeeded in clawing its way into Globo's prime viewer time, and although it managed to do so in 1990, it was thanks to a completely unexpected situation, through a project that had already been rejected by Globo for not conforming to its standards. But it was a very competitive project precisely because it presented a different standard of production from that of Globo. In the *Pantanal* sequence, on the contrary, Manchete went in the direction of excessive experimentalism,[18] which cost them all the ground they had gained.

But the expression "standard of quality" does not adequately transmit the deeper idea of complex strategic and structural determinants that define a specific pattern of cultural production capable of loyalizing a part of the audience, thus transforming it into a captive audience that the broadcaster can negotiate on the advertising market. The expression "techno-aesthetic standard" was inspired by Dominique Leroy's lecture (1980), in which, in quite a different context and following a theoretical perspective completely beholden to the structuralist tradition, he defined the concepts of techno-aesthetic systems and structures.[19] But I maintain my own original conception of a configuration of techniques, aesthetic forms, strategies and structural determinations, which define the standards of cultural production historically determined within a company or enterprise or by a particular cultural producer for whom this standard is a source of barriers to entry.

This approach also incorporates the neo-Schumpeterian discussion of the concept of learning. We know the technical development of television, being exogenous to the sector, fundamentally depends on financial factors. The option, for example, of installing a more or less flexible direct transmission system for local journalism is a strategic decision constrained by the financial capacities of the enterprise. But once this innovation is adopted, a learning process (learning by doing) is initiated, so that the enterprise can develop a competitive know-how advantage. This is important above all for the systems of programme production. The fact, for example, Globo had opted from the start to produce on video allowed them to develop their own language, extremely well adapted to the medium of television, which differentiates it in the international market. What was initially a limitation (the financial inability to produce in 35mm like Hollywood producers) becomes today, especially as a function of the technical progress of video systems, a competitive advantage (brand image, capacity to explore synergies in the video distribution sector) (Bolaño, 1991).

But this conclusion brings us to another interesting question: the importance of in-house production, not just for the economies that vertical integration enables or for the possibility of exploring synergies thanks to a horizontal diversification strategy, but above all for the perspective it opens up in constituting a proprietary techno-aesthetic model that can translate into both barriers against effective or potential competitors, and an offensive weapon, for example in the international market. In Brazilian television, which always had this characteristic, an importation strategy could only be imagined by very weak capitals, forced to make do with a more restricted market segment, which demonstrates the weight of the barriers to entry in this industry. On the other hand, this characteristic is doubtless one of the most important elements in explaining the international success of Globo, even in a situation in which it develops a tendency (evidently contradictory) to constitute just a few hegemonic techno-aesthetic models worldwide, competing in each national market.

The techno-aesthetic model is also the principal means each broadcaster possesses to maximize the reduction of the random character of cultural product performance, by ensuring the loyalization of a segment of the audience. But this loyalization is always problematic: the audience is always a floating average distributed differently among the broadcasters depending on the particular time slot, day of the week or event, depending on the nature of the audience product that, once again like labour power, is not the fruit of a conventional production process. It is more like a force, an energy that capital appropriates, but that is not removed from the individuals.

We saw, in the first chapter, that for Habermas, the qualitative difference of Marx's analysis derives from the inherence of labour power to the subject; thus the analysis of the dual nature of the product allows it to describe capitalist development, simultaneously from the viewpoint of capital and of the lifeworld of the producers, such that (and here a previously cited concept bears repeating) "the categories of 'action' and 'function', of social integration and systemic integration, are inextricably interwoven with salaried labour" (Habermas, 1981, vol. 2, p. 474). Something similar takes place with the audience product. Its inherence to the subject intermingles its analysis with questions linked to the determinations imposed upon it by capital and the state and the advent of the symbolic needs of the subjects themselves.

I hope this helps to clarify the superiority of the Marxist method even over that of Habermas who, despite noting, in *The Theory of Communicative Action,* as I have already pointed out, that the audience also determines the Culture Industry (which is, shall we say, very much in agreement with his theoretical proposal), fails to make explicit that this is due to the inherently contradictory nature of capitalist information itself.

Towards a regulation-based analysis

At this point it is interesting to restate the steps taken up until now, in order to form an analytical framework capable of taking concrete case studies of communications systems organization into account. We know the Culture Industry is a creation of capital and the state and has as its objective the performance of symbolic mediation work between these instances of power and the masses of voters and consumers, as opposed to other institutions of symbolic nature, such as churches. We have seen in detail that this objective must be defined in terms of a conflict between two general functions, advertising and propaganda, which reflects the contradiction between capital and the state that characterizes the capitalist mode of production.

In order to fulfil these functions the Culture Industry must be capable of attracting the attention of the audience, which means that certain psychosocial needs of the public itself must be satisfied by it. This brings up a third function (programming) that must be fulfilled by the

Culture Industry from the moment more organic forms, related to popular culture, of creating meaning are displaced and appropriated by it. Furthermore, this appropriation is a permanent process that develops according to a circular movement of constant interaction between mass culture and popular and resistance cultures. I hope to have made it clear that it is the need to fulfil, in these terms, the programming function that calls for the mobilization of a special type of labour, the characteristics of which are highly relevant to the study of the communication and culture economy.

The global alternative I sought to offer here to the analytic perspective is germane to these studies that incorporate all the advances they have made (and especially the analysis of the capital/labour contradiction in the cultural and communications sector) into a more complete theoretical framework and which, in addition to the issue of mediation and the third function of the Culture Industry, emphasize the central theme of competition, often neglected in the communication and culture economy. The concept I have formulated of techno-aesthetic standards seeks to complete the movement from production to competition, aiming towards a complete analysis of the set of determinants of the real dynamic of the Culture Industry and the mass communications media.

However, the underlying microeconomic perspective in my solution is not restricted to that. It incorporates a series of elements explained in this and other works (see in particular the discussion on technological trajectories in Bolaño, 2004, Chapter 3). I sought to make clear that it is the specificity of mediation and its fundamental importance in the current practice of developing the system that, by enabling this conversion, significantly, from the symbolic capital invested in the sector in economic capital, creates an interest in individual capital in cultural production, which, by the way, adds a new element to the contradiction between the interests of capital and of the state. This is demonstrated by the liberalization movement and the introduction of publicity in European TV, interesting because it signifies the introduction of the logic of competition at the heart of a Culture Industry that historically functioned under the control of the state, favouring the propaganda function over the advertising function.

The objective of this item is to propose an analytical framework capable of integrating all these and other elements that, as a whole, will enable the study of any specific communications system, in terms of its structure as well as its dynamic. The three following frameworks are meant to graph the greatest possible number of determinants of the structure and dynamic of the principal mass communication media and the different cultural industries up to the advent of the internet and the general paradigm of digitalization. Chapter 6 will complement this discussion based on an examination of the political economy of the Internet.

This is evidently a simple artifice of which the only objective is to facilitate the representation of a much more complex model. There is little point in reaffirming the need not to give this type of modelling a greater importance than it really has: to present a certain number of functional connections between agents in a global theoretical framework that is far from functionalist.

In other words, the diagrams presented are only useful at a certain level of abstraction and should be viewed as a simplification, for the sake of convenience, of a much more complex reality in which the relationships between the actors are always characterized not by the functionality/non-functionality pair, but by contradiction. Nevertheless, it is precisely the functional relationships that are represented in the diagrams. The objective is to trace lines of analysis that enable us to find, in each particular case, a sectorally, temporally and spatially determined mode of regulation, the contradictions of which must be fully explained.

With the three diagrams below, I believe it is possible to classify most culture industries in terms of their intra- and intersectoral dynamics, which are separate from the mainstream classifications of the communication and culture economy, without necessarily excluding segmentations previously established, for example, based on the characteristics of the labour processes, but before incorporating them into an analytical framework meant to be more general. I will concentrate specifically on what I have called the "analytical model for the audiovisual" (Figure: 5.1), since the other two ("simplified for the audiovisual including radio" and "simplified for newspapers, books and magazines") are similar to it, rendering their more detailed analysis redundant (Figures 5.2 and 5.3).

An analytical model for the audiovisual

Let us take the first of the three diagrams. The middle box represents the four types of television (commercial, public service, segmented and interactive), which correspond to the second, third and fourth generations of the audiovisual according to Salaün's classifications (1989). The small triangles represent the individual capital enterprises investing in

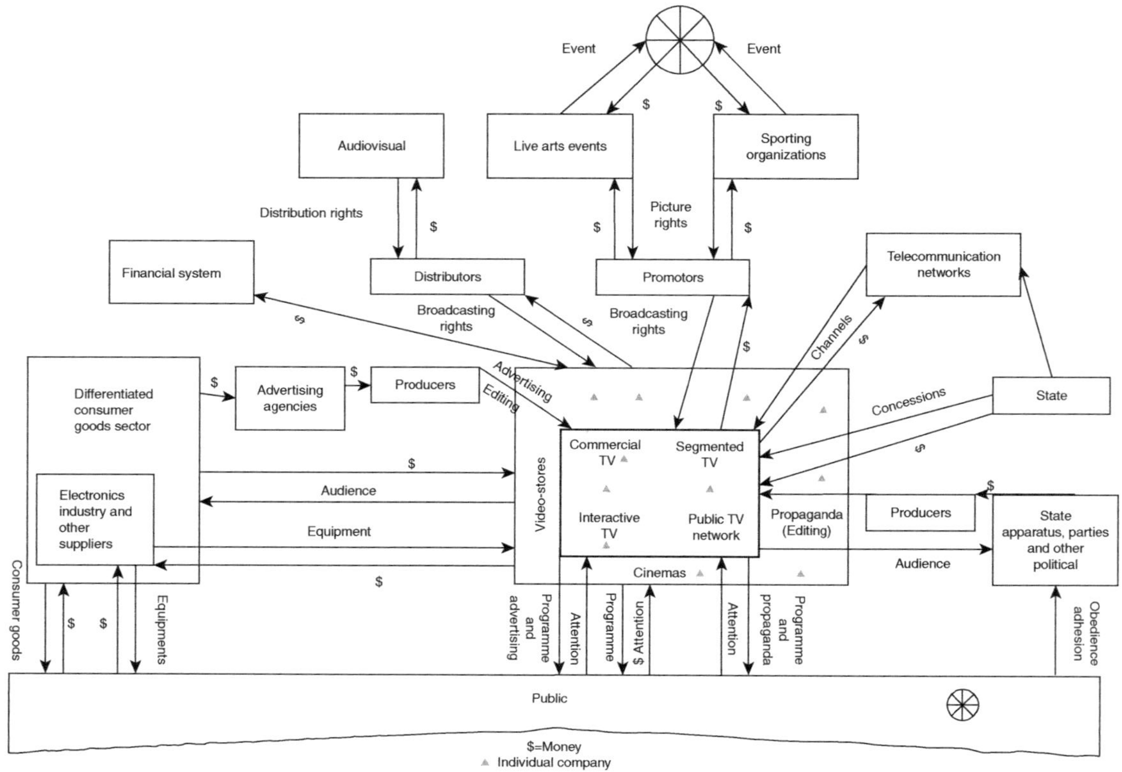

Figure 5.1 Model of analysis for audiovisual sector

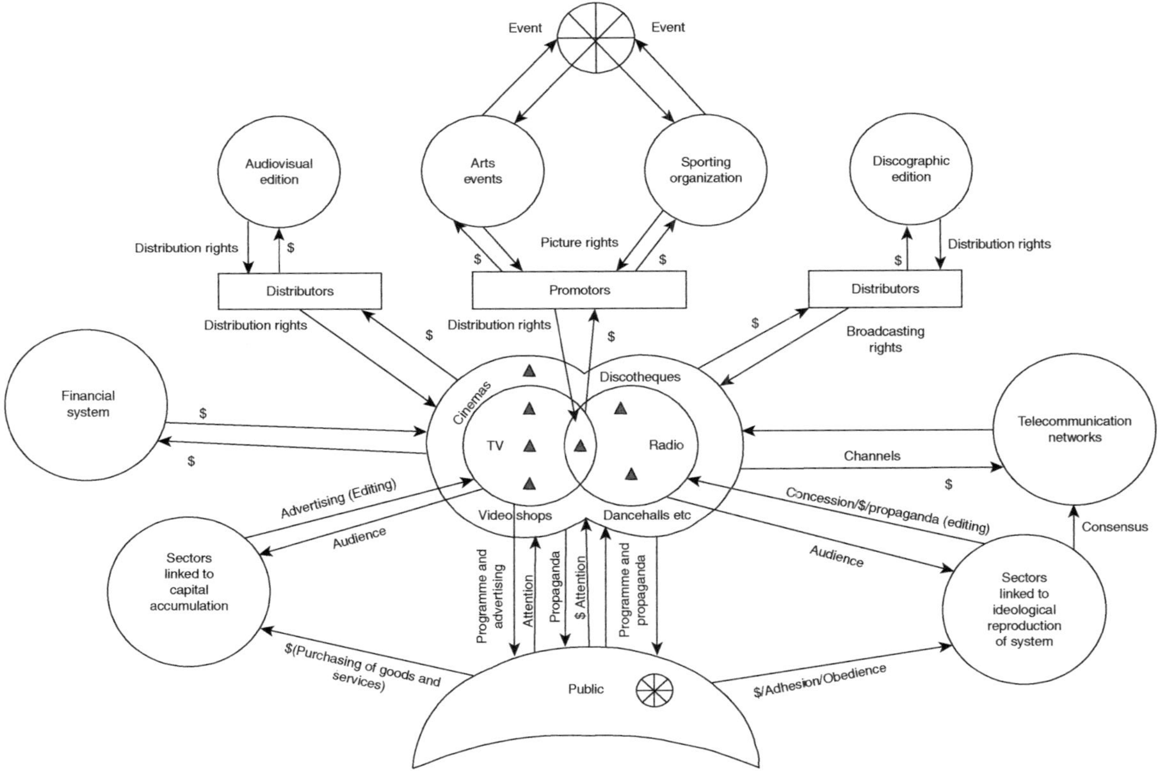

Figure 5.2 Model of analysis for audiovisual sector, including Radio

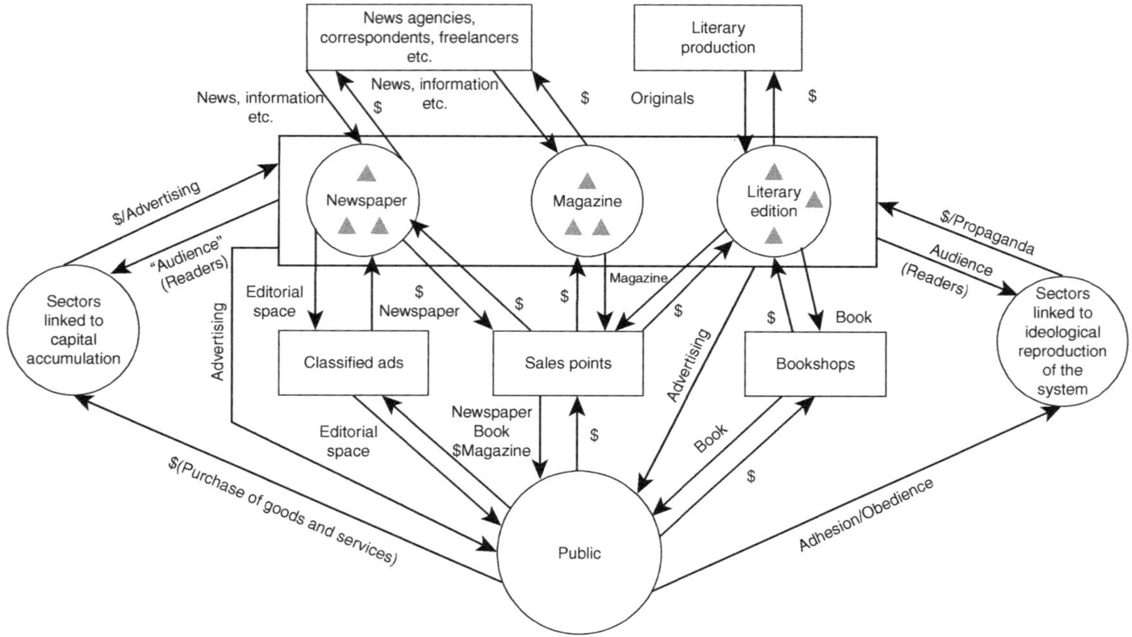

Figure 5.3 Simplified analysis model for newspaper, books and magazines

the sector. This first box is included within another that also adds other distribution spaces for audiovisual productions in a strict sense (film and video productions), film projection theatres and video stores. The upper section of the graph represents what we might call the "audiovisual complex", which includes the sectors of audiovisual publishing, the arts and live presentations and event promoters, responsible for the intermediation between production and distribution, and which take on crucial importance, above all with regard to film distribution, organized under the form of an oligopoly functioning on a worldwide scale, but also of the organizers of large events and large sports federations that monopolize the negotiation with broadcasters and TV networks.[20] For obvious reasons I did not consider in this diagram the entire chain of small and middle-sized negotiators, managers, agents and lawyers whose function is essentially to reach agreement on the distribution of the prices that promoters finally negotiate with the networks. My objective here is to present an overall framework of the intersectoral structures,[21] leaving a more detailed analysis of each specific sector out of the equation.

The important fact that should be highlighted in the analysis of this quadrant of the diagram is that all the flow lines within the "primary market" are lines of money or rights. In fact, it is the broadcasting rights and not the programme itself that the station acquires. The transfer of the programme product to the audience product is necessarily made under this legal framework. This means that, in order to pass from the limited level of a microeconomic concept to that of a macroeconomic concept relating the whole of the audiovisual sector[22] with advertisers from the greater differentiated consumer goods sector (and, therefore, with the macroeconomic dynamic of monopolistic capitalism) and with the state and other political institutions (hence with the macro political dynamic), this transfer must be made through the legal system.

In other words, the passage from a microeconomic analysis of the processes of programme or event production to the macroeconomic and macro social analysis of the link between the processes of capital accumulation and the ideological reproduction of the system requires a level, which we could refer to as "meso-economic", in which unification is achieved, due to the programming task performed by television (or radio) of the different cultural productions (which then become cultural production in the abstract), which cannot be effected without the intervention of law. This is a classic process of private issuing of a circulation right on the basis of a capital datum (programmes). On this level, state action is limited to the setting of rules to ensure that the private creation of commercial rights is possible, and that those rights can be negotiated on the market through the intermediation of money. In this case the state acts as a simple legal agent for private rights, which in turn leads to the expansion of the circulation marketing sphere.

But this function of the state is subordinate to its principal function as a licensing power. This is where the constitution of regulatory agencies comes into play, such as the FCC in the USA or the CSA in France, given that the function described above could theoretically be fulfilled by the classical forms of legal organization that can no longer take on this issue when the state directly assumes control over the system or assumes the role of a licensing power. In these cases, the constitution of specific apparatuses for the control or regulation of the system becomes indispensable. The French case demonstrates, for example, a close relationship between the privatization of the audiovisual and the constitution of the independent instance of regulation, as Emmanuel Négrier noted. If the idea of creating an audiovisual authority separate from governmental power gains popularity in France with the *Paye Report*, from 1970, in the Office de Radiodiffusion Télévision Française (ORTF) statute, it was only in 1982, under the three-pronged condition of the affirmation of the strategic importance of this industrial sector, the questioning of the role of the state in controlling communications and the legitimization of private audiovisual management, that it was able to become a reality. "It is precisely from the moment in which the legislator consecrates the idea of a possible privatisation of the audiovisual, in 1982, that the creation of an instance of regulation becomes necessary" (Négrier, 1989b, p. 91).

Thereafter, citing J. Chevalier, Négrier explains that this creation can be seen, in comparison with the prior situation in the country – where the state exercised an audiovisual monopoly using a specific apparatus (the ORTF, subordinate to the Ministry of Communications) – not as democratization but rather as "the declination of the classical principal of the democratic decision" and as a way to contain the traditional powers of democratic control of the administration (idem, p. 92). I hasten to add that this argument cannot be used in the Brazilian case, in which an independent instance of this kind could constitute a significant counterweight, not only to the unchecked power the executive has in the licensing of frequencies, but also to the enormous interests of the legislature, where a large portion of the representatives of the people consist of radio and television licensees. This constitutes one of the gravest publicly acknowledged distortions of the organization of the Brazilian political system. But the French (or European) case is another matter.[23]

It is not possible to discuss here the highly interesting European case. The main point to emphasize for the moment is that the differences between Brazil and France, or among state-run, private or mixed audiovisual systems of organization, are the different sectoral modes of regulation. The diagrammatic model that I have described hopefully hopefully the capacity to serve in the characterization of any specific case and, consequently, in comparative analysis. Later on I will return to this, using Italian television as an illustration.

On the right side of the diagram we have the state and the political institutions, as well as a special industrial sector – that of the telecommunications networks. The state appears twice as a licensing power, which shares some attributes with certain capitalists: in one case, those linked to its function of ensuring the general external conditions for the accumulation of capital and, in the other, those that form part of the monopoly of symbolic violence it holds. In the first case (telecommunications), the analysis is no different from that conducted by Marx for the transportation and communications sectors in *Capital* and in the *Grundrisse*, which we have already considered. Let us add simply that within a national telecommunications system competition is also present, whether it is that exercised between capitals participating (or hoping to participate) in it, or between the various state apparatuses involved (e.g. between France Telecom and TDF in France until the incorporation of the latter by the former) or between the specific interests of the state and capital in the sector.

A further point worth mentioning: the technical discussions among the different telecommunications actors are frequently political discussions. This means that the determining role in this sector over the audiovisual is not limited to questions of a "technical" nature. They are also eminently "political". Unfortunately, it will not be possible here to offer a more detailed analysis of the telecommunications sector. This would require a detailed study of the relationships among the many actors present in this sector – not limited to national transmission monopolies or near-monopolies or to the worldwide oligopoly of equipment manufacturers in the sector. Such a study would need to embrace inter alia private satellite operators, private cable systems operators, the municipalities to which these networks are linked and the different programme providers, together with other related sectors such as information technology and TV itself.

When I speak of licensing I am of course referring to the more general case, which obviously includes the situation in which the operation of the system is performed directly by the state itself. Whatever the case, licensing power, both in telecommunications and in the audiovisual field, defines certain "serfdom" relationships. These are particularly evident in the distortions of the organization of the Brazilian political system, where licensing is deployed as an instrument of political negotiation. This occurred during the long debate in France over the role of the mass communications media in the coverage of the Gulf War, or in the famous case of the BBC's behaviour during the Falklands War. Other examples are the legal mechanisms available to the state to requisition free broadcasting time in certain circumstances from commercial TV broadcasters. It is on this basis that the issue of television independence should be discussed – not as the attribute of a determined institutional form.

On the left-hand side of the diagram are the industrial sectors linked to the audiovisual as advertisers or equipment suppliers. The latter is a conventional intersectoral relationship, reflecting that between the audiovisual and the financial system represented in the same quadrant. The most remarkable aspect of this part of the graphic is the triangle that brings together the audiovisual and the audience, and what I will call the "extended differentiated consumer goods sector". This is an expression defining the set of advertisers and which merits a brief explanation. I mention "consumer goods" because the group dynamic is still the one defined in, for example, Marx's or Kalecki's reproduction models. But this is an "extended" consumer goods sector because it comprises certain commercial, service and even general public banking service sectors, some capital goods areas such as agricultural, transportation and other equipment (all serialized capital goods could in effect be considered, but in general this only applies to highly segmented broadcasts, the existence of which is basically theoretical or of limited statistical significance). Finally, what characterizes this sector is a competitive dynamic focused on differentiation, which generally eliminates the non-oligopolistic sectors. The only exception would be paid announcements by associations of artisans or small capitalists (bakers, etc.).

The large leftmost triangle is opposite another (state and institutions of a political/audiovisual/public nature), with which it shares a common side describing three theoretical possibilities of group structures. The simplest structure is that of paid television, in which the programme is sold to the audience like any other product. The limit case of this hypothesis is the pay-per-view system. But we also have two other possibilities in which the relationship between the audience and television is itself "mediatised": conventional public service television, in which the viewer pays a fee to the state in exchange for the right to access the system, and traditional commercial television, in which the public only pays for the acquisition of the receiver apparatus and electricity costs. Among these three "pure" models any combination is possible. In European countries, for example, the three cases cited are shown to exist, while in Brazil the fee to use a TV set does not. Public service television, prevented by law from access to advertising, can only be grant-financed. This precludes it from engaging in more ambitious strategic action, effectively condemning it to projecting an image of independence and heroism (sometimes leading to disillusionment) enjoyed by an audience of 1%, 2% or at most 3%.

While in each case the viewing audience receives programmes, big business appropriates viewers' attention to serve its own interests. Even in the less evident case of exclusively paid television, the audience and its characteristics are important in the negotiations between networks and programme and event providers. In the case of a public monopoly with a single channel, the audience continues to be a determinant, even when it is not measured and does not generate discussion about the "ratings dictatorship".

What is of greater interest to us is the advertising/programming/propaganda conflict indicated in the diagram containing the two large triangles mentioned above. In practice, it is obviously not easy to make a clear distinction between these three components. The increasingly frequent use of advertising methods in political campaigns is evident; the same is true of institutional propaganda activity or public relations exercises by companies. The same programme can include increasingly explicit publicity/advertising not restricted to propaganda. Nowadays the predominance of advertising is a worldwide trend.

I hope to have made clear that the theoretical distinction between these three elements is fundamental, since it is the only way to explain the contradictions that arise between political and economic institutions, between each of these and the audience and, perhaps, between the imperatives of capital accumulation, ideological reproduction of the system (which is not evidently an exclusive attribute of either propaganda or advertising/publicity, arising first in a space of contradiction between economic and political institutions and not simply between capital and the state) and symbolic reproduction of the lifeworld of the individuals who form the masses with which the state and capital are anxious to communicate. In actual fact I am no longer concerned with finding an abstract relationship between the different logics of advertising, propaganda and programming, but rather with discussing the possibility of its articulation, in terms of functionality, non-functionality and regulation relationships, on a more specific level of analysis. The excellent study by Musso & Pineau (1990) on Italian television may help to clarify this point.

These authors, in my view, make very clear the movement from a stabilized institutional setting (from the post-war period onward) to the crisis (in the 1970s and 1980s) and, later, to the stabilized configuration based on new institutionalized commitments from the second half of the 1980s). The long period spanned by the administrations of Filiberto Guala and Ettore Bernabei is marked by RAI's absolute monopoly and the "pedagogical model" of television, a tool of the Christian Democrats' political hegemony. This is a configuration in which propaganda is almost totally predominant, forcing advertising to use other non-television related channels. As a result of the student and union struggle against the control of information by the Christian Democrats, a range of reform proposals began to appear, to counteract the monolithic nature of the public monopoly. After the historic strike of 1969 this movement culminated in 1975 with the reform law and the *lotizzazione* (division into plots) of RAI, instituting what could be referred to as a "new propaganda regime". The RAI crisis was nothing more than a part of the crisis arising from Christian Democrat hegemony and the entire political pact in place since the end of the Second World War. Note that this process was similar to what happened in France at the same period, where the initial configuration of the system was also marked by the hegemony of the "pedagogical model" of Gaullist television, which suffered growing criticism, culminating in the events of May 1968 and leading, among many other things, to the first "audiovisual reform" in 1974. But this is the point where the similarities between the two cases end, with each of them following separate paths in the efforts to reform their national television systems.

Transformation of the system in Europe is not restricted to politics. From 1971, the Italian public monopoly was undermined by a developing private sector that knew how to exploit the gap between the advertising needs of companies and the limitations imposed by the structure of the public television system. The appearance of cable and the relaxation of controls on the airwaves, and the appearance of Berlusconi's national and international empire (which began with pirate radio and TV stations) marked the end of an entire regulation system rooted in propaganda. It is interesting to note that the structure that was developed after the 1976 constitutional court decision, characterized by the proliferation of small local stations subordinate to large advertising agencies (which operated as programme distributors) was remarkably similar to that displayed by the Brazilian market in the 1950s and 1960s. This in no way represented a threat to the all-powerful RAI.

The process of concentration was extremely fast and by 1979–1980 the large literary publishing capitals begin to show interest in the sector. From this point on a transition took place in the private sector: basically a system of perfect competition (weak barriers to entry, precarious and constantly-challenged leadership positions, predomination of the public sector in the definition of programming policy, etc.) gave way to an extremely concentrated oligopolistic structure. In this process the public sector itself was under heavy pressure and felt it necessary to react. The previous arrangement among the political parties participating in the *lotizzazione*, instituted with the 1975 reform of the RAI, was forced to change and, finally, television as a pedagogical instrument had to give way to television as a Culture Industry, leading to "the abandonment of the reform of the public monopoly and the legitimisation of commercial television, all in favour of the mixed system" (Musso & Pineau, 1990, p. 55).

The stabilization of the system, starting in 1985, took place under completely new political and market conditions, whether from the viewpoint of public relations/propaganda, from that of the relationship between capital and the state in the sector or from that of the market and the competition process. The RAI had thus to learn to operate within a competitive system. The result was the constitution of an oligopolistic market dominated by two large companies – one private and the other public – in which advertising began to play a predominant role vis-à-vis propaganda. It was, in short, the instalment of an entirely new institutional configuration, as well as a new mode of information and culture regulation. The big difference from the situation in France was that the legislator hardly intervened at all in the regulatory process, which was basically conducted by the judicial power.

It was clear that this new situation could not be taken as definitive. On the contrary, the existence of an important sector of small local enterprises, small networks, cross-border stations, etc., characterized a much more dynamic structure than that existing in the post-war era – not because of the danger that small capital could probably represent to RAI or Berlusconi, but rather because of the variety of possibilities for entry and development that a large capitalist enterprise interested in this market would have. Movements of this kind were described by the authors in more recent periods (after 1985) and the sharpened international competition and introduction of technological innovations broadening the horizons of segmented television caused problems even for companies that succeeding in building substantial barriers to entry. The precariousness of this stabilization was also accentuated because "politics permeates the Italian audiovisual space and contributes to permanently redefining its frontiers. Thus, in the face of a duopoly, certain pro-Christian Democracy industrialists attempted to create a private network in order to re-establish a balance of influences" (Musso & Pineau, 1990, p. 118); not surprisingly, given the closeness between Berlusconi and the key Socialist Party heavyweights. It is not necessary to refer here to the discussion between the Italian case and what happened after the "*mani puliti*" case ("clean hands" was a nationwide Italian judicial investigation into political corruption held in the 1990s), Berlusconi's election as Prime Minister and his later downfall. We can, however, safely go along with this author's conclusion. Economics and politics are always dynamic and states of stability can be defined as "moments of transition into crisis". Even firmly consolidated positions, such as that of Globo in Brazil or RAI in Italy, are always a source of contention. Analysis of regulation during times of stability is only justified if it is linked to analysis at times of crisis, in the same way as the study of market structures and barriers to entry is only of interest if it is viewed from the dynamic perspective of competition.

The dynamic of the complete model

The second diagram, which I have called the "Simplified Model for Audiovisual Including Radio", is a simple extension of the first for the overall audiovisual sector. The model is simplified (compared to the first) in order to save space, but the previous discussion still applies. A detailed analysis of the radio dispute would add little to our discussion here. It should simply be stressed that the diagram proposed was unable to embrace the direct relationship forms between the medium and the audience, which are of the greatest importance for radio, although they are not ignored by television (especially local or regional television). A good portion of the economic and social specifics of radio come from this "interactivity". The issue is of key importance and, although it is not well presented in the diagrams, it has not been entirely neglected in my global analytical framework.

To save space, the diagrams do not include the horizontal relationships between audiovisual production, discographic production, the performing arts, the financial system, etc., or the contribution of research institutes to the advertising sector. Again, this is not the result of a deficient theoretical framework. I have already mentioned the importance of research institutes in the definition of the audience product. On this point I need only highlight the importance of considering all the types of intersectoral relationships in the study of actual cases. These are of particular importance for understanding the functioning of the culture industries, the issues of intermediate competition[24] and multimedia concentration. It is a difficult issue to represent in diagrams that use one or more of these kinds of framework as a mere analytical artifice. Thus, we could begin our study of the mass communication media in Brazil by defining the principal multimedia clusters in the country and by rapidly determining the different forms of intersectoral relationships and synergies, with the aim of evaluating the competitiveness of each of them in each specific market and within the Culture Industry as a whole. For this, the diagrams presented here could be of significant use, together with other conventional analytical tools (audience ratings, enterprise income, expenditure data, etc.).

The third diagram complements the two previous ones by integrating newspapers, magazines and books (in reality, three general forms of published products), which represent a much broader range – from the pamphlet to the scientific journal, a form quite similar to the book, with comics somewhere in between – as well as their respective "chains" constituted by news agencies and subscribers (who, in reality, complement the significant production of information performed by magazines and above all by newspapers) and literary production (in which the labour, as we have seen, is mainly artisanal, although situations involving producers of bestsellers, poetry or doctoral theses can also be considered. These are the longest-standing sectors in the Culture Industry, the relationships of which with the audience are generally much more conventional that those of radio and television, although all alternative forms of relationship that are not that of the simple sale and purchase of a product can be seen, including the free distribution of newspapers and other printed material exclusively for the purpose of publicity, advertising or propaganda. Whatever the case, the discussion presented previously on advertising/propaganda/programming remains valid.

On the other hand, the direct economic relationship between the audience and the advertising medium (classified ads) is of major importance to newspapers and helps, inter alia, to encourage the formation of a network of small businesses specialising in the collection of this type of material from the public. The importance of this sector is such that it gives rise to small and medium-sized journalistic enterprises specialising in the publication of this type of material in large cities. Another key characteristic of this segment is the substitution of telecommunications for a retail system consisting of a network of small-scale vendors (bookstores and newsstands). These constitute a competitive market, in common with other types of businesses such as retailers of CDs, videotapes or DVDs for mass consumption.[25] Other forms of distribution such as mail-order and in-home sales are also common. Telecommunications systems are used in the sector not as a distribution medium, but for "inter-enterprise" (e.g. between the newspaper and the news agencies) or "intra-enterprise" communications (e.g. for the simultaneous printing of a newspaper in different locations) – a form of communication more in keeping with telephone use than with broadcasting. Unlike with radio and television, the state does not appear in this segment as a licensing power, but rather in a more conventional role (e.g. as a kind of censor).

I do not wish to get caught up in the minutiae of the aforementioned sectors. The communication and culture economy is quite familiar with the issues involved. The three diagrams presented above encompass most of the so-called "content industries", lacking only: (a) some of the so-called "new media", such as videotext or teletext, which sit in the intersection between content industries and networks, as is also the case with interactive TV, included in the first diagram; and (b) other sectors which are not "industrialised", such as unique works of art or video art. At this point, it is not my intention to present an exhaustive framework, which would be neither possible nor desirable. Furthermore, the inclusion of these sectors would be incapable of reflecting the general conclusions we have reached here. It would be more interesting to review the global functioning of the model, taking once again the audiovisual example. The diagram on the next page should help to explain this approach (Figure 5.4).

The different technological trajectories of the audiovisual – film, mass, interactive, segmented TV (cf. Bolaño, 2004, p. 89, 93–98) – are represented in the central circle by the curves around which are positioned the different individual capitals, represented by the triangles. The two bold lines constitute the first level of determination of the technological trajectories that define the technical virtualities, the effectiveness of which depends on the second set of determinants, represented by dashed lines. As we have seen in Chapter 2 (ref: Flichy and Salaün), the definitive configuration of a new mass communications medium depends not only on its technical virtualities, but also on its acceptance by the public and the end-use to which it will be put, in addition to the financing model that will finally be adopted, and that will enable the reproduction

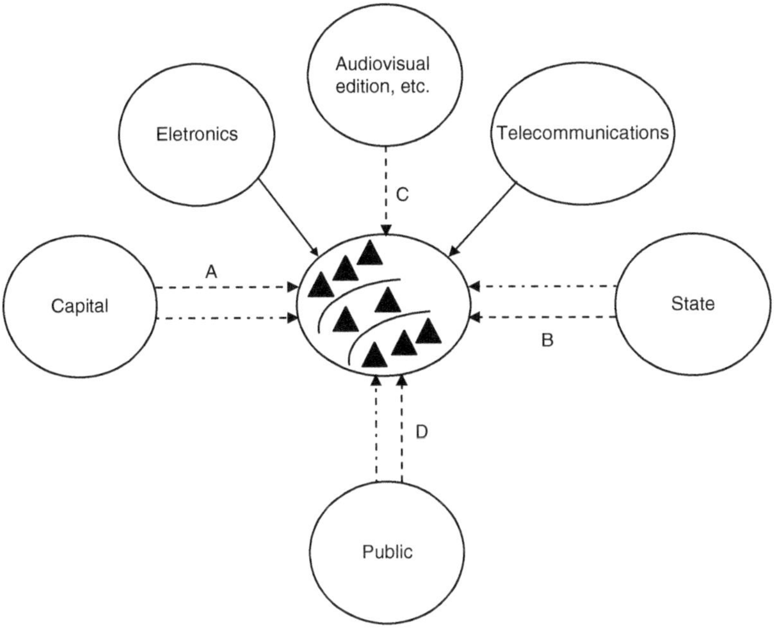

Figure 5.4 Synthesis of audiovisual dynamics structure

of the type of social relationship that the technical interaction/use proposes. The three principal forms of audiovisual financing are publicity, parafiscal charges and direct purchase by the audience.

These levels of determination depend primarily on the definition of hardware, its economic format and the type of social use involved.[26] The telecommunications, broadcast and teledistribution models are, for example, linked to types of technology, social use and forms of financing which are as different as television when defined as "interactive", "mass" or "segmented". But the crucial element, which characterizes the so-called content industries, is represented by the four dotted lines, linked to (a) the functions of capital accumulation in general and (b) ideological reproduction of the system, which the Culture Industry fulfils in capitalism, and (c) the production and (d) the consumption of culture.

Each of these four axes aligns with different theoretical contributions, most of them discussed here: (a) multiple authors who follow the foundational contributions of Baran & Sweezy or Smythe, as well as many neoclassicals and elements involved in the advertising market; (b) the more classical Marxist analysis of ideological apparatuses and hegemony or the majority of the Latin American theories of dependence or cultural imperialism; (c) the different schools, critical or neoclassical, of the communication and culture economy. In terms of the fourth dotted line (d), we can cite the various studies on the reception of the media, both in the "structural" (French) and the "content" (Brazilian) aspects, which are not a topic for study in this book since they exceed the limits of my competence, wrapped up as they are in disciplines such as psychology, psychosociology or anthropology. However, the general issue of what I have called "programming function" is crucial, as I hope to have made clear in the previous chapter, for the global application of the theoretical framework proposed here, which seeks to consider the whole of the contributions cited, refuting some and incorporating others in a coherent and non-eclectic way.

Let us take the vertical axis (C/D) of the model. Note that the audiovisual (or *flot* culture) is, first, the element of mediation between the production and the consumption of culture. It is this fact that transforms television into the "dominant media", to use Flichy's expression: this is the condition for access to the market of the various cultural productions, which assures them notoriety. The radio and television programmer holds the crucial decision-making power over what should or should not have access to the public and, consequently, over what will or will not have social validity from a mass culture perspective. The ability to ensure prestige and notoriety television is not limited to cultural productions; rather the relevance of all social occurrences is largely measured by the space they occupy on television. This is what will decide, ultimately, which artists are best, which politicians are most important, which crimes are most shocking, etc. The power of manipulation that this situation provides is indisputable, although many mitigating factors exist that refute any Orwellian arguments on the subject.[27]

In any case, television functions vis-à-vis the other sectors of cultural production as an oligopoly, thus maintaining the hegemony of the Culture Industry in most capitalist countries, enjoying advantages when bargaining with the world oligopoly involved in the film distribution – a sector that manages to preserve its autonomy in relation to the mediation power between the production and consumption of cultural goods held by TV and that confers on it a particularly high accumulation potential.[28] Something similar seems to occur in the relationship between radio (although much less concentrated than television) and the music industry. Flichy affirms, for example, that the participation of the music industry in radio programmes increased in the USA from 47%

to 80% between 1950 and 1963, reducing in parallel the percentage of in-house production as the result of the increasing competitiveness of television companies (Brazilian TV is a good example of this).

It is in this relationship between cultural producers and the culture-consuming public, mediated by the radio and television apparatus, that the different techno-aesthetic standards I spoke of previously are defined. Each of the individual capitals in the *flot* industry, with the backing of research institutes and a permanent dialogue with advertisers (including the state) and advertising agencies, defines a determinate action strategy in relation to the culture-consuming public, which will define their demand to the producers of the publishing sector. The latter offers a variety of options that the work of programming combines within a structure, according to the defined strategy. It is in this way that the different competing techno-aesthetic standards are constituted, which, as a whole, will form a techno-aesthetic regime within which the broad reproduction of symbolic capital will take place.

We have already seen that what television offers to the public is a mixture (whether it is easily differentiated or not is unimportant) of advertising, propaganda and programming. These are three concepts that have less to do with the empirical reality of day-to-day TV programming than with the definition of the functions that programming is destined to fulfil in the processes of capital accumulation and the ideological reproduction of the system. Dotted lines A and B represent the very differentiated demands that capital and economic institutions on one side, and the state and political institutions on the other, make on the Culture Industry (or the audiovisual, in this case), which serves as a secondary element of mediation between these instances of power and the public.

We can now return to any of the three previous diagrams and observe that, both on the part of capital and the state, there is an expected feedback from the action of the Culture Industry on the public (acquisition of goods and services on one hand, obedience on the other). The public is expected to react in a particular way to the stimulus given to it through advertising and propaganda. The entire system is organized in a way that guarantees this result. Each individual consumer goods sector expects, ultimately, when advertising its products, an increase in sales (of course there are other strategic objectives in play, but this does not change the fundamental question), though advertising can obviously fail to produce the expected results. In fact, as we have seen, the function of publicity and advertising is, together with the credit system, to diminish the rotation time of capital, reducing uncertainty in terms of the realization of capital gain. But there is no fundamental, infallible law that ensures that advertising will be efficient if it lacks efficiency at the micro level. A small recession can undo the effect of all the advertising in the world. A television system can be organized as it was for decades in Eastern Europe, basically outlawing advertising, which was forced to take refuge in other spaces, which generally proved to be less efficient for the required purposes.

When we refer to advertising we are in effect referring to a condition of functionality that may or may not be fulfilled, depending inter alia on the structure and global dynamic of the system. The same can be said of the propaganda and programming functions. Thus a techno-aesthetic standard very disassociated from the needs of the public may not gain social validity – or may do so only marginally. Theoretically a dysfunctionality of this type can be considered even for a techno-aesthetic regime as a whole, although the probability that this occurs in reality may be practically nil, at least under current conditions.[29] We can speak, therefore, of three general conditions of functionality, the effectiveness of which cannot be ensured a priori. Moreover, another problem needs to be considered: that of the compatibility of these three functions, which also cannot be taken for granted. For this to occur, regulatory mechanisms are needed which are able to ensure the reproduction of all of them. In short, a sectoral mode of regulation is called for, with authorities and others institutionally committed to enforcing it (e.g. the Federal Communications Commission in the United States or the Conseil National de l'audiovisuel (CNA) in France).

The interests at play in each case are extremely complex: advertising agencies, advertisers, institutes, the state, political groups, social organizations, consumers, the different sectors of cultural production, the different communication media that vie for the attention of the public and people's free time and, above all, the advertising pie, the producers of electronic and telecommunications equipment, the institutions that dispute the hegemony of the symbolic order, the popular and resistance cultures, the various capitals, monopolistic or otherwise, that act or wish to act in each of the sectors mentioned, the star system. In addition to this, in thinking of this extensive game of interests, the different levels (local, regional, national and international) on which it is constructed (Bolaño, 2003) and the different levels of concentration of the different sectors must be taken into account.

Each national communications system will acquire, in a determined period of history, a specific configuration. Thus, Gaullist television in France, as with Italian TV in the same period, looked to propaganda as its primary function, prohibiting commercial advertising. This was opposite to what was occurring in television in General Franco's Spain, which, though adopting the statist model of fascism, was a pioneer in the introduction of commercial advertisement-based television in Europe. In England, unlike the vast majority of European countries, the mixed system (state/private) had already been introduced in the 1950s. In the USA, Brazil and the Americas in general the commercial model is predominant, although historically significant cases of state systems have existed (Argentina and Venezuela) and public service has also occupied (extremely limited) space in many of these countries. In addition, just as there are no two identical national systems, commercial models are also extremely variable: in the USA, for example, the rules limiting monopolies, restricting multimedia concentration, favouring local production, etc., are very strict, while in Brazil the most no-holds-barred form of capitalism predominates. The examples are numerous.

The analytical frameworks presented above provide a model that is malleable, flexible and adaptable to the study of each particular case, in each country, in each Culture Industry, in each combination of specific factors and in each sectoral regulatory mode. As with any regulationist model, what the frameworks are able to provide is a snapshot of a stable configuration, determined historically, the internal contradictions of which will at some point lead to a crisis – from which will rise a new stable configuration with new contradictions and so forth. This regulation-crisis-regulation movement has taken place, worldwide, in the case of the Culture Industry, for around a century, characterized by a tendency to form three social logics (publicity/advertising, propaganda and cultural production) in which the latter is subsumed by the others (a natural occurrence if we agree with Bourdieu that the holders of symbolic capital are a dominated fraction of the dominant class) and, most importantly, the first becomes progressively more hegemonic in relation to the second, confirming the theses of the sharpest theoretical critiques of capitalism on the expansive character of the logic of capital.

6
Subsumption of Intellectual Work and the Political Economy of the Internet

The essentially linked nature of the political domination, economic exploitation and ideological reproduction processes of the capitalist form of information has not changed because of the development of information technology and communication, although the most interesting aspect of the internet is its potential to democratize information, encourage horizontal communication and connect society in a way that is more independent and relatively invisible to the state and economic powers.

In reality, nothing is univocal in capitalist development and the same factors that drive it open up possibilities for transformation, although at present the great revolutionary force, the working class, are suffering their greatest ever defeat at a global level as well as a profound and relentless restructuring of the world system. However, the emergence of the internet raises the issue of joint action by society and its organizations in the pursuit of a fairer social order and greater autonomy with regard to the economy and the state. Here the internet promises interactive global communication and to be a community creator.

We should not expect too much from this potential because the asymmetries are a structural part of the internet, ensuring the existence of a complex hierarchy in which individuals and especially organizations who wield greater economic, political or symbolic capital prevail. Additionally, economic interests are increasingly hegemonic and essentially all the logic of action within the internet is essentially competitive and individualistic. However, we know that there is a political culture in the network that still favours actions that are not economically motivated. Also, the design itself and its form of expansion guarantee its users a certain autonomy which is naturally differentiated and asymmetric, whether they are companies, individuals, criminals or NGOs. There is room, in any case, for counter-hegemonic political action, which also derives from the contradictory nature of the information of which I spoke earlier.

Above all, the interactive nature of the internet can be a key element in the rescue of organizational functions and the agitprop of the unofficial and non-commercial press, to obtain an independent press committed to social movements. In this sense, what is important is the idea of "creating community" and connecting global interest groups in order to provide impetus to localized political action. The local–global relationship is essential.

While capital is being globalized, national resistance has become increasingly less effective in response to what has become known as neo-liberalism; thus it is only natural that the resistors have started to organize and act on a global level. And this is where the internet can make things easier. But for it to have any meaning other than purely "symbolic", and be able to show any effectiveness, it is necessary to set specific policies in motion in the place where they will be most effective.

The virtual is not a substitute for the real; it only provides a new dimension, or in other words, what today is conventionally called virtual space is nothing but a new dimension of reality, a second nature, which helps us see the relationship of the potential liberators offered by the development of the productive forces, and the limits imposed by exploited production relationships within which technological progress occurs. Based on this, it is possible to go beyond the detection of a simple parallelism in the field of mass communication, to move into a discussion centred on structural determination and historical freedom, and find that the problem that interests us lies within the method of production itself.

Here the question can also be considered from the convergence point of view. Consider initially the case of cultural work. The issue of culture can be, and traditionally is, posed in two different ways. It can first be understood from the point of view of the opposition between culture and economy, taken as separate spheres, between which there is a relationship of tension as well as determination. In a general sociological perspective, under certain circumstances the cultural producer and artist are defined as intellectuals in the traditional sense, or as Gramsci puts it, as "organic" intellectuals. In this case, cultural work has an ideological function, which is the construction of hegemony of a particular class or a counter-hegemony linked to an alternative society project. The concept of "national popular culture" is considered as such. The ruling class, as we know, is that which can transform its particular interest into the national interest and, by extension, their particular class of culture into hegemonic culture, socially recognized at national level as the superior model and as a standard.

On the other hand, culture can be seen in an anthropological sense as a set of social practices that encompass economic practices and the culture produced by the people, not necessarily the people as a nation, but the people as a community, which defines itself through deep cultural identities to endogenously guarantee the symbolic reproduction of the lifeworld. In this sense, one cannot speak in principle of a cultural producer separate from the community, or cultural work as a special work. The community produces its own culture. However, we can also talk about class culture in this case. The definition of class given by E. P. Thompson (1981), for example, is along the same lines, and Hobsbawm (1987) shows very clearly the existence of a working-class culture in 19th-century England, globally opposing the predominant bourgeois culture. The same can be observed, for example, with the anarchist workers who made up the industrial working class in Brazil prior to 1930.

A new phenomenon has arrived in the 20th century that profoundly alters the data in that equation: the Culture Industry. It creates a mass culture that is not quite bourgeois; it is essentially popular in the sense that it opposes the erudite. Rather than being bourgeois, the Culture Industry reworks popular culture and transforms it into mass culture, which, in turn, dissolves and subordinates all forms of class culture, from folklore to the erudite, which then become cultures of resistance.

That culture of the masses, whose paradigm is television in general, developed in response to needs expressed by the capitalist mode of production itself from the way it was structured throughout the 20th century. We have seen throughout this book that this issue can be thoroughly understood through discussion of the contradictions of information, in particular in its development, to the degree of abstraction in which one can speak of functions, of the publicity–propaganda opposition, within which the first, publicity, is linked to the process of capital accumulation, the competitive capitalist and mass consumption, which in turn is connected with mass production and, more specifically in the 20th century, with the so-called Taylorist-Fordist model with large unions, etc., while the second, propaganda, is linked to the needs of ideological reproduction of the system at the level defined as a function of the state, or else political legitimacy to rule, in which the mass democracy model also triumphs (after the defeat of the fascist alternative, also of the masses, of state organization under capitalism), of the mass parties.

We saw that there is solidarity, and at the same time, tension between these two functions of the Culture Industry, the specifically capitalist form of cultural production, hegemonic in the historical conditions of monopoly capitalism. To fulfil its dual role, that is, for the Culture Industry to effectively mediate between capital and state on the one hand, and the mass that constitutes the public on the other, the Culture Industry needs to respond to the need to produce meaning in the lifeworld, at which publicity and propaganda are aimed, once the mechanisms of symbolic reproduction that exist in popular culture, in the second sense mentioned above, are destroyed by the processes of "colonization" that the Culture Industry itself performs on the *Lebenswelt*, to put the issue in Habermasian terms.

To the extent to which it is succeeding, the Culture Industry is, in fact, promoting the unification of these two concepts of culture and creating a national popular culture, in the anthropological sense of the term, which serves not only the needs of legitimizing domination, but more importantly, the manipulation of needs with a view to continuing and increasing capital accumulation.[1] To fulfil this third function, the Culture Industry needs to be capable of creating an empathic relationship with the public, transforming it into an audience.

The typical figure of the cultural worker as that of the popular artist is doubly dispossessed. On the one hand, he is separated from the public. To gain access to the public, the artist is required to submit himself to a technical and economic apparatus within which he becomes a producer of surplus value. On the other hand, the artist's work creates boundaries, subsumed by capital which also comes to rationalize cultural production in a broad sense, causing the classic effects of specialization of labour, unemployment and the creation of an army of reserves which marked the emergence and expansion of the working class.

The problem is that this process of subsumption of cultural work by capital has limits that cast doubt on the possibility that real subsumption can be imposed in the same way as it was on material production. That limit, responsible for the hallmarks of cultural production (randomness of production, economic strategies to overcome it, need for renovation, maintenance of very specific market structures), is seen by the French school of political economy of communication and culture, as noted in Chapter 4, as derived from a heritage of unique art which marked the emergence of bourgeois art in the Renaissance period.

My own explanation of the phenomenon is, I repeat, different: the cultural work has a symbolic mediation role between the institutions of power and the public because the cultural worker is, in itself, an element that has emerged from popular culture and has, therefore, the ability to communicate with the people, to create an effect of empathy that cannot be otherwise achieved.

Clearly, an entire orchestra can be replaced by a single electronic organ, but the needs of the lifeworld are so complex that this process, so far, has encountered insurmountable limits, preventing the knowledge of popular artists from being expropriated to the same extent as occurred with the craftsman at the stage of what I called, in Chapter 1, "primitive accumulation of knowledge". This is not a feature of artistic work, but of all cultural mediation work, such as that of the journalist or the educator. What then can we say about the entire so-called intellectual work?

Intellectual work

We know that the division between manual and intellectual work is older than capitalism,[2] whose starting point, however, lies precisely in the expropriation of artisan knowledge and therefore in the replacement of that division, which had been partially erased by craftsmanship. In any event, this division acquires a specific character in capitalism, because it occurs not only in the macro-social sphere but also within the production process itself, alienating the manual worker and depriving him of the possibility of using his mental capacities and of having a complete view of the entire production process. Similarly the intellectual foregoes the ability to act directly on the means and objects of labour, stunting a part of his creative potential.

Marx dealt with the disastrous consequences of the division of labour in detail, clearly focusing on manual work. We are very familiar with the dangers of specialization for the individual worker, deforming both body and mind and effectively stupefying them, while the worker becomes more effective collectively and enriches capital. Today we know that this is also true for intellectual and bureaucratic work, causing other forms of stress, atrophy, other occupational diseases and alienation. This has been especially evident since the moment when capitalist development led to the expansion of all manner of work involving design, control and organization, the growth and proletarianization of the so-called "middle class", drastically changing the existing social structure from the beginning.

The process of subsumption of conceptual, intellectual and bureaucratic work by capital is historically specific and acquired new momentum, reaching a qualitatively and quantitatively superior state, with the development of information technology, telematics and office automation. At the same time, the introduction of information technology in conventional work processes, robotics, etc., has led to a growing intellectualization of traditional proletarian labour, which, unfortunately, has nothing to do with overcoming the alienation of labour. It is more to do with the change of direction of the alienation and the reinforcement of the worker's boundaries with the advancement of the exploitation of their mental energies and capacities, in addition to their physical energies and manual creative abilities. This fundamentally changes the social structure and the form of basic capitalist social relations.

Software is the method the system has found to frame the mental work, to turn it into a pattern and exploit its potential for capital. Thus it is that knowledge, once the property of the isolated intellectual worker, becomes an element of constant capital, similar to what happened to manual labour with the emergence of machines. There is a convergence of trends in the development of the subsumption of labour in the processes of cultural production and intellectual production in general, that extends to large sections of the traditional working class, posing the same questions on mediation and boundaries that we talk about when speaking of cultural work.

The "quasi-intellectual" concept of Cesareo, under these conditions, does not fully reflect what occurs, as it is no longer just about replacing the old-style intellectual with a new "alienated" intellectual. The trend now is of a general intellectualization of the work process, evidenced by the disqualification, parcelling and subsumption of all types of intellectual work. At a time when manual labour can be widely replaced by machinery, there is a requirement for the working class to primarily mobilize its mental energies, causing hypertrophy of certain intellectual abilities to the detriment of others, new forms of alienation, deepening social exclusion, with complete immiseration of those who fail to adapt to change and, at the same time, growing unemployment of skilled people and, in short, an uncontrollable rise of all the widely known social (and mental) conditions that characterize the end of the 20th century and the beginning of the 21st: spiritual poverty, insecurity, violence at all levels, loss of sense of existence, drug addiction, micro-social forms of corruption, etc.

The situation is classic with regard to the creation of a working class (now intellectualized in the sense described above) whose subsumption by capital is increasing (although we cannot say what the limit of this process will be) in parallel with the formation of a reserve industrial army fitted to the new structure of the system, with an increase in relative misery, concentration of wealth, centralization of capital and increased competition in every sense. In this respect, the beginning of the 21st century is similar to the 19th century: (neo) liberalism is dominant, the Keynesian interventionist state is retracting, the welfare state is being destructured and, with this, the general law of capitalist accumulation is once again being crudely imposed, again confirming the until-recently discredited predictions made by Marx. This is not simply a return to the past, however; the central problems posed by the 20th-century monopoly system remain intact, so that at this moment, and until a new mode of regulation is stabilized that is capable of generating widespread development without exclusion, it combines the worst of both worlds.

As we saw, the rise of the Culture Industry during the 19th century is linked to what Habermas calls "structural change in the public sphere", i.e., the neutralization of its critical characteristics and its capacity for political action in favour of manipulative communication methods (advertising and propaganda), as a reaction to the potentially explosive nature that it began to attain from the moment of the transformation from the liberal state into a democratic state of the masses, removing restrictions imposed by the former's participation in non-proprietary and unenlightened layers. What we see today is a new restructuring of the public sphere, which incorporates the exclusive and critical nature of the classical bourgeois public sphere, maintaining and reinforcing, for most of the world's population, the paradigm of mass culture and the nation state (Bolaño, 1997).

The internet is the most important example of this trend. Offered initially as a non-hierarchical revolutionary structure, a communication between free and equal individuals, today it is clearly shown to be something that consists of a complex and extremely asymmetric network of players, where the ability to communicate and have access to relevant information depends precisely on those elements that in the past ensured access to the liberal public sphere, namely economic power (ownership), political power and knowledge, in that order. Today's profound transformation of all communication systems is not aimed towards advancing democracy, but towards the constitution of a world in which power is increasingly concentrated, making critical "communicative action" viable again for certain sectors of the world population, the vast majority being excluded but nevertheless excited by the prospect of regular participation in increasingly innocuous electoral processes (even with regard to national policy), where even here the power of decision is found elsewhere.

Thus, both material and symbolic production today converge, pointing to the establishment of total capitalism, in which nothing escapes being a commodity, and the production of value and surplus value. Furthermore, if this is true, it should be noted that the development of information and communication technologies points to the overcoming of the separation between work and life, thereby reinforcing the alienation, but also demonstrating the possibility of a real transformation in the direction of socialization via work, in a non-capitalist way. Additionally, to the extent that this development is linked to a situation in which certain material needs would be potentially satisfied, this opens liberating possibilities that were previously unimaginable. In this sense, it is necessary to fight for self-determination of leisure time, against the divisive and individualizing tendencies that capitalist management signifies.

The political economy of the internet

Development of the internet is rooted in the larger transformations experienced by the different communications sectors during the European broadcasting reform of the 1980s, and the global restructuring of telecommunications in the 1980s and 1990s, linked with the transition to a new regulatory model more suited to the new structure of capitalism which developed during the crisis of the accumulation model after the Second World War. Thus it is that communications in general take on a central role in the new accumulation model. Dan Schiller places the issue within the global telecommunications revolution in the 1990s, and summarizes it as follows:

> First, the network system-building boom was of a magnitude that the world had never seen. Old networks were upgraded to support novel services, while capacious new systems sprang up at every level, from local loop to global grid. Equally significant, however, was a second feature of the emerging regime. Policymakers the world over simultaneously abandoned public-service policies for market-driven tenets and acceded to the integration of networks on a transnational scale. National welfare controls over this critical infrastructure dropped away, while disparities in access widened.
>
> (Schiller, 2000, p. 2)

For Schiller, the internet would be the catalyst for a period of political and economic transition towards a "digital capitalism" after its subordination by market logic. In fact, there is a fundamental change in the organization of the internet when changing from a state-military-academic mentality (as in the classic North American innovation model driven by the military-industrial composite in response to the demands of the State Department) to another, academic-commercial mentality after the privatization of the mid-1990s.

It is not only a change of logic from state to private, but, on one hand, that of a public economy based on state investment to a market-driven one according to different modes of commodification, and on the other, from a political-military defence logic, to one of privatization, regulation and economic globalization supporting capitalist restructuring and maintenance of US hegemony in international economic relations. This general movement is part of the transition from the Cold War to the imperial model of sovereignty spoken of by Negri and Hardt (2001).

In the first chapter of his book, Schiller traces the historical path of development and the privatization of telematic networks, especially the internet, in the USA from the 1950s to the 1990s. The state logic of liberalization from the 1970s is well summarized in the following excerpt:

> Around 1970, short-term lobbying to secure piecemeal regulatory changes shaded into long-term strategic planning. At about that point executives and government bureaucrats recognized that the stakes in this arcane area of policy were huge – that continued U.S. corporate stewardship of the exploding information technology industry might renew waning U.S. global political-economic power. This outward-rippling expansion led towards comprehensive restructuring of the world's information infrastructure.
>
> (Schiller, 2000)

A crucial moment in this process, as we know, was the telecommunications reform in the USA in 1984 with the breakup of AT&T, which would trigger a liberalization and privatization movement on a global scale under pressure from the US government and international institutions like the World Bank, the International Monetary Fund and the World Trade Organization (WTO).[3] The abrupt rupture of the old model in the USA, the UK and Third World countries including Brazil (despite the delay with which the process took place in Brazil compared to other Latin American countries), contrasts with the slow and heavily controlled changes in Western Europe.

The internet victory in 1995 and Clinton and Al Gore's Global Information Infrastructure Project (GII) would eventually undermine European resilience. Europe would go on to liberalize the telecommunications sector in a more incisive manner in the hope of positioning itself more competitively in the "new economy", and in the technological development of specialized areas such as the internet. The debate over the format of digital TV that arose because of the expansion of the digitalization model clearly shows that the hegemonic European (and Japanese) intentions did not disappear with the end of the discussion over HDTV[4] at the beginning of the 1990s.

This search for competitiveness by Europe typically occurred during the return of American hegemony that was put under pressure at the time of the crisis in the 1970s and would be re-imposed during the Reagan administration in the monetary, political and military areas, but with doubts about the real economy given the progress made by Germany and Japan, chiefly in the automotive and electronics sectors. The transformation of the development method would come about rapidly. Precisely at the moment in which the hegemony of the dollar was restored, the crisis affected principally Japan, but also Europe, heavily impacted by unemployment and the complex process of German reunification. This transformation, therefore, would be once again led by the USA, particularly after the implementation of the restructuring policy of the Clinton administration.

In contrast, as might have been expected, the European Information Society project, from the Anglo-Saxon liberal perspective of the "New Economy", is nothing but the European way of entering into this huge game in which the initiative lies with the USA, whose telecommunications, IT and content production industries, to say nothing of biotechnologies, will widely lead the new accumulation system. The development of telematic infrastructures, under these conditions, supports the enterprise networks linked to the evolution of capitalism in the period of globalization, leading to the transformation of the world economy with the internet performing a central role, or digital capitalism in the words of Schiller, a process that involves major changes in all sectors of the communications economy.

Looking at the possibilities offered by technology, the distribution of information provides a double perspective. First, the commercial perspective which is of immediate interest to the state (at least in the central countries, especially the USA) and the market, and second, linguistic exchanges within the lifeworld. The historical development of the internet, in which the commercial logic becomes increasingly important, fails to eliminate the non-commercial market. On the contrary, it appears as a fundamental attraction for connecting individuals who pay the telephone companies and access providers (or agree to receive advertising in exchange for free or cheap access), in search of not only marketed content and commercial facilities, but also the possibilities of remote communication and integration.

There is, therefore, a contradiction in the system, comparable to that which is present in all development of the productive forces under capitalism, which manifests itself today in the growing process of subsumption of intellectual work by capital, linked to the development of information and communication technologies and the telematics networks. These are in reality two complementary movements. The general intellectualization of labour and its organization in networks also corresponds to an intellectualization and connection of the consumer to the global network. The mode of consumption, like the mode of production, becomes more communicational and computerized, altering social relations and the structure of the lifeworld of large segments of the world population included in the processes of capital reproduction. More information and communication in the workplace and in the lifeworld can become, under certain conditions, more information and communication in the service of a liberating, alternative and anti-capitalist project.

This is not, however, the hegemonic trend, but the creation of a knowledge economy, focusing on the subsumption of intellectual labour and the privatization of knowledge through the development of patents and intellectual property affecting all national systems of education, science and technology.[5] For the practical operation of the relations between state, university and market, which underlie the development of the internet from its inception, the business relationship between the military sector and academic laboratories is the basis for the subsequent privatization of the network, which in turn means the final step from one logic to another, purely commercial logic, involving the sale of patents, merchandise or audiences in the advertising market.

However, beyond the models of mass internet and e-business there is a large public demand which is not limited to students, professors and university researchers, but also includes social movements, NGOs and public administration, whose telematic communication needs are very different to the purely commercial ones that are prevalent today in the internet. This demonstrates the continuity of public and state interest in the system.

Internet convergence: An analysis model

The diagram below is an overview of the general organization models of the telecommunications systems, their major structural features with regard to the communication paradigm, the financing model and the relationship with the end user plus their relationships with suppliers of software, hardware and content production. The first line represents broadcasting (radio and TV), a core element of the "mass communication" paradigm. Conventional telephony, the traditional opponent of this model, is shown on the second line, defining a completely different communication paradigm with a finance model that is also different from the first case (Table 6.1).

In this regard, the diagram is self-explanatory. Note only that, unlike the first case, sectors linked to the production of content are not tied to this paradigm, given that the industry limits the offer of this infrastructure to private interpersonal communication. This is the basic model studied by the economics of telecommunications, which is fundamentally concerned with transmission, pricing issues, universalization of services, so-called cross-subsidies, etc. From the point of view of this discipline (first column), in principle everything could be reduced to such issues. In fact data transmission systems, from the telegraph to the telex and fax, would not pass this limit until computers became networked, revolutionizing the methods of transmission, access and management of databases. This is the new model, shown on the third line.

The central part of the diagram shows the areas of software and network equipment providers, of content production in the different cultural industries, the management of databases and end-user equipment. In this latter case, it is a part of the electric and electronic industry, which also specifically includes the production of audio and video equipment, not shown in the diagram, but which must be taken into consideration in the analysis because it is important in the user's relationship with the Culture Industry in its entirety as a system.[6]

The different convergence possibilities have an impact on these historical models, with repercussions for the communication paradigms, funding models, ideological function, etc. We may put forward here the working hypothesis that the three background logics (mass communication, interpersonal communication and access to databases), linked to three basic financing models, remain valid as analytical tools. Without entering this discussion in depth, the convergence systems that pressure the model should be noted.

Table 6.1 Communication industry: Historic models and connected sectors

	The Telecommunications Economy				
	Telecommunications: Historical models:	**Sectors producing linked content**	**User Interface**	**Communication Model**	**Finance Models**
The Communication and Culture Economy	Broadcasting	Culture Industries	Radio/TV	Mass Communication	– Publicity – Public Budget – Taxation
	Voice Telephony	-------	Telephone	Interpersonal Communication	Tariffs
The Information Economy	Data Transmission	Management of Databases	Computer	Man – Machine interface Access to Databases	Sale of Information – Commerce

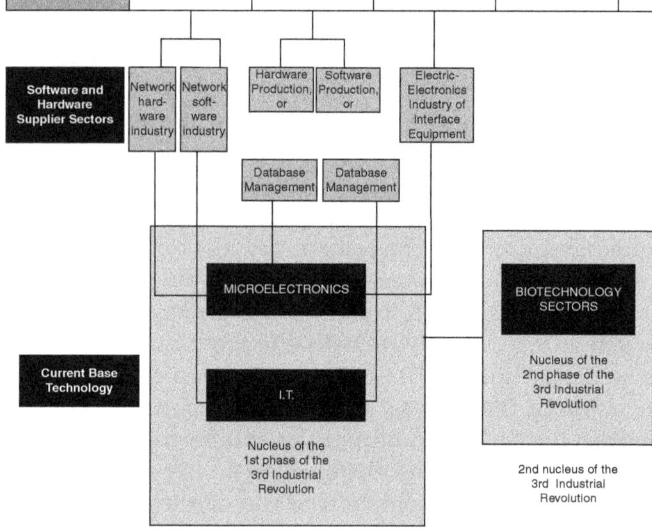

1. Broadcasting itself is the convergence of telecommunications, communication and culture that radically transformed, in its time, the Economics of Communication and Culture.
2. The TV segment reinforces this form of convergence (telecommunications, audiovisual), thereby significantly altering the communication paradigm and the audiovisual financing models.
3. The computer networks systems, particularly the internet, represent a possibility for convergence between telecommunications and IT, giving unprecedented impetus to the development of data transmission systems and access to databases that promote a revolution in the economics of information. The internet also promises to reshape voice telephony, which has not yet happened on a large scale.
4. The postal system has been greatly impacted by the development of interpersonal communication methods (e-mail, chat), enabled by the network and by the expansion of logistical requirements related to electronic commerce.
5. The internet promotes a third fundamental change in the economics of communication and culture in becoming an alternative mass media as well as a place of convergence for all the industrialized cultural production.
6. It is also necessary to mention the audiovisual-IT convergence of video games and the explosion of online games, which is an economic and cultural phenomenon of enormous magnitude.

This analysis model will help us interpret two interesting contributions in the study of the internet economy, presented below, which, in turn, will help us refine the proposed analytical instruments.

Internet economy: Two important contributions

In 1999, a group from the Graduate School of Business of the University of Texas at Austin, brought together through the Center for Research in Electronic Commerce and sponsored by Cisco Systems, began developing an empirical investigation proposing a classification of the internet economy based on economic indicators, which is interesting for our purposes.[7] The following diagram and table summarize the main aspects of the report provided online by the authors, including general quantitative data.[8] To produce its Internet Economy Revenues Indicator (IERI) and its Internet Economy Jobs Indicator (IEJI), the group divided the internet economy into four layers[9]: (1) infrastructure providers (network hardware and software, PCs, servers, fibre optics, backbone providers,

ISPs); (2) development of infrastructure applications (including software development, multimedia applications, network consultants, online training, etc.); (3) internet intermediaries; and (4) commerce.

Layer 3 contains companies that are exclusively linked to the internal net market (pure internet players), who do not generate transaction receipts (transaction-related revenues) of the type generated by trading companies at the top layer where companies selling their products or services directly to consumers through the network are located (e-tailers that sell books, CDs, computers, airline tickets, etc.). Layer 3 is made up mainly of content carriers or providers, internet advertising agencies and virtual shopping, while Layer 4 consists of sellers acting through e-commerce.[10]

Classification of activities related to the internet economy by layer

Layer One: The Internet Infrastructure Layer

- Internet backbone providers (ATT, MCI, Embratel)*
- Internet service providers (AOL, UOL, Zaz)
- Networking hardware and software companies (Cisco, Lucent, 3Com)
- Fibre optics makers (Corning)
- PC and Server manufacturers (Dell, Compaq, HP, Itautec)

Layer Two: The Internet Applications Layer

- Internet consultants (Nua, Forrester, IDC)
- Internet commerce applications (Netscape, Microsoft, Sun, IBM)
- Multimedia applications (Real Networks, Macromedia)
- Web development software (Adobe, NetObjects, Allaire, Vignette)
- Search engine software (Inktomi, Verity)
- Online training
- Web-enabled databases (Oracle, IBM DB2, Microsoft SQL Server)
- Online transaction processing
- Network support services

Layer Three: The Internet Intermediary Layer

- Market makers in vertical industries (VerticalNet, PCOrder)
- Online travel agents
- Online brokerages (E*Trade, Schwab.com, DLJDirect)
- Content generators (Cnet, ZDnet, Broadcast.com)
- Portals/Content providers (Yahoo, Excite, Geocities, Terra)
- Internet ad brokers (Doubleclick, 24/7 Media)

- Online advertising (Yahoo, ESPNSportszone)
- Virtual shopping

Layer Four: The Internet Commerce Layer

- E-tailers (Amazon.com, eToys.com, Barnes & Noble, etc.)
- Manufacturers selling online (Cisco, Dell, IBM, Compaq)
- Airlines selling online tickets (Continental, Delta, United)
- Fee/Subscription-based companies (e.g. thestreet.com, WSJ.com)
- Online entertainment and professional services (games, online journalism, pornography)
- Delivery services (UPS, Fedex, Airborne)

Source: Center for Research in Electronic Commerce, Graduate School of Business, University of Texas at Austin.
(*) We have taken the liberty of adding some companies present in the Brazilian market to the original list, as well as some additional information (Table 6.2).

The authors consider the separation between layers 3 and 4 to be very important. We can interpret the issue in our own way by saying that the companies in Layer 4 that market their products through the network constitute a market locus. Any productive capital, direct or through an intermediary (commercial capital), will come across the problem

Table 6.2 Economic internet indicators, by quarter

Layer	Revenue (in U$ million)			Jobs		
	1998 Q1	**1999 Q1**	**(%)**	**1998 Q1**	**1999 Q1**	**(%)**
Layer I – Internet infrastructure providers	26,795	40,139	+50	472,617	656,551	+39
Layer II – Internet application development	13,925	22,487	+61	407,858	563,124	+38
Layer III – Internet intermediaries	10,992	16,666	+52	355,358	444,302	+25
Layer IV – Internet commerce	16,508	37,540	+127	506,693	900,882	+78
Internet economy	64,000	104,969	+68	1,572,999	2,301,707	+46
Internet Economy – Annual projection*	301.4 bi	507.0 bi	+68			

of realization at a certain point in its circulation. What occurs with companies who provide their goods and services through e-commerce is that, under these conditions, commodity relationships cease to be immediate. There is a technical means of communication involved in the (remote) relationship between buyer and seller, whose expansion leads to the emergence of a new type of intermediary (similar to commercial and financial capital, for example), a provider of communication media within the network, as well as the infrastructure (layers 1 and 2).

The possibility of replacing the physical intermediaries by virtual network intermediaries is a fashionable topic when making predictions about the future of the world economy in the context of the internet economy. The widespread consensus is more or less that the broker loses ground with the internet. According to the Texas group, what happens is that the internet needs a new category of intermediaries whose role is heavily based on knowledge and information. "We affirm that a deployment of the network or an implementation and popularisation of its access through the increase of its base infrastructure is a fundamental precondition for the consolidation of this new category of intermediary. This is also the vision of the U.S. administration." (U.S. Government Working Group on Electronic Commerce, 1999, ♣).

Regarding companies in Layer 3, this is a new type of mass communication whose action is funded indirectly by advertising or other forms of tiered payment, and not through direct payment by the user as in the case of mass television. The authors of the report in question mention the following: selling publicity space (advertising); online mapping services (membership subscriptions), as occurs for example with network pornography where access to the bulk of databases is done through assignments; and fees and commissions. Apart from this there is the growth of network support for products distributed free over the internet (mainly software), such as Microsoft Explorer and Netscape Navigator, plus the latest fashion in operating systems, Linux from Red Hat. In these cases the public receives the principal service free, which in this market is the logical approximation to the *flot* culture of the communication and culture economy.

This is not true with the cultural industries on Layer 4 of the model, whose operating logic is similar to that of segmented television (through surcharge) and not mass television. The authors do not make the distinction, but this is crucial: there are two types of companies in that layer, cultural industries and others. In the network the latter are engaged in electronic commerce in a general way that does not alter the traditional definition.[11] When a large industrial or services company invests directly in Layer 3 of the internet economy, this should be seen as a diversification of activities, such as when there are changes in the administrative structure of a holding company: it becomes more complex, but that is all. The situation is different when a major newspaper or television broadcaster invests in the network. In this case, it is not just entering a new field of activity, it is a strategic repositioning of the company within the Cultural Industry as a system.

Another interesting classification for our study comes from Phan and N'Guyen (1999), who shed light on fundamental elements of the internet economy and the social logics involved. The authors generally follow what Kavassalis and Lehr proposed in 1998 with regard to the separation between transport and guide or routing (of information) on the one hand, and services and applications on the other, between them defining the difference between systems that provide support for the services, and the information and intermediary services themselves. The first group includes the physical infrastructure providers, backbone suppliers, Internet Access Providers (IAPs) and local connections. The infrastructures are provided by the operators, who control some of the public telecommunications networks. With regard to the provision of infrastructure for educational and research institutions, in each country the public authorities assume its financing and hand over its management to an institution such as the American NSF, the Brazilian National Education and Research Network (RNP), fronted by the Internet Steering Committee or the French equivalent RENATER. In the case of private users, larger ones have direct access to a backbone, while small businesses and the general public have to use the services of an IAP / ISP.

According to the authors,

> in the USA the large "backbone" owners (WorldCom, Sprint, AT&T, GTE, purchased by Bell Atlantic) do not make much money despite the recent practice of making small ISPs pay for access to their networks. Elsewhere, most of the interconnection agreements are founded on the peer principle, in other words, the mutual exchange of traffic flow without financial compensation, which cannot in any way guarantee high earnings.
>
> (Idem, p. 105♣)

This low profitability for IP transport service is a problem for large operators,[12] even more so because of their inability to form a cartel against the users at the moment when they "faced the entry of new competitors willing to invest in IP capabilities and to smash prices to make their investments profitable". Since 1997, operators like WorldCom, Global Crossing, Qwest and GTS have "multiplied their transatlantic connection projects to increase IP transport capacity and threaten the cartel of the historic operators or 'heavies' with regard to underwater cables", which is part of a larger strategy, aimed "especially at large companies with the highest international traffic expenses" which could significantly affect the earnings of the historic operators. Thus, there would be a paradox related to the internet economy, formulated by the authors as follows:

> The efficient operation of IP networks and the funding methods applied...do not allow the internet to generate the same financial flows as the phone, which are based on the optimization of hierarchical and centralized infrastructure and tariffs. This situation is advantageous for users and justifies the extraordinary growth of the Internet, but poses a problem for investors who expect returns.
>
> (Idem, p. 117♣)[13]

As for the ISPs, the system of charging users was seriously threatened when a text published in 1999 talked of the expansion of free internet access, a trend that has not increased to the extent expected by the authors, but has never gone away. The trend among these companies is significantly towards concentration. While at the end of 1995 there were, according to the Gartner Group, over 2,500 ISPs in the USA in a market estimated to be worth $ 550 million at the end of 1999, America On Line (AOL) had already established itself as a world leader, with an installed base of approximately 18 million customers. "But there are still many small providers in limited geographic areas which are gradually bought out by major ISPs" (idem, p. 106).[14] The conclusion is that access provision doesn't seem to be "a very profitable activity" either:

> The superiority of the internet is notable from the point of view of users – based on asynchronous communication – in relation to the telephone network, regardless of whether there is payment or not. Transportation and switching costs over an IP network are nearly independent of usage and all users can share it at any time. Furthermore, the occupancy rate of the circuits is relatively high: not so for the phone, which also has fixed costs, the reservation of a

> complete circuit dedicated to the conversation to the exclusion of others, thereby creating a momentary shortage which can be limited through tariffs. This tariff is however a source of income for telecom operators that does not exist for ISPs.
>
> (Idem, p. 109)

Despite that, the business of providing access continues to attract companies looking to sell content services, advertising finance or commercial exploitation of clients, since "the possession of a broad customer base could in fact represent an advantage for access providers in their dealings with service providers or advertisers" (idem, p. 107). This is clearly the same logic as creating a commodity audience, presented in the previous chapter.

Phan and N'Guyen include servers in the Internet Intermediary Layer, to use the terminology of the University of Texas, (over 70% of which run UNIX online access systems), client interfaces (including browsers), plug-ins, search engines, secure transaction systems (e.g. encrypted, that the Texans include in Layer 1 of their internet infrastructure) and payments, etc.

Of the browsers, Microsoft Explorer, which in principle was offered free on the net and then integrated into the Windows operating systems (95, 98 and NT), emerged as a competitor to Netscape (the commercial version of Mosaic), which was also free until 1996, when Netscape Communicator was launched. The entrance of Explorer caused significant market loss for Netscape, which was forced to become free again. The company then initiated a court action against Microsoft for anti-competitive behaviour, a strategy also followed by AOL after acquiring Netscape, who also sought indirect forms of financing such as advertising and the "supply of advanced internet services together with Sun, Microsoft's declared adversary" (idem, p. 111).

Apart from the ability to create and present websites as well as to navigate them, which is the main function of the browser, thanks to the open nature of the system other applications can be integrated, such as Java applets, or Adobe's PDF using Acrobat Reader (from Adobe itself). Similar systems are used for music (such as MP3), multimedia animation (Flash or Shockwave from Macromedia) or video (Quicktime or RealPlayer). The economic logic for the distribution of these plug-ins is described by Phan and N'Guyen as follows:

> The reading software is usually free, at least until the system becomes a market standard and display of the files is paid for. This allows

> the provider to develop the broadest possible users "club". If this style of presentation is successful, the provider can make a profit from the business by selling display software to those who want to use its functionality. This financing method is effective in encouraging "sophisticated users" to propose new display services, and allows these suppliers to develop them. Such services do not need to be used by all members of the net, but their viability may depend on their success. Thus, all network members contribute to the evolution of what is offered by the internet through its usage, participating in the competitive selection of the solutions offered for free. It is learning through diversity that allows each to choose the service that best corresponds to their needs.
>
> (Idem, p. 111 ff.)

Now we need to consider the commercial layer, as defined in the University of Texas study: the production of content (written or audiovisual media) – for which the network appears as both a threat (for the opportunity offered to evade Copyright Systems) and a promise (to the extent that it creates a powerful new distribution channel) – and e-commerce itself. The first case includes the dominant groups of the written media (such as Hachette and Havas in France, Bertelsmann in Germany and Dow Jones in the US), "who increase the value of their inventories through the net", and the audiovisuals who only recently started to adopt an active policy of internet presence.[15] The economic logic of this sector can be summarized as follows:

> Most sources of information available on the Internet are free. However, some information or services providers use "pay per view"... Others offer unlimited access to a limited number of subscribers... The Financial Times and Les Echos, which have a less price sensitive clientele, charge per viewed item, while the Wall Street Journal, which has the same type of clientele, prefer a $59 annual charge.
>
> (Idem, p. 113)

The authors note that a pure and simple e-commerce logic is generated for the sectors of the online Cultural Industry concerned with monetary transactions, in which the internet players place their greatest hopes in the possibility of the intermediary's charging a fee for the service provided and thus creating an unquestioned source of income, similarly to what happens with the sale of tangible goods or services by companies that divert some of what they offer to the network (distributors of computer equipment such as Cisco or Dell Computers, travel agencies and banks).[16]

Finally, the authors refer to those enterprises engaged in electronic trading and packaging, known as "portals":

> Such portals are therefore in a position similar to that of a television station, or a set of thematic broadcasters, as they are based on giving access to a greater or lesser number of services. However, the portals have two peculiarities. First, they are faced with an almost infinite number of service providers. Their added value therefore will be not only to provide nice query interfaces... but also, and especially, in the selection of privileged content, sometimes with exclusive access. Second, the packagers, through interactivity can "target" offers depending on the client profile. This makes them true intermediaries between supply and demand of content.
>
> (Idem, p. 115)

Thus, by integrating various functions, portals can extract revenue from different sources: the advertising market (insertion of banners), the information or online transaction providers who pay for the right to "reference" and sometimes for exclusivity over the portal and customers, who sometimes pay for personalized services.

> This multiplicity of income sources is no guarantee of strong profitability, but does rouse the interest of financial operators. Indirect funding from advertising... or the paid reference currently represents privileged funding sources. Publicity converts the Internet into mass media, where this mode of financing is normal.
>
> (Idem, p. 115)

The authors cite the study of the Internet Advertising Bureau, according to which the sale of advertising space on the net in 1998 amounted to US$966 million, versus US$266 million made in 1997 by Aftel (of which US$63 million was Yahoo, US$43 million NetCenter, US$36 million Infoseek and US$35 million Excite). After the acquisition of Netscape by AOL, new forms of advertising arose such as windows associated with the browser or other plug-ins. The big advantage of advertising on the net is the enormous possibility for segmentation, much more so than that found in traditional media.

> Unlike in the press and audiovisual, Internet advertising can be segmented provided the surfer leaves traces of the sites they visit. These

> traces are found in the statistics of the access providers…, managers of sites, [and] there is also specialized software, such as cookies, that allow service providers to find information about previous customer connections. This information can thus be used to develop personalised marketing…The suppliers of free access…will widely develop this practice to compensate for lack of profits related to free access.
>
> (Idem, p. 116)

There is no specific entry cost for the creation of a portal.[17] The essential thing is to acquire notoriety, which facilitates the entry of well-known brands, from any sector, into the business. Microsoft, for example, exploits this advantage. Other portals capitalize on the management of virtual communities (Geocities) or commercial internet access (AOL). Most often it is the association with a search engine (such as Yahoo, Excite, Lycos, NetCenter, Alta Vista). The link with a browser is, in all cases, the real key to success, "which explains why most established portals are based on historical internet search engines, being complementary to the browsers whose capabilities they extend" (Phan y N'Guyen, op. cit., p. 116).

In the opinion of the authors, for vendors of online services the portals would eventually acquire an importance similar to that of the hypermarkets for manufacturers, in reference to the strategies for product exposure. Today we see that the situation is more complex, with search engines such as Google becoming popular, which could not have been foreseen just a few years ago. The economic model of the web is still far from stabilized, but what has been said up until now provides the outline of this model in the implementation phase of the internet with regard to mass demand. The trend in the early 2000s is vertical integration between content providers, between content providers and portals, or even between both of these and access providers.

However, there is also a market for companies that see in the IP protocols a way to renew their IT equipment and take advantage of savings from network connection with a view to creating intranets and business to business trade. This is where the future of the internet lies, according to the authors. The key success factors are no longer vertical integration and size, but innovation and customer service. The self-referenced dynamic of collective technical progress, a characteristic of the network, is a powerful innovation mechanism, capable of jeopardizing Microsoft's attempt to capitalize on savings from the effects of the network.

> The "economic model" that will be offered by suppliers of products and internet services will depend on this "battle for the standards": whether through widespread outsourcing vis-à-vis the Redmond company or a competitive open system where the production of standards again becomes a public commodity, but, the provision of the service will continue to be the stage for a highly competitive industry. That is the real challenge facing the Internet, the last avatar of the telecommunications networks.
>
> (Idem, p. 120)

The social logic of the internet and the GNU/Linux system

The first diagram below condenses the elements of the different economic models and social logics that exist in the internet economy, based on the study by the University of Texas and the text of Phan and N'Guyen, comparing them to the analytical and theoretical framework developed in this book. The second diagram is self-explanatory and represents the network as a hierarchical access matrix with the players involved and functions performed.[18] (Table 6.3, Figure 6.1)

There are four social logics linked to the operation of the network:

1. CMC, where C can be e-C (electronic commerce or commerce of information itself) and M can be e-M (e-money);
2. Classical advertising logic (selling audience);
3. Provision of corporate services (business to business);
4. Internal interactive communication with the lifeworld (Table 6.4).

With regard to the first case, we could map the whole network by determining the existing financing mode (or modes) for each case and from there the characteristics of the market structures, business strategies, innovation methods, etc. If we think of all the sectors and markets that participate in the network in some form or other (or are part of the network itself), we can imagine an array of products and markets, including any number of variables. The issue becomes even more interesting through the existence of e-C and e-M.

The second case can be clearly understood from the economics of communication and culture, following the theoretical framework presented in this book and in Bolaño (2004a). Note that when we speak of internet of the masses, we are not just talking about this second form, very similar to the so-called mass TV, but also partly of the first, which is closer to segmented TV or the publishing market. This is the

Table 6.3 Key to diagram

Capitais Individuais	Individual Capitals
Convenções	Conventions
Fluxos partindo do Público	Flows from Public
Fluxos partindo dos Vendedores	Flows from Sellers
Fluxos partindo dos ISP	Flows from ISP
Fluxos partindo dos Provedores de Infra-estructura	Flows from Infrastructure providers
Público	Audience
Dinheiro	Money
Atenção	Attention
REDE	NETWORK
Informação/Publicidade	Information/Publicity
Comércio eletrônico	Electronic Commodity
Mercadoria	Merchandise for Commodity
Acesso	Access
Provedores de Infra-Estrutura de Redes	Network Infrastructure Providers
Estado	State

internet as Culture Industry. It is juxtaposed to the internet as a market in the broadest sense, as in the business to consumer systems (Logic 1) or business to business (Logic 3).

In the case of the fourth social logic presented, the issue is extremely complex, even surpassing the limits of the political economy. To reinforce the ideas presented in this regard throughout this chapter on the contradictory and potentially liberating network (insofar as it provides an interactive censorship-proof channel of communication between individuals, marked by a free distribution of information which, according to Barbrook, does not become information merchandise, but is invested with a natural gift[19]), I return to Brecht's Radio Theories. Let's start with this revealing quote from 1927:

> The fact is that opportunities always hit us in the face but we do not take advantage of them. These cities that you see rising all around you have certainly caught a completely exhausted bourgeoisie by surprise, worn out by deeds and misdeeds. While this bourgeoisie controls them, they will be uninhabitable. The bourgeoisie values them simply by considering the perspectives they can logically offer. Hence the exorbitant overvaluation of all things, not just of the organizations that close in the "opportunities"... In these cities all manner of artistic production begins with a man who approaches the artist and says he has a hall. The artist then interrupts the work he has undertaken

> for another man who said he had a megaphone. Hence the profession of an artist is to find something that justifies the hall or megaphone without reflection of their construction. It is at the same time both a difficult and unhealthy profession.
>
> (Brecht, op. cit, p. 6♣)

Brecht sees the radio as a political and educational means with a huge democratic and interactive potential, but limited to the objective conditions of its existence in a society that does not allow that potential and all its consequences to be effective. He illustrates his position by referring to an old story of a Chinese gentleman who was confronted with the presumed superiority of Western culture because of

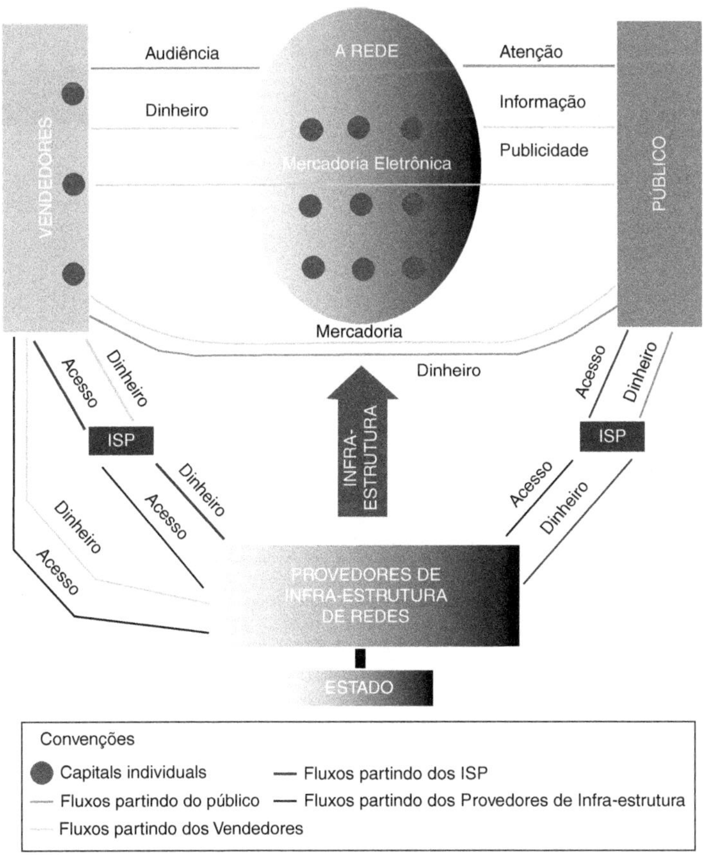

Figure 6.1 Mass internet: Intermediation models

Table 6.4 Hierarchy of internet access and players

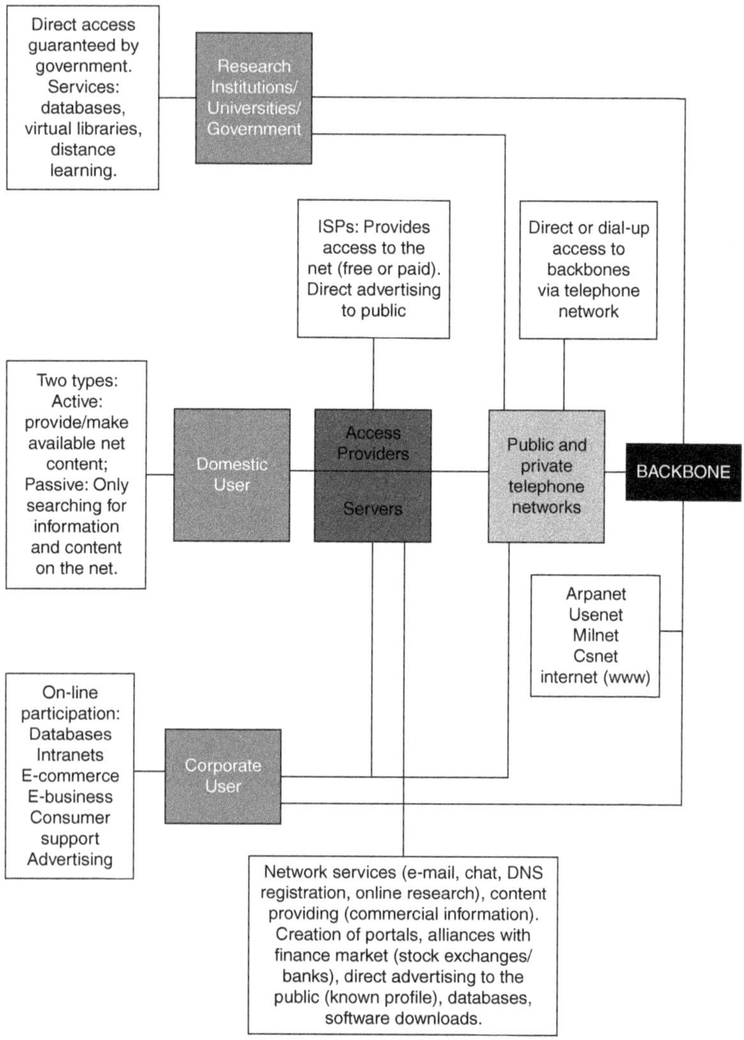

the existence of marvels such as railways, automobiles or the phone, to which he replied, "I am sorry to say it but we have already forgotten about that." Brecht uses that story to illustrate the impression that the radio is "immeasurably old" or antediluvian.

If so, the same is even more true of the internet, whose hastily presented revolutionary aspects already existed in radio, as imagined by the young Brecht in defending, for example, "a sort of listener rebellion, their activation and rehabilitation as producer" (idem, p. 10♣). Is that not, in the end, the great promise of GNU/Linux today? Or when he notes the need to transform the radio from a distribution apparatus into a communication device, claiming that broadcasting should make exchange possible, or that it is necessary to "avoid the power of disconnection by organising the disconnected" (idem, p. 14), or that "the public not only has to be educated, it also has to educate" (idem, p. 14), etc. These statements are examples of much later debates about digital inclusion or on the contradiction between public service and commercial service in the communications media.[20]

It is beyond the scope of this text to discuss in detail the subject of GNU/Linux and the free software movement and its meaning. This is a complex issue, linked to the broader issue of intellectual property.[21]

What can be said here is that the emergence of free software breaks new ground for public policies of digital inclusion. The freedom of distribution, modification and copying allows, among other things, economy in the acquisition of informational systems. Reducing the costs of computerization of government agencies could free up resources for investment in digital inclusion projects. More than that, the development of free software is an alternative to the current organizational model of the computer industry which is based on rigid patent rules, high implementation costs, and an expenditure structure for the consumer and early obsolescence strategies that imply a strong digital exclusion. Apart from allowing a great saving for the state because there are no licence fees, the use of such software in government agencies and digital inclusion programmes could ensure a positive dynamic of local knowledge production.

The GNU project was launched in 1984 and aimed to develop an operating system compatible with standard UNIX systems. Linux is a fast operating system modelled on UNIX and is constantly being improved. However, UNIX is proprietary software with a closed source and still marketed today. Its history, meanwhile, is important to the open software movement. UNIX has its beginnings in the mid-1960s, when researchers at the Massachusetts Institute of Technology (MIT), General Electric, Bell Laboratories (Bell Labs) and American Telephone and Telegraph (AT&T) decided to create a time-sharing operating system: Multics. One of the Multics developers, Ken Thompson (Bell Labs), withdrew from the project, starting a competitor based on the same ideas and baptised UNIX by Brian Kernigham (Bell Labs).

> In 1973, Dennis Ritchie, another Bell Lab researcher, rewrote the entire system in a high level language called C, developed by him for a PDP-11, the most popular microcomputer of that era. Having a system written in a high level language was exceptional and may have been one of the reasons for acceptance of the system by users outside Bell. AT&T participated in the system in the period from 1977 to 1981, making some specific modifications and released System III. In 1983 [...] the famous UNIX System V was released commercially. Today, this system is the international standard in the UNIX market, being marketed by various large companies.
>
> (Bareinboim, 2004♣)

The Free Software Foundation[22] (FSF) was created in 1985, initially bringing together a few programmers who shared free software and tools with open source code. The initial idea was to produce an operating system based on UNIX.

> But how can Linux be based on a commercially expensive system with closed source? The answer lies in another programme called MINIX. MINIX is a free UNIX clone whose source code is available. It was created for strictly educational purposes for anybody who wants to run a UNIX compatible system on their computer and learn how the inside of the operating system works. It is worthwhile mentioning that it was written from scratch and despite being a clone of UNIX contains no AT&T code and can therefore be freely distributed.
>
> (Bareinboim, op. cit.)

Finally, in 1991, a young computer science student at the University of Helsinki by the name of Linus Torvalds developed a more advanced system than MINIX, a kernel (core operating system) called LINUX, registering it in the General Public License system (GPL). In a note to a newsgroup, Torvalds says:

> As I mentioned a month ago, I'm working on a free version of a MINIX-lookalike for AT-386 computers. It has finally reached the stage where it's even usable (though may not be, depending on what you want), and I am willing to put out the sources for wider distribution. It is just version 0.02 but I've successfully run bash, gcc,

> gnu-makee, gnu-sed, compress, etc. under it. comp.os.minux Linus Torvalds[23]

Since then, Linux has come to be circulated by a huge group of developers linked across the network and bound under the rules of the GPL, constantly improving the program with a philosophy of social inclusion. As early as 1992, with the spread of the internet, a movement was formed around a "freedom of knowledge" ideal for the development of a comprehensive and multi-functional operating system called GNU/Linux. The objective of the GNU's Not Unix project is the production of software that can be improved and distributed for a growing audience. Since then the FSF have tried to assert their rights in the production of free software through the GPL.[24]

The basic premise of free software is widespread usage so that it may benefit needy communities and developing countries.[25] The free software will contribute to the construction of basic information infrastructure and training in the use of IT for local development and digital inclusion policies. Therefore,

> free software needs support and maintenance, just as owned software does. The use of free software in call centers and digital inclusion units can be a great incentive for the emergence of many local companies qualified to configure and even develop solutions tailored to local business interests and government agencies. The two most important advantages in the use of free software for local economic and social development are open source and the absence of royalties for its use. Open source allows any skilled programmer to create the solutions that best meet the needs of its customers. The absence of royalties allows the local support and development company to keep hold of all the income generated.
>
> (Silveira, 2003, p. 17–48♣)

Free software as an alternative model

The strategies of the computer industry to maintain prices over time, despite productivity achievements in the sector,[26] are well known, limiting massification and boosting consumption almost exclusively in the included social sectors while preserving monopoly profits and market control. Thus, through an iterative process of planned and linked innovation in hardware and software, the IT industry drives early obsolescence of equipment. This prevents productivity gains from resulting in an effective reduction in prices, breaking with the diffusion model of social use of new products, typical of the post-war expansion period, which led for example to the widespread use of radio and, more or less, television too, even in countries with major social disparities such as Brazil.

Additionally, the current functioning of all the communication industries (telecommunications, information technology, telematics and content industries) follows a pattern opposite to that of the welfare state period, marked by the politics of public service broadcasting and universal access in telecommunications. The transformations in the current production restructuring, with the privatization and the introduction of competition in the various markets, will lead to a fierce concentration of capital, contrary to the neoliberal proclamation, as described by Narváez (2002). To cite just one example, in the software and network services market, "Microsoft and Oracle account for 87% of sales, 99.4% of revenues and 91% of the market value" (idem, p. 108 ff.♣) in 1999. In the area of internet hardware, there is a predominance of five companies (IBM, Lucien, Intel, Dell and Cisco), but each has a different specialization, assuming monopolistic or quasi-monopolistic control over a specific market segment (servers, networks, processors, PCs).

A similar phenomenon occurs with telecommunications, and the Brazilian position after the privatizations of the Fernando Henrique Cardoso government is paradigmatic, since the whole process (from the fragmentation of the Telebras system to the granting of concessions to mirror companies, including the definition of concession bands for mobile telephony) was designed on the basis of the illusion, explicit in the preamble to the General Telecommunications Law, that it would ensure wide competition and be able to protect the interests of consumers and universalization,[27] which so far has not happened. Instead, what can be seen is the absolute control of each of the country's three regional fixed telephony markets by a single company, leaving the mirror companies completely marginalized, while the mobile phone sector is quickly consolidated nationwide. The opening phase of the competition began in 2003 and contrary to what was imagined, has effectively led to increased concentration and tacit agreements in relation to long distance operations.

In conclusion, we can say that from all angles the current structure of the communications sectors tends towards concentration and, further, to preserving a model of exclusion through price, in complete contrast to the model of inclusion of the Fordism period. The old television of the masses, the model for that stage, basically only requires a one-off payment from the consumer for the acquisition of the equipment (whose life cycle also follows the traditional lines of massification referred to previously) and the monthly electricity payment to the utility company. In contrast, internet access today, for example, requires the purchase of a much more sophisticated device (and a number of peripherals) and is subject to a recurring process of planned obsolescence (which keeps the effective price immune from the dramatic cost reductions possible under the current technological revolution), payment for electricity and telecommunications (privatized or at least acting according to private logic for better performance, eliminating, for example, the previous practice of cross-subsidies that guaranteed a certain level of globalization that is today considered detrimental to the proper functioning of market forces) and payment to access providers and other services.

It is clear that one can think of a rupture of that model, given that it is not in any way a technological determination, but fundamentally one of economic decisions derived from the hegemony of liberal thought in the period of crisis of Fordism and the market power of certain companies in that process. The technology itself, in reality, could even indicate a greater efficiency of a different type of system organization, as evidenced by the expansion of Linux, for example. In a special publication of *Reportagem* (May 2003, p. 50–60), Lia Rodrigues paints a fairly complete picture of the arguments for the Linux model, which can be summarized in the following topics:

- Free software allows a huge cost reduction for companies and other institutions who upon acquiring a copy of such a program, depending on the licence type, acquire the right to install it on any number of machines without any additional payment, as occurs in the hegemonic model of Microsoft, which survives through the sale of licences to use its patent protected program. Nothing prevents the free software from being freely distributed, as in fact happens in many cases.
- This means a shift in corporate expenses from licence fees to hiring IT service companies and personnel for the development and improvement of programs, as the logic behind this model is that the opening up of the source code allows each user to make any changes it considers appropriate to the program.[28]
- From the point of view of the state, it may also mean a major saving in the cost of IT, both for purposes of compliance with public service

> and also for the public policy of digital inclusion by eliminating the royalty payment for proprietary software, and at the same time stimulating national training in software production and, therefore, the development of technology.
>
> – The free software also breaks with the strategy of early obsolescence of equipment for incompatibility with the latest versions of proprietary software as was discussed recently (each new Windows version needs a machine with more memory to run satisfactorily), allowing the reuse of old computers in projects that do not require the latest technology.
>
> – The security of public systems would also be increased, according to Mario Teza, one of the interviewees, who said "buying proprietary software is like buying a lock: whoever knows the code can break its security. In the world of free software it is much more difficult for this to happen because the system logic is centred on the user – each site has its own security logic" which in turn makes it more resistant to virus attacks, since "it is not attractive to make a virus that can attack only one environment".
>
> (Rodrigues, 2003♣)

The movement in favour of Linux is reminiscent of the early internet when all software was free and users were, for the most part, pioneers of technology development working in universities and research centres, where they managed to build the entire network culture, influenced by the libertarian ideology of the social movements of the 1960s. If the massification of the internet and its marketing, especially from the mid-1990s, represented the victory of the business model, the current success of Linux, and the challenge for Microsoft, restores the hopes of these young pioneers while pointing to a more inclusive system structure, not necessarily contrary to its organization as a market economy but instead governed by a kind of anarchic, antimonopolistic liberalism and strongly committed to so-called civil rights.

From our point of view, it is interesting to emphasize that the first three highlighted points, in particular, point to the existence of an alternative information and communication technologies (ICT) development model that is economically viable and potentially inclusive, which could reinforce the idea of applying the internet under the concept of public service, the idea coming from past discussions in Europe on the organization of radio and television systems. The possibility of a funding model that can guarantee universal access from the perspective of a public service is fundamental to a true democratization of ICT, which so far has not happened. In this respect, the struggle for free software is important, since it does not lose sight of the fact that the priority is to build a massive system (even more massive than that arising from the privatization of the network after 1995), a promoter of digital inclusion as a part of social inclusion in a broader sense.

Conclusion and Prospects: Communication and Capitalism in the 21st Century

The idea of competition and disputes is deeply ingrained in the ideological mindset projected by the Culture Industry, which stimulates the ostentatious display of symbols of wealth and differentiated individual consumption. Differentiation is the necessary assumption of homogeneity fabricated by mass culture, whereas individualism is the opposite of massification. In short, it is the relationship between these opposing concepts (differentiation/homogeneity, masses/individuals), under the primacy of technical progress and efficiency (instead of ideology) on which the Culture Industry is based. This industry is destined to serve as a general competitive space for wide-ranging monopolistic business sectors (differentiated consumer goods, commerce, banks, companies producing manufactured goods and running certain services, etc.).

Even state monopolies, as well as some businesses for which the product differentiation strategies are not important, look to the Culture Industry as a vehicle for institutional propaganda, to provide a social legitimacy which, in the final analysis, is no more than a competitive strategy for consolidating and preserving space in the face of potential competition and the vicissitudes of the political game. It is, in summary, a key component in the competitive game among different political groups anxious to conquer the hearts and minds of citizens, mainly through the medium of television or, failing this, through other cultural industries.

The increasing internationalization of television, resulting from the internationalization of business, new technological developments and the characteristics of the medium, have transformed it into the "dominant medium". Television has also become a wide open space for broad sectors of monopolistic businesses to compete with one another in the world arena. This entire competitive universe is part of the more general rivalry among the different geo-economic and geopolitical areas of capitalism in the global quest for power. The telecommunications network belonging to national states, for example, whether in the capitalist system or not, is a mechanism for pursuing and attracting business. It also serves to propagate foreign policy and enables states themselves and groups with access to the media with vast and varied audiences to relay their messages to different parts of the world.

Two types of determination can be identified in the development of the world telecommunications system, although making a distinction between them is only feasible as an analytical device. One type belongs to the side pursuing the struggle for political and economic power on a global scale; the other favours an ideological relationship between the masses (receivers) and the national and international powers (transmitters). The development of television, together with the entire Culture Industry, is to a great extent, in different countries, a subsidiary product of the development of telecommunications (and of other technologically dominant sectors), and relates to the second type of determination above, although in the final analysis the first is always a factor.

TV broadcasting has been basically assigned this function: to establish a viewing public, a mass audience, and to induce it to gradually conform with the requirements of the economic and ideological reproduction of the system. Ideology is always present, both directly through ostensive action (although evidently contradictory) of the state and the groups which dispute hegemony in the political area (propaganda), and indirectly through the dissemination of a way of life adjusted to the mass consumer society (advertising). In the most general terms we can argue that the Culture Industry is part of a system of communications which is the material manifestation, in the historical conditions of monopolistic capitalism, of the contradictions of information discussed early on in this study.

The Culture Industry is the most advanced, specifically capitalist form of the cultural production most typical of monopolistic capitalism, whose full constitution was only completed after the Second World War with the expansion of television. According to Beaud, Flichy & Sauvage, this is "the only true cultural industry", a description which, as we have seen, comes from Adorno, for whom television represents a fundamental leap compared to what went before. Adorno's was a pioneering analysis, at a time when the industrialization of culture was still restricted to the reproduction, diffusion and distribution of cultural products. With television and the entire system that it leads, cultural creation itself has been subjected to a similar, although not identical, capitalist logic which preceded the production of other goods. I say that it is not "identical" because there are limits to the subsumption of cultural work, which are linked, as I have attempted to make clear, to the mediation function of the Culture Industry to which, in common with any institution of a symbolic kind, it must conform.

To this internal limitation of the capital–labour relationship in the Culture Industry must be added another, linked to the existence of other cultural forms and other social institutions, which not only compete with it for the hegemony in the area of sense production, but also impede advertising-related or propagandistic use of the mass communications media, which are after all obliged to respond in some way to the social and psychological needs of the consumer audience. This phenomenon is linked both to the expectations of individuals in relation to the products they are offered by the various media competing with one another, and to the existence of a public sphere in which these fulfil, in monopolistic capitalism, a role similar to that which newspapers fulfilled in relation to the old bourgeois public sphere.

However, there is a crucial difference between this public sphere and that organized by monopolistic capitalism, in which the former effectively relinquishes its place to an efficient, although contradictory, activity spurred by the mechanisms of advertising and propaganda. The contradictions of information are manifested in a different way at this stage of the organization of the system, highlighting the question of the media's manipulative potential. The main objective of Chapter 2 of the present study was to explain the changes which occurred in the system and that finally generated what we know as the Culture Industry. It was not, at that point in the study, appropriate to discuss the question of its limits. The main objective of the first two chapters was to deduce, using a derivationist-type theoretical strategy, the propaganda and advertising functions of the Culture Industry, starting from the most abstract level of the analysis of the form. Thus I defined these functions as roughly linked to the decisions which are imposed by the opposing and complementary logics of business and the capitalist state.

After doing this I returned to the subject of the limits, on one hand treating the characteristics of work processes and valorization in the Culture Industry and the "barriers" to their inclusion, and on the other hand what I called the "programming function". The larger theme of culture and the new public sphere was not a principal objective of this study. I was basically interested in studying the Culture Industry and its relationship with all the modes of capitalist production.

Using a strategy of exposition derived from the contradiction between the advertising and programming forms of information, the two general functions which the Culture Industry has come to fulfil under monopolistic capitalism, I began, after reviewing Marxist literature on the subject, to discuss the characteristics of employment in the cultural sector, which led to the theme of the "programming" function as an alternative theoretical proposition, and from there I finally moved to the question of limits. The last part of Chapter 5 returned to the subject of the links between propaganda, programming and advertising at a much lower level of abstraction, with the aim of formulating an analytical framework applicable to the study of concrete cases of organization of national communication systems and specific cultural industries.

Confidential intercapitalist, mass marketing information, and information at the heart of the labour/work process, are all logically organized in hierarchies which reflect the needs of the state and business in terms of the structure of the mass communications media. Expanding information technology, the development of telecommunications and the constitution of the Culture Industry are integral parts of larger communications systems being formulated at international level. The Culture Industry, the specific form of cultural production under monopolistic capitalism, is becoming increasingly the key operational link between big business, the state and the masses. Information technology and telecommunications also form part of the global communications system.

The Culture Industry is the least internationalized of these three parts, since it depends on local culture and lifestyle; it must also respond to the needs of symbolic reproduction which originate in each audience or specific social group rather than in the state or the business world. Communication with this population is a basic need for the state and monopolistic business enterprises. The competitive struggle among large multinational companies means that they can only function by taking "local" circumstances into account.

Miège claims that the need to respect all kinds of cultural specificities in communications restricts the possibility of creating economies of scale, and that despite the increase of monopolistic concentration and the transnationalization of production and consumption in most branches of the Culture Industry in the 1970s and 1980s, national production remains high, and market structures, at least in France, are similar to those described by Flichy (1980), which as we saw are characterized by the existence of many small companies working alongside dominant large oligopolistic businesses. For Miège (1990, p. 172) this is manifested by the difficulties of big business in "developing methods of industrial rationality", all of which are related to the discussion on the specificities of cultural production that are ultimately linked to the need for a special type of work not totally reducible to the abstract labour required by the symbolic mediation function.

The importance of this mediation has caused the Culture Industry itself to be transformed into a specific arena of competition among certain capitalist blocs which have engaged with the sector with a view to exploiting its business potential. Thus within each cultural industry, different businesses are likely to seek differentiation strategies which facilitate the segmentation of their activities according to the desires of the target public for something different, and businesses therefore work hard to define a variety of different techno-aesthetic standards for this purpose.

An unprecedented expansion of the Culture Industry took place in the post-Second World War period, led inter alia by the rapid emergence of so-called "television for the masses". With the advance of internationalization and heightened competition in the TV sector in the 1970s and 1980s, the homogenization/diversification dialectic led to the emergence of certain global techno-aesthetic standards, which coexisted with a number of others of more localised significance. This accorded with the changes occurring throughout the entire system, leading to economic globalization and fiercer disputes in all areas between large companies and power blocks. This was also the case for the entire set of cultural industries, including segmented TV, an innovation dating from the 1980s which has expanded globally, and which has played a key role in internationalizing a major part of the television industry, but without restricting the role of the nationally run companies which generally dominate mass-audience television.

Notes

1 The Contradictions of Information

1. What the transportation industry sells is change of location. The useful effect is inseparably connected with the process of transportation, i.e., the productive process of the transport industry. Men and goods travel together with the means of transportation, and their travelling, this locomotion, constitutes the process of production effected by these means. The useful effect can be consumed only during this process of production. It does not exist as a utility different from this process, a use-thing which does not function as an article of commerce, does not circulate as a commodity, until after it has been produced. But the exchange-value of this useful effect is determined, like that of any other commodity, by the value of the elements of production (labour-power and means of production) consumed in it, plus the surplus-value created by the surplus-labour of the workers employed in transportation. This useful effect also entertains the very same relations to consumption that other commodities do. If it is consumed individually its value disappears during its consumption; if it is consumed productively so as to constitute by itself a stage in the production of the commodities being transported, its value is transferred as an additional value to the commodity itself.

   (*Capital*, Volume 2)

   **Capital, Volume. I–III*: 2010; based on the First English edition of 1887 S. Moore & E. Aveling, Trans. Moscow: Progress Publishers (Original work published 1867).
2. It is precisely from the discussion of this observation that Harvey (1989) develops his thesis on the "time-space compression" accompanying capitalist development, becoming more pronounced in the present period, which he calls "postmodernism". Harvey is, of course, not the only Marxist writer to have been seduced by postmodernism. Frederic Jameson also embarked in this territory in a now classic article (1984), setting off a debate in the pages of the *New Left Review* in which Latimer (1984) and Eagleton (1985) participated. See also the earlier version of Jameson's article (1982), published in 1985 in *Novos Estudos Cebrap*. Notwithstanding a number of interesting insights in the work of these and other postmodernist authors, I consider this theoretical perspective to be essentially misguided. Unfortunately, it is not possible within the scope of this work to consider the problem in all its depth. I will confine myself to discussing, later in the text, the better known contribution put forward by François Lyotard (1979). *Marx, K. (1973) *Grundrisse: Foundations of the Critique of Political Economy* M. Nicolaus, Trans.: Penguin (Original work published 1939–1941).
3. In any case, to the extent that this equality, already at the level of appearances, is merely formal, the neoclassical economists' assumption of perfect information, one of the pillars of that theoretical model, is certainly called

into question. In reality, such a restrictive assumption must be proven in fact before being accepted as a principle; otherwise, the assumption of the perfect rationality of agents will be seriously questioned, regardless of any reference to expectations or to the logic of capitalist calculation and its inherent instability, to mention just two of Keynes' excellent arguments. But if the possibility of distortion of information is inherent from the beginning, forming part of the basis of the capitalist mode of production in the most general sense, the burden of proof rests on those who assert the possibility of perfect information.

4. I should clarify, meanwhile, inspired by the reading of Fausto (1983, Chapter 1 and Appendix 1), that this definition, which is intended to adhere closely to the expository method of Marx in *Capital*, should not be confused with any type of anthropologism. Man, with all the attributes of a subject, is only found in Marx at the level of utopia. There is no predetermined human subject, since the subject in capitalism is not man, but capital. Capitalism, with all that preceded it, constitutes the prehistory of the subject. This is not the proper place to discuss Marxist utopia and its inconsistencies, but it must be said that it has a role to play in the synthesis of theory, the same role as that of spirit in Hegel's dialectic. Socialism, however, is not a historical inevitability, since the process of history is a process of struggle which depends on the correlations of forces and demands in concrete situations. Marxist theory is engaged: it seeks to participate in the social struggles that will lead to the fundamental rift in which the fully constituted subject will take destiny into its hands and begin to write its history. At that point, we will pass from the realm of necessity to the realm of freedom, from prehistory to the history of the subject. However, in turning away from anthropologism we do not thereby fall into anti-anthropologism. Indeed, in the Marxist method, the subject is and is not present at the beginning. It is not determined, as in humanist and anthropologist discourse, but is presupposed. The subject appears at the beginning in the form of its predicates. There is no generic, complete human being. Rather there are workers, capitalists, slaves, feudal lords. Marxist discourse is a discourse that does not determine, but rather presupposes the subject, thereby also distinguishing itself from anti-humanism and anti-anthropologism. That is why it makes no sense to question Marx's work in terms of its more or less general anthropological principles, as did Baudrillard, for example, in his 1972 and 1973 papers. Marxian discourse does not work with principles but with presuppositions – presuppositions that will be negated over the course of the process of exposition, highlighting the ideological character of bourgeois principles. Thus, the principle of equality becomes a principle of inequality, freedom becomes "unfreedom" and property becomes dispossession. Marx pursues the idea contained in the bourgeois principles, but by giving them a content that contradicts the idea, he reproduces the internal contradiction to which they are subject, demonstrating their ideological character.
5. There is a paradox here, according to Lyotard, since scientific discourse, which suppresses narrative within its domain, requires a grand narrative, or metanarrative, to legitimize itself. Connor concisely exposes the fallacy of this paradox:

> It is clear that Lyotard is speaking here of two very different types of narratives, one that seems to include poetry, singing, pageantry, ritualised performance, the other showing the features more usually associated with narrative – temporal extension of causally-linked series of events and their movement toward resolution. In fact, if we decline to accept the designation of "narrative" for the type of linguistic exchange practiced by the Cashinahua, and similar, non-scientific language games, Lyotard's paradox evaporates.
>
> (Connor, 1989, p. 31)

6. The conservatism of Lyotard's solution is, furthermore, well known. See, e.g., Eagleton, 1985, p. 63, also quoted in Harvey, 1989, p. 210, and especially Habermas, 1980. Connor also criticizes Lyotard on the point just noted, averring that the expansion of information technologies tends in precisely the opposite direction to the situation of perfect information that Lyotard posited (Connor, 1989, p. 33). But Connor's most interesting critiques refer to the implausibility of Lyotard's vision of the current state of scientific knowledge (p. 35 ff.), concluding that "Lyotard's model is doubly totalising for it depends not only upon a vision of the total collapse of metanarrative, everywhere and for always, but also upon an unshakable belief in the absolute dominion of metanarrative before the arrival of the postmodern condition" (ibid., p. 36).
7. The imputation of all power to the state, ignoring this micro-social determination of the power of capital over living labour, is as mistaken as ignoring the fact that the state itself possesses its own economy and economic rationality, not to be confused with those of capital, as was convincingly demonstrated by Therer (1989, 1991, 1992).
8. Indeed, considering that corporate publications are directed at three distinct audiences (company personnel, the general public and other companies), which involves three types of communication that are nonetheless often poorly differentiated (in addition to the function of promoting certain forms of administrative associativism), it is often difficult in practice to distinguish the true character of a company's internal communication directed at its workforce. While this may ultimately lead to problems of an analytical order, it does not alter the basic theoretical problem I am addressing: viz., the fact that there is no mediation in the communication process within the labour process.
9. In fact, Marx's solution has a decisive advantage in relation to that of Habermas: viz., it arrives at the synthesis that the latter attempts without the need to adhere to such idealizations as "ideal speech situation", "systematically distorted communication" or "uncoerced will formation" (which even a Habermasian like McCarthy criticizes – 1987): concepts which fundamentally serve to construct an ideal type that allows Habermas to isolate the contradictions inherent in the *Lebenswelt* itself (and whose existence he does not deny) with the goal of constructing that system of dichotomies (understanding-event, critical society-state) whose Kantian basis Sfez (1988), among others, has identified, and which will allow him to reduce all contradictions to the Durkheimian binomial of social integration–system integration. He thereby accomplishes nothing more than trading the Marxist

utopia (which has, in fact, a role in the synthesis of theory – cf. Fausto, 1983, Chapter 1, Appendix 1) for the utopia of a communicative action free of external restraints (which also plays a role in the synthesis of theory – cf. McCarthy, 1987), which allows him to substitute the problematic analysis of "pathologies of communication" for Lukacs' theory of consciousness in the analysis of reification.

10. The same could be said of the capitalist state, which as a material institution also features the internal contradiction that as a central element in articulating the macro-social conditions that ensures the system's reproduction, reproduces within itself a set of interpersonal relationships whose character is defined not only by the internal needs of the logic of the state itself, but also by the lifeworld of the individuals that participate in the state apparatus, who hail from the most diverse social strata and are grouped in a hierarchy that reflects, in essence, the hierarchy of the social body itself. Poulantzas, for example, makes this very clear (Bolaño, 2003b). From our point of view, it is interesting that the communicative process within the structures of the capitalist state is also characterized by immediacy. Moreover, here the wage relation is also a precondition of the power relation.
11. For an extensive critique of the notion of an "information society", see Lyon (1988). For an overview of the theorists of "post-industrial society", to whose work we can trace the positions of both the postmodernists and the information society theorists, see Frankel (1987).
12. > It is through competition that the laws of the system are made effective.... At the same time, it is at the level of competition that the contradictions of the mode of production intrude, interruptions which nonetheless are corrected by internal mechanisms of the system that are also manifested through competition.
    >
    > (Fausto, 1988, p. 1315)
13. We may anticipate our argument in saying that this contradiction between advertising and propaganda is crucial in the characterization of that intermediate sector of capital constituted by capitalists who control the mass media and thus find themselves at the centre of a complex web of interests, while at the same time competing among themselves for the appropriation of a portion of the social surplus. This problem will be taken up again later.
14. According to Habermas, however, this reformulation of the problem remained captive to the interests of a specific class (as at the founding of the bourgeois public sphere, when the bourgeoisie could be considered a revolutionary class in the Marxist sense) – in this case the industrial proletariat.

2 Monopoly Capitalism and the Culture Industry

1. Here it is worth referencing the Brazilian case and the start of the import substitution process with the policy of burning surplus coffee production, where Furtado, in his classic *Economic Formation of Brazil*, had already identified a Keynesian-type action even before publication of the *General Theory*.
2. This idea of "compensatory action" by the state (and of its causes and consequences) is very aptly put by Dieter Heideman: "the compensatory

activities therefore recognise social differences and take the form of benefits or losses, depending on the particular conditions of each citizen. By ensuring ownership and social differences, which demand special rights, the state preserves the society of classes". (Heidemann, 1983, p. 94). To perform these and other tasks, the state requires all citizens to pay taxes:

> all are forced to take responsibility using a portion of their means for the maintenance of government agents, through the imposition of law, support for ownership and the promotion of waged labour. For forcing all citizens to pay taxes, the state makes some pay for the security of ownership and others for the insecurity of their existence.
>
> (Ibid., p. 95)

3. It is worth mentioning that this displacement of conflicts and the form of reification (seen by Habermas as "pathologies of communication", as previously mentioned) are closely related to the end of the "utopia of social labour" which is the basis of the welfare state, as well as of fascism and communism, proving that "the utopian direction changes from the concept of work to that of communication" (Habermas, 1987, p. 114). For Habermas, what disappears under these new conditions is not the relationship between historical thinking and utopian thinking that characterizes Western modernity, but this utopia of social labour:

> the utopia of social labour lost its persuasive power – and not only because the productive forces lost their innocence or because the abolition of private ownership of the means of production obviously did not result in self-government by the workers. Above all, the utopia lost its point of reference in reality, the structuralising and socializing force of abstract labour.
>
> (Ibid., p. 106)

It is precisely these new conditions imposed by the social welfare state that have proliferated in the advanced capitalist countries since the war and that, at the same time, neutralize the explosive potential of the class struggle and create new potential for conflict, pronouncing the end of the utopia of social labour, or the end of the "totalising ideologies". (Habermas classifies these totalising ideologies into two representative groups, first by the "The French Revolution which was fought under the banner of bourgeois ideals [and] inaugurated the epoch of ideologically determined mass movements" and then by "modern reactions" that followed it and that "ranging across a broad spectrum of scientific – mostly pseudoscientific – popular views, from anarchism, communism and socialism, through syndicalist radical-democratic, and conservative-revolutionary orientations, to fascism and National Socialism. This was the second generation of ideologies that arose on the ground of bourgeois society". What the two had in common was the fact that "unlike the classical bourgeois ideology, [to which the author limits the ideological critique of Marx, Habermas, 1981, vol. 2, p. 353–354] [...] work up specifically modern manifestations of withdrawal and deprivation – that is to say, deficits inflicted upon the lifeworld by societal modernisation", and, despite the differences in content, adopt the form of "totalising conceptions of order addressed to the political consciousness of comrades and partners in struggle" – Habermas, 1981, vol. 2, p. 353–354). This is not, however, the end of the utopian force to come out of the Enlightenment project. With the end of these ideologies and with the transformations that shift the utopian direction towards the concept of communication, new perspectives are opened for a return to the Enlightenment project based on the concept of "communicative action aimed at understanding". This is the political project of Habermas and the basis for his critique of postmodernism.

4. As Maria Arminda Arruda (1985) clarifies, until 1890 there was little advertising by retailers and it had a minor role in the distribution of products. Arruda presents an interesting definition of the periods, classifying advertising into three types (artisanal, agency and business) according to the phases of capitalism (competitive, transition – during the formation of monopolies – and monopoly). In the first case, production is amateur, without division of labour and without the intervention of an agent, and strictly speaking may not even be classified as advertising because it takes the form of "simple appeals that do not play a role in the reproduction of the system" (p. 49). In the second case, there is separation between producer and agent, with the emergence of agencies. Although in that situation advertising will go on to acquire "a growing significance in capitalist reproduction", it does not achieve a division of labour. Finally, in the third phase agencies are set up as companies, division of labour emerges, the part of employees in the development of advertising messages is amplified, management and production functions are definitively separated "predominantly using persuasion techniques borrowed from social sciences, and advertising becomes essential for the reproduction of capital" (p. 50). We will return to this subject and the work of Maria Arminda Arruda later. For now, note that in the above citations Habermas takes a fairly conventional view of competition, similar in this respect to that of Baran & Sweezy, which I will discuss at another time.
5. Habermas goes on to discuss the issue of public relations, concluding that in the form of institutional propaganda, on the one hand,

   > The sender of the message hides his business intentions in the role of someone interested in the public welfare. The influencing of consumers borrows its connotations from the classic idea of a public of private people putting their reason to use and exploits its legitimations for its own ends. The accepted functions of the public sphere are integrated into the competition of organised private interests

   and, on the other hand,

   > in the measure that it is shaped by public relations, the public sphere of civil society again takes on feudal features. The "suppliers" display a showy pomp before customers ready to follow. Publicity imitates the kind of aura proper to the personal prestige and supernatural authority once bestowed by the kind of publicity involved in representation.
   >
   > (Habermas, 1961, p. 193–195).

6. For the periodic staging, when elections come around, of a political public sphere fits smoothly into the constellation representing the decayed form of the bourgeois public sphere. Initially the integration culture concocted and propagated by the mass media, although unpolitical in its intention, itself

represents a political ideology .... The collapse of political ideology as diagnosed decades ago by Mannheim seems to be only one side of that process in reference to which Raymond Aron speaks of the *Fin de 1'Age Idéologique* (End of the Ideological Age) altogether. The other side is that ideology accommodates itself to the form of the so-called consumer culture and fulfils, on a deeper level of consciousness, its old function, exerting pressure toward conformity with existing conditions. This false consciousness no longer consists of an internally harmonised nexus of ideas, as did the political ideologies of the 19th century, but of a nexus of modes of behaviour .... Advertising is the other function that has been taken over by the mass media-dominated public sphere. Consequently the parties and their auxiliary organisations see themselves forced to influence voting decisions publicistically in a fashion that has its analogue in the way advertising pressure bears on buying decisions .... The temporarily manufactured political public sphere reproduces, albeit for different purposes, the sphere for which that integration culture prescribes the law; even the political realm is social-psychologically integrated into the realm of consumption. (Habermas, 1961, p. 215–216)

7. In his 1981 work, his interpretation of the reasons for the fragmentation is related to the issue of structural differentiation of the *Lebenswelt* – see p. 355–356 whose Kantian root has been criticized by various authors involved in the *TCA* debate.
8. It is worth noting that this complementarity between fragmentation of the social body and a unification of the mass media is at the core of "traditional management" of the "symbolic politics" studied by Sfez (1988), which discusses the representativist and expressivist theories of communication. On the one hand, the representation "is a useful means of linking the stochastic and atomised elements to obtain the bond that life in society requires, namely, hierarchies and vertical and horizontal ties". Such a conception of communication leads to the multiplication of the "symbols and symbols of symbols, to try and reconstruct the concrete reality of individuals and groups", forming "subjects who are represented but with territorial and social cuts" such that "what should be included ... falls outside the binding mechanism. Society works ... but away from the subjects that continue to be atomised". Thus, the "billiard ball model", communication seen from the linear and mechanistic angle, tends to the formation of token symbols or signs taken as atomistic realities" (Sfez, 1988, p. 76 ff.). On the other hand, the expression is "internal link and full participation"; it

   > repairs such divisions presenting a bond of another kind: a symbolic one tending to the convening of culture, traditions, memories of the past ... Those images are indeed ambiguous and polysemic, and the more so that they are, the more likely that individuals will identify with them. Each individual or group is imprisoned by that to which they are internally linked.

   Between this concept and that described in the previous paragraph there is a "mutual restraint" (in the "traditional science of communication") once the management of a representativist model requires the support of an expressivist vision "that animates its rigid structures", while the latter, where each self-generated unit reflects the social totality, requires some type of mechanical linkage for the management of these units, such as that given by the first type of model (Sfez, 1988, p. 76 ff.♣). Thus, the communication criticism by Sfez matches the vision of a social process, which on one hand fragments individuals, reclassifying them according to a hierarchy and social structure where they appear external to it, and on the other, requires unification through ideological mechanisms to justify the systemic unit as social.

9. In the terms of Sfez, we can say that the action of advertising is typically an action that reaffirms the mechanistic view of communication. It classifies and prioritizes atomized individuals in search of greater "efficiency".
10. High and middle bourgeoisie plus "fractions of the wealthier working classes" remain, without essentially affecting the lifestyle of the working class.
11. 1936 is when the first version of the work that came out in Germany in 1955 was published. The Brazilian version is in the collection *Los Pensadores,* Abril Cultural, São Paulo, 1980. The first version was published in Brazil by *Brasiliense* in 1985, together with other selected works.
12. The next part of the question on "creative independence" makes the second problem quite clear:

> very simply, a quick historical overview shows, first, traces of an independent creator whose means of expression are inseparable from the creative activity itself.... Then, those of an artist for whom the dissemination or reproduction of their works puts them in a negotiating position with public or private broadcast structures (...galleries for painters, theatres for actors, editing houses for writers...). This situation leads simultaneously to the first forms of partnership between creators, and above all, to the formation of copyright companies whose functions of defence and management of the interests of cultural workers allows some regulation of the system relations between them and dissemination companies.... But this situation, as well as the payment by *cachet* system is not only maintained, but also thrives to the extent that capitalism invests in the artistic sphere.
>
> (Huet et al., 1978, p. 131)

The authors conclude that if the maintenance of a rights negotiation system between these associations and the capitalists involved in the production and dissemination of cultural goods serves the workers, once their participation in the reproduction is allowed it is, in fact, of strategic interest for capital itself:

> this system is the apparent guarantee of the independence of artistic creation and therefore gives it a valuation that preserves the fiction of a unique and specific use value at the moment when real production modalities are increasingly trying to integrate the cultural worker in a process of collective and anonymous work.
>
> (Ibid., p. 132♣)

13. Where there is an attempt "not so much for total control over the cultural worker by the editor, but of real new production through the formation of a collective workforce that includes the singer, songwriter, author, arrangers,

musicians, sound engineers, artistic directors, etc..." (Huet et al., 1978, p. 132).

14. Flichy also refers to the theme in the following terms:

> While salaried labour became widespread with the expansion of capitalist production, artists continue to be paid according to various forms of copyrights and royalties dating back to the emergence of the right of representation in the 19th century. This system ... really only benefits a small minority of *vedette* thus dividing part of the capital gain .... This system offers a double benefit for the publisher. It decreases their initial investment and turns the remuneration of artists into a variable cost. On the other hand, look at the privileged position of the author in the production process, the uniqueness of their creation. For the artists, who are paid some form of income, the creative activity appears to flow spontaneously from the nature of the artist, from their innate gifts and not as the result of selling their labour.
>
> (Flichy, 1980, p. 39♣)

15. This "usurping" relates to the idea of "primitive accumulation of knowledge" that I spoke of earlier and refers to the appropriation of artisan knowledge by the capitalist in the transition of the craft to large industry, as well as to the longer process of the appropriation and transformation of popular culture into mass culture. Without entering into the discussion of these issues, Enzensberger once again captures the essence of the issue when he says that "On the analogy of the economic development of capitalism, which was indispensable for the development of the industrial revolution, the non-material productive forces could not have developed without their own capital accumulation" (Enzensberger, 1971, p. 32).
16. For the first time in history, the media are making possible mass participation in a social and socialised productive process, the practical means of which are in the hands of the masses themselves .... In its present form, equipment like television or film does not serve communication but prevents it. It allows no reciprocal action between transmitter and receiver. (Enzensberger, 1971, p. 15)

3 The Culture Industry and Its Functions

1. What is specified with the characterization of this two-way dynamic is the fact that Culture Industry does not occur in only one area of the public sphere in monopoly capitalism. Other foci of social value determination such as family, political parties, unions and non-governmental organizations should be added. It is clear that the role of the Culture Industry in these is of fundamental importance since it fulfils, in monopoly capitalism, an articulation function similar to the one fulfilled by the press at the time of the restricted public sphere of the liberal state. It is clear also that there is no parallel in history in terms of the power of manipulation available to the media today. But that same history demonstrates that there are objective limits to the Culture Industry's manipulating potential, imposed by social order determinants in the broadest sense of the term.

2. The closest reference to the topic, in his well-known 1969 book, goes no further than the affirmation that the information apparatus works "by cramming every 'citizen' with daily doses of nationalism, chauvinism, liberalism, moralism, etc. by means of the press, the radio and television ... the role of sports in chauvinism is also of primary relevance" (Althusser, 1969, p. 63).
3. In his classic 1978 book, Poulantzas goes back to the topic of ideological apparatuses, to which he dedicates one of the three items in the introduction, where he seeks to highlight his new position on Althusser's ideas. For Poulantzas,

   > the conception that supports the distinction [valid only from a descriptive and indicative point of view only] between repressive state apparatuses and ideological state apparatuses deserves ... profound reservations ... In the way in which it was systematized by L. Althusser, it supports itself on the presupposition of the existence of a state that would only act and function through repression and ideological indoctrination.
   >
   > (Poulantzas, 1978, p. 35♣)

   He states that, besides these two forms of action (repression and ideology), the state also acts in a positive manner, introducing itself "even in the nucleus of the reproduction of capital itself". Also the relationship between the masses and the state

   > always possesses a material basis. Among other reasons, because the state, working for class hegemony, acts in the unstable field of balancing negotiations between the ruling and the subservient classes. Thus, the state is constantly taking a series of positive material measures for the popular masses, even if these measures reflect concessions imposed by class struggle.
   >
   > (Ibid., p. 36♣)

   The mistake of understanding state action only from the point of view of repression–ideology pairing would lead, according to Poulantzas, to break down the exercise of power into two groups of apparatus in an almost nominalist and essentialist manner, by reducing the specificity of the "state economic apparatus". On the other hand, the separation would have "the merit of broadening the state's sphere, including in it a series of hegemony apparatuses, generally 'private', and of insisting on the ideological action of the state" (ibid., p. 40♣). That same ideological action, on the other hand, also presents a positive character in Poulantzas' conception; to him the state does not produce a unified discourse with the function of masking reality, but various discourses "embodied differently in the diverse apparatuses according to the class they are destined for" or a discourse that is "segmented and fragmented according to the power strategy directives", with the purpose of specifically showing its tactics "with a view to organizing the dominant classes".
4. The great empirical goal of the authors is the TV organizational model that prevailed in Italy and France during the post-war period and that, especially beginning with the 1968 events in France, began to receive criticism not just from the Left, but also from entrepreneurial sectors and advertising media interested in introducing commercial television. Cesareo seeks to show that

the organization of state TV in Europe essentially serves capital: "experience confirms that... through public management... the use by the class that controls the means of production and distribution can be conserved. On the other hand, public management organizations always found a way to provide for space for private capital, and to collaborate broadly with it" (Cesareo, 1974, p. 59♣). He speaks of "only one model" of television in the capitalist system, characterized by four elements: unidirectionality of communication, labour division in the artistic production process, centralized decision-making and rupture of contemporaneity. Even if these characteristics are unquestionable, they do not justify the idea of a single capitalist model, given that besides not making any difference in relation to the socialist countries' systems (cf. Costa, 1986, p. 27), they do not portray the current problematic. Cesareo himself, in line with this reasoning, recognizes that "the ruling classes were not able to balance the political demand of tax collection, efficiency and pure profit derived from the internal logic of the apparatus. And this has been one of the permanent reasons for the crisis of the 'model'" (Cesareo, 1974, p. 59♣).

5. Note the similarity of these ideas with those of Granou discussed previously. But here there is progress in comparison to the French author, who has little good to say about mass media.
6. Thus Cesareo reaffirms the idea of a single capitalist model present in his 1974 book. He makes clear, however, that the state introduces an element of contradiction within the model itself: the way is left open for the penetration into the apparatus of different and new control methods. Such methods require a similar bureaucratic organization as that needed for the management of the state, which sometimes conflicts with the bureaucracy of enterprise and the organization of work imposed by the production strategy. The emphasis on political control and bureaucratic norms and personnel management, that appears determined by political "equilibrium", reduces the function of the apparatus and can conflict with the enterprise's "pure" productive criteria. Here the contradiction between the "public" and the "commercial" can arise, but within the general logic of the current "apparatus structure". In fact conflicts tend to constitute part of a structure, within a framework of relationships that can be modified without changing the main framework of the "model". (Cesareo, 1979, p. 45♣).
7. Cesareo analyses the crisis of mass media, which he defines at two levels: the need to expand the production scale to ensure a more competitive presence in the market and that of the consequences of internal ruptures of the hegemonic structure's cohesion, derived from the inability to create adequate and differentiated models of behaviour applicable to different social conditions, in a situation in which "the collective texture of relationships and behaviours tend to break up here and there", with the development of "subversive" behaviours with strong social impact. Since the apparatuses fail to deal with social processes from which those behaviours rise, pressure for decentralization and reforms to the apparatus increase, such as occurred in France and Italy after the social movements of the 1960s, including the historic RAI strike. Strongly influenced by that situation, Cesareo speaks of a process of public awareness and committed intellectuals, supporting the idea of apparatus reform but without noting the pressures on the system arising

from the progress of capital due to marketing, privatization and against the public service system. Those pressures would increase all over Europe, resulting in complete transformation of the audiovisual landscape during the 1980s.

8. There is a coincidence between that new Latin American school of thought and the theoretical approach defended here, to the extent that both oppose the cultural dependency theories. Yet, while Martín-Barbero and García Canclini follow a newly coined predominantly anthropological school, the alternative proposed here starts directly with the Critique of Political Economy, affiliating itself, in terms of Latin American economic thought, with what we could call the Unicamp school (see Bolaño, 1996a) which in my opinion makes the most consistent internal appraisal (structuralist, as opposed to monetarist) of ECLA/CEPAL, although it is not so well known with regard to (sociological) dependency theories. In any case, it is part of my broader academic project (although not of this book) to look for a connection between the theoretical proposal defended here and that of so-called Latin American cultural studies (without eclecticism, based on the concept of cultural work and its mediation function, as I shall define in due course). This approach will also obviously demand the reinitiation of an international debate, taking special account of the views of the British school, between scholars of political economy and those of cultural studies.
9. Renato Ortiz speaks of two schools of thought in the studies on the Culture Industry and mass media whose common thread is the question of dependency: the first "favours an analysis of transnational conglomerates that operate from the core countries, showing how at world level the communication process is unilateral and is distributed according to political and economic interests" (Ortiz, 1988, p. 185♣). Ortiz cites, among others, Schiller's oldest book and the classic study by Varis and Nordenstreng on international flows of programmes, whose results are summarized in the article included in the collection organized by Jorge Wertheim. The second aspect focuses particularly on the impact of cultural imperialism in Latin America and seeks to understand how media communications evolve in a situation of dependency, with "cultural colonialism" and "alienation" as their main themes. Ortiz cites, in this case, Luis Ramiro Beltrán & Elizabeth Fox and Dorfman & Mattelart, as well as Caparelli (1982). As far as our interests are concerned this distinction is irrelevant.
10. Ortiz arrives at a similar conclusion to mine and, by coincidence, also cites Avila's work:

    > the argumentation is enunciated as if the development of Culture Industry were its reason to be external to the axis of Brazilian capitalism. That is why it is common to read in the literature on mass communications, the idea that market society will build, in reality, a "consumption ideology" and not a real development of the productive forces, presenting themselves as something external that is introduced to the masses by multinationals using marketing techniques. Thus we would have in that sense the creation of an induced popular mass culture in which the Culture Industry would really be an atavism in relation to the natural course of Latin American history.
    >
    > (Ortiz, 1988, p. 189 ff.♣)

11. Under these conditions, Latin American nations become "mere recipients" of imposed "alien values" that lead to passivity and aggravate the social inequalities typical of underdevelopment, when a consumer ideology (of commodities, information or entertainment) that is incompatible with the lifestyle of the majority of the population disintegrates an entire previously existing culture of consumption (Sarti cites Sunkel and Fuenzalida) and triggers "a process of frustration that ultimately leads to collective aggressiveness as an escape valve" (Beltrán). The lack of information would be another feature of dependent societies in which the "atrophy of the capacity to inform" coexists with "substantial infrastructural hypertrophy of mass media" (Pasquali).
12. The result would be a "double alienation" imposed on Latin Americans. As explained by Dagnino, Latin American cultural and intellectual production is alienated first by its status as a product of the integration of Latin America into the international capitalist system, and used to seeing the world as capitalist by definition. Second, it is alienated because the dominant ideology is defined outside of the region, in the system's centre of power where the model to be imposed on the dependent countries is developed (Sarti, 1979, p. 236♣).
13. Sarti agrees with Weffort that the basic imprecision of the concept of dependency resides in the vacillation between an approach centred on the nation idea (the starting point of dependency theorists) and one centred on class (on which these authors tend to focus). That vacillation, which is the basis of the dialectic between internal and external factors in the determination of capitalist development, was responsible for the significant debate on dependency theories from which, according to Sarti, the cultural dependency theories emerge with no fixed parameters. Sarti cites a passage by Fernando Henrique Cardoso (1971) in the debate with Weffort, where he declares that "it would be naive to pretend to transform the notion of dependency into a totalizing concept" and points out that "to the extent that it is proposed as an element of Marxist theory of capitalism [expansion of the capitalist production mode towards the periphery of the system], the 'dependency theory' considers the articulation of classes in each dependent society as essential" (idem, p. 242♣). The cultural dependency theories therefore represent "backwardness in relation to the matrix", since they ignore those that are postulated and adopt dependency theory "as a theory to explain Latin American reality in a globalizing and mechanical manner and take it to the level of ideological superstructure. They fall into flagrant economicism when arguing that the superstructure in Latin America has to be dependent, because that is simply what their economy is – dependent" (ibid.).
14. "The distinction between production technique and sales technique was confused.... The cost of production of many items... is attributed principally, to the production of ordinarily meretricious sellable appearances" (cited by Baran & Sweezy, 1966, p. 137♣).
15. "The information, entertainment and 'educational' material transmitted to the audience is an inducement (gift, bribe or 'free lunch') to recruit potential members of the audience and to maintain their loyal attention." (Smythe, 1977, *Canadian Journal of Social and Political Theory*, vol. 1, no. 3, p. 5).
16. Note that when he speaks of monopoly capitalism, Smythe refers exclusively to the USA, affirming that in Europe, "the state was resistant to the

advancement of monopoly capitalism". Such traditional resistance is giving way under the onslaught of pressures from the centre of the monopoly capitalist system (Smythe, 1977, *Canadian Journal of Social and Political Theory*, vol. 1, no. 3, p. 2.).

17. For a critical presentation of Say's Law see Miglioli, 1981, Part 1.
18. For a clarification of the concept of savings, see Conceição Tavares, Assis & Teixeira, 1982.
19. In this regard, the article by Cardoso de Mello of 1977 is quite enlightening.
20. These include, outside the field of Marxism, authors that regard advertising as a mechanism to create norms of consumption, such as Kaldor, Galbraith or Vance Packard, who perceive that advertising possesses "a desire to manipulate individuals and create artificial needs in consumers with the purpose of dominating the public's consciousness and perpetuating the current system" (Arriaga, op. cit., p. 38♣).
21. Zinser's affinity to Smythe is more explicit. After defining the mass media as "economic entities whose purpose is profit and whose function is to contribute to the reproduction of capital" (Zinser, 1980, p. 99♣), Zinser defines "audience commodity" as Smythe does, defining the programme as an "audience production input", and as a "gift to the audience" with the purpose of capturing its attention. For Zinser, the programme contents are

    > certainly alienating, but not because they respond to a purpose of ideological character, but because in their own logic the production of alienating images is inserted [he does not explain what he understands by that] through which he hopes to not only attract the receiving audience, but also to render it more receptive to the advertising message.
    >
    > (Ibid., p. 100)

4 The Political Economy of Communication and Culture

1. I do not mention, for example, Nadine de Toussaint's pioneering work (1978) or Bonnel's interesting contribution (1989); and I touch only tangentially on Dominique Leroy's research.
2. Labour that is exchanged for capital, that is capable of producing added value.
3. Goods paid for through expenditure, that do not function as capital.
4. It is interesting to reproduce here Ramon Zallo's criticisms of the authors' concept of cultural labour. Zallo, in addition to judging the interest of the definition of "indirectly productive" work to be doubtful, considers the distinction between productive and unproductive labour to be insufficient in the definition of artistic work, given that, as the authors themselves point out, the wage relation is not the standard in cultural industries. He cites a quote from Marx in which the latter affirms that "categorising labour as productive or unproductive is totally irrelevant" in the analysis of independent work. He states that writers or artists are not producing either salaried or unproductive work, but are independent producers of goods offered to commercial or industrial capital. According to Zallo, although it is difficult to compare the different activities involved in the production of these goods in "phase one" of that workflow, which, as we have seen, is not a

unified process, that is not the case from the moment that the work is integrated into a capitalist production process. This capitalist process supposes "a (percentage) fixed cost variable that, for the publisher or producer, is part of the constant flow of capital circulation. There is no uncertainty in the valorisation process" (Zallo, 1988, p. 48 ff.).

5. With regard to the unique character of the product, Flichy (1980, p. 40) gives the example of filmmaking. Here, since it is obviously an industrial and collective production process, division of labour is clearly established from the beginning. Uniqueness is frequently achieved through the "starification" (by analogy with valorization) of "a creator who attests to the unique character of the film".
6. Flichy appears to exclude radio and television from this definition, since they are characterized "by the obsolescence of their products, continuity of programming, the breadth of coverage and the intervention of the state in their activities" (Flichy, 1980, p. 55). Later he suggests that in these sectors the principle of uniqueness does not apply. We will fully analyse their differences, compared with editorial type cultural production, later in this book. In his article, produced in association with Paul Beaud & Monique Sauvage, Flichy is clear that randomness does not apply to television, which has highly developed forecasting methods, and a captive and globally stable audience (Beaud et al., 1984, p. 198). Zallo correctly points out that Flichy's position, subsequently adopted by the GRESEC in their second book (Miège et al., 1986), does not hold up: competitivity in the radio and television industries reintroduces unpredictability (Zallo, 1988, p. 51).
7. The criterion of reproducibility, on the other hand, is central to the authors' classification of cultural production into three groups, these being: "reproducible without the intervention of cultural workers" (musical instruments, photographic prints, new audiovisual products); "reproducible with the intervention of cultural workers" (sound recording, book, film); and "semi-reproducible" (prints, crafts, video art). The first two are industrial production processes, while the third is artisanal production. The industries in the first group are material production industries, while those in the other two are "content" based. This taxonomy, clearly insufficient, will later be abandoned by the GRESEC, so it is not worth going into it any further here (for additional analysis, see Zallo, 1988, p. 30 and s. & p. 47 ff.).
8. The inclusion of the press in that definition is confirmed much further on, when Flichy, referring to the topic of multimedia conglomerates, emphasizes the existence of "a very strong bond within wave culture between the press and broadcasting" (Flichy, 1980, p. 195).
9. "A TV broadcast, by definition, is consumed at the moment of its broadcast... [and] does not constitute a single work, intended to be viewed several times" (Flichy, 1980, p. 55).
10. Ramon Zallo takes on a critical analysis of that classification (Zallo, 1988, p. 150 ff.) and proposes a much more complex taxonomy, based on a fairly detailed analysis of work processes and of valorization (ibid., p. 63–71). He identifies a set of five sectors, ranked according to their "degree of capitalist industrialisation": pre-industrial activities (large-audience cultural events); discontinuous editing (printing, sound recording, cinema, videography); continuous editing (printed newspapers); continuous broadcasting (radio

and television, including cable and satellite television); and a segment covering new production methods and computerized or telematic consumer services (computer programmes, teletext, videotext, data banks). Zallo dedicates a chapter to each of these in this important work. He also introduces two "intermediate" cultural sectors: advertising; and cultural sectors housed within industry generally, such as graphic and industrial design or video production. Zallo's taxonomy is most thorough and provides a fairly detailed analysis of each of the various cultural industries, including non-industrial sectors of cultural production. GRESEC II, for its part, offers a dynamic analytical perspective that translates into an extremely insightful appreciation of the historical evolution of the authors' area of interests. They are not aiming to carry out an exhaustive segmentation of cultural industries; they want to evaluate the current and possible future states of the French audiovisual industry. There are no fundamental differences between the two proposed classifications. There are more points of agreement than disagreement between Zallo and GRESEC II, and the differences are quite specific, relating to particular aspects of the French classification method. Zallo accepts the French group's general concept of "social logics", which he seeks to correlate to his own concept of sectors (cf. Zallo, 1988, p. 50 and s.).

11. This leads to the paradox that it is precisely those companies – which one would hope to offer scheduling with stronger local news and cultural content – that are forced to source their programmes from large national and international producers.
12. At a later stage, based on research by Patrick Pajon into video games and home microcomputers in the USA, the authors affirm the existence of a "search by the new industries for the most appropriate operational models for management of creativity...at the outset, every solution can be considered, although in the longer term the editorial model seems likely to prevail" (Miège et al., 1986, p. 87). The sectors studied by Pajon were using three management models: (1) an "integrated style, where the key actor is the project-editor, a sort of artistic director who provides the internal link between creators and technicians on the one side, and the management and marketing teams on the other" (ibid., p. 85). In the eyes of the public, this person appears as the sole creator and guarantor of the artistic quality of the product; (2) an "intermediary mode in which the editor interacts with design teams external to the company, who are paid entirely by royalties, managed and recruited by a talent development department" (ibid., p. 86). Here, the artistic quality is guaranteed by endorsing and publicizing the creative team. Finally, there is (3) the editorial model, in which the editor simply purchases or commissions the programmes. This broad choice of functional modes allows small production units to establish themselves, a phenomenon that, according to the authors, is not limited to this new sector, but applies to "practically all the audiovisual communication industries" (ibid., p. 88). This last observation can be considered in the light of my earlier comments about the need for creative renewal, "artist nurseries" and other hubs of creativity, which lead to large capital working alongside and coexisting with smaller investors. It is the smaller capital that generally takes on the risks of the creative activities. We will return to this point later. Expanding sectors typically see a removal of barriers to entry, with a resulting increase in the number of

companies in that market. There is another element that helps explain the proliferation of small units in the US domestic microcomputer market, however. Not only is the cost of production equipment falling, but we see a new phenomenon that the authors suggest is contrary to all other new industries studied: "expensive and sophisticated equipment" is replaced by "highly specialized personnel, who acquire their training essentially 'on the job' " (ibid., p. 85). Despite this, the fundamental key is that the strong global expansion of the sector, including the emergence of new private channels within traditional television in Europe, led to an unprecedented increase in demand for programmes. This led to a significant increase in audiovisual production. Barriers to market entry within the sector were reduced, which consequently created development opportunities for small and medium enterprises. The new video games sector is a similar case: a market that rapidly expanded to massive proportions, equally demanding rapidly increasing supply.

13. In addition to this collaboration with independents, Flichy highlights the decentralization of the editing or production functions as another method used by large groups to avoid inertia. He gives the example in book publishing of Hachette, which gives great autonomy to the publishing houses it buys (Grasset and Fayard among others), also increasing the already large autonomy of artistic directors on the recording side.
14. The authors also provide some elements important to the specification of what I used to call "quality standards" (Bolaño, 1988) but now prefer to call, as we shall see below, "techno-aesthetic standards". To quote Beaud et al: "between the need to respect consumer habits and the desire to make 'cuts' to gain or regain viewers, and retain or increase its own resources, the production system must keep a place or have contingency available for possible innovation" (Beaud et al., op. cit., p. 191). The authors dismiss the concept of competition in favour of a "production system", ignoring, and seemingly unaware of, the intimate relationship between production and competition that the techno-aesthetic system seeks to clarify. There can still be no question that the "desire to retain or gain audience" is based on a notion of competitive struggle between television companies. This seems to me a more correct understanding of the important topic of innovation in the sector, and the limits and barriers it can face depending on planning needs.
15. This argument about restriction of innovation is linked to the idea that the principle of production unpredictability does not apply to TV, as I noted above. "The stability that emerges from everyday audience ratings actually provides a very solid forecasting tool... that may be another obstacle to innovation" (Beaud et al., 1984, p. 198). According to the authors, there are four questions to ask in order to gain an understanding of how the innovation-planning dialectic resolves itself historically: (a) where are innovation risks taken (types of services, programme genres, companies, company sector and level of responsibility)?; (b) what forms has it taken historically (new or unusual formulas, unknown or "notorious" actors)?; (c) what conditions have historically led to it appearing at a given point in time (new technology or techniques, better equipment, definition of a new professional type, changed relationships between the different players)?; and (d) what was the decision-making process that allowed it to be

accepted? I do not see any way to properly introduce this important set of issues other than through a research programme that clearly addresses the issue of competition and competitivity in the television sector. In this short (but provocative) article, the authors can only ask these questions, without reaching any answers.

16. Concerning the first part, Salaün uses Louis Quéré as a basis on which to claim that the media are not just a means of airing views, but also a "space where a society defines itself and builds its symbolic language". By saying that, Quéré adds a subjective dimension to Habermas' concept of *public sphere*. He criticizes the German philosopher for having called the mass media, at the end of *Structural Change in the Public Sphere,* "a perversion of the ideal of reference" (Salaun, 1989, p. 48 ff.). And indeed, as we saw earlier, as long as Habermas adopts, to any extent, the liberal ideal of the bourgeois public sphere, he can only see the Culture Industry as an aberration. For Salaün, the solution lies in the welfare state, following Rosanvallon and especially François Ewald, who devised a toolkit for social management, set in a context where social rights are based on a notion of collective responsibility, so that "the social contract supplants consensus". Viz., "the need for social management is really no longer disputed. Negotiations held between the different factions and interested parties concern the scope and methods of this management, including the place the State should have in it" (Salaun, 1989, p. 51). This means that the individual, as well as being a citizen and a private person, takes on the role of "social subject" (employee, unemployed, student, consumer, etc.). "A new concept was born, the public service: a protean place where several logics intercept, but overall a social management space" (ibid., p. 53). The public sphere, broken up into public services, can therefore no longer be seen as Habermas envisaged it. Certainly, the modern media continue to be "the principal site of "publicity" (that which has become public). But they, too, are a public service" and, following Quéré, "a space where society represents itself symbolically, which allows the individual to feel themselves to be an integral part" of it (ibid., p. 56 ff.). For this public space to be able to fulfil its function of legitimation, it must be "freely accessible and comprehensible to all members of society". For Salaun, that means "in bourgeois democracies, widely disseminated media must exist. So, the public sphere must be created as a public service." He then asks the natural economic question arising from this, simply and essentially correctly: "either the market is capable, through its size and organization, of being commercialised at minimal cost to the end user, or it must resort to public funding" (Salaun, 1989, p. 57).
17. Salaun cites as examples the writer and the independent composer.
18. As is the case with scriptwriters, filmmakers and musical performers.
19. Zallo subsequently provides more evidence, both among the new media (he mentions TeleText) and the more traditional industries (citing books, vinyl records and audiovisual publishing).
20. "The set of branches, segments and ancillary industrial activities that produces and distributes goods that: have symbolic content; are designed for creative work; are organized by capital that can be evaluated; are targeted at consumer markets; and that have a function of social and ideological reproduction" (Zallo, 1988, p. 26).

21. Republished in English under the title "The Production of Belief: Contribution to an Economy of Symbolic Goods", in Collins et al. (1986).
22. Herscovici presents the idea as follows:

> the appreciation of the symbolic value of a work of art can only occur within that space. This means that, by nature, that appreciation is subjective, since it depends on the operation of this field of production. That approach refuses to recognize an intrinsic value to the work of art... on the contrary it emphasizes the relationship between artistic appreciation and the development of taste... The basic working principle of that space is the rejection of normal economic practice. All the actors, artists, cultural producers (art gallery and theatre directors etc.) and consumers have to appear to be "disinterested"; cultural activities may only appear to be searching for gain of a symbolic nature. The internal logic of this field only allows, as its prime motivator, this symbolic accumulation.
>
> (Herscovici, 1990, p. 113)

23. Concerning the theme of necessity, it is worth citing Enzensberger's correct perspective. When discussing the question of consumer manipulation, he affirms: "a widely accepted thesis states that modern capitalism survives thanks to the exploitation of false needs. This is a half-truth... The force of attraction of mass-consumerism is not based on the dictates of false needs, but in the falsification and exploitation of completely real and legitimate needs, without which the parasitic process of advertising would be superfluous" (Enzensberger, 1971, p. 37 and s.). He adds that the same can be said of mass media, which "does not owe its irresistible power to some clever trick, but to the elemental force of deep social needs, which are manifested in the current vicious form these media take" (ibid., p. 3–8). Citing Henri Lefebvre, Enzensberger clarifies that "consumption as a spectacle promises the disappearance of the shortage", a fallacy only conceivable if it refers to a mass need. "This utopian need genuinely exists. It is the desire for a new ecology; for the removal of the barriers raised in the current environment; for an aesthetic that is not limited to the sphere of 'artistic beauty' " (ibid., p. 40). As far as the media go, "there are other collective desires that are equally powerful and unequivocally emancipatory. Capital often identifies them more quickly, and evaluates them better, than its enemies do, but only so as to capture them and strip them of their explosive force: these desires are the need for participation in the social process, at local, national and international level; the need for new forms of interaction; the need for liberation from ignorance and patronisation; the need for self-determination" (ibid., p. 41).
24. In the same work (1990), for example, Herscovici defines two types of cultural product, the first characterized by a very low reproducibility (numbered editions and Arts), in which artistic work represents 60% or more of the cost of production; the second, highly reproducible (all publishing and press sectors), in which artistic work is only involved in the manufacture of the original design, representing no more than 20% of production costs (p. 112). On the other hand, if it is true that "only non-artistic work (technical, administrative and commercial work) can be transformed into an abstract" (p. 116), it follows that this abstracted labour represents no less than 80%

of production costs in the sector of cultural production that can properly be termed capitalist.

25. Although it may be correct to speak of a dialectic of homogenization and differentiation in mass culture, the terms Herscovici uses to put the question do not seem entirely appropriate. First, one should not seek the logic of distinction within the offer or supply, but primarily within the reception of cultural products. It is a known fact that the same product, marketed to distinct socio-economic groups, will be received quite differently. All studies on how mass media are received make that fairly clear. In this way, supposed "ideological neutrality" (an unfortunate term, because it is open to interpretations quite different from Herscovici's intention) only exists from the point of view of the mass media itself. Besides that, including from the supply side, the logic of differentiation has produced something more than just the existence and continuation of "restricted markets generating strong marks of distinction". There is, in fact, a tendency towards segmentation of the public that partially reverses the trend towards uniformity; this opens the door to the birth of a whole new generation of audiovisual concepts (television segment), as we shall see with Salaun.
26. It is clear that the advertising function is not equally important for each of the various cultural industries, although it is crucial for the Culture Industry as a whole. In any case there are also other forms of capitalist cultural production that do not take part in the logic of advertising. That is not the aim of this study.
27. The authors of that passage later attempt to generalize "Baumol's law", when discussing the issue of rising costs in the audiovisual sector: "The 'Baumol effect' is spreading ... The audiovisual sector, even though it has an approximately industrial structure, retains a clear affiliation with the live show. The same causes obviously produce the same effects" (ibid., p. 194). Dominique Leroy (1980, particularly Chapter III) carries out a deep analysis of Baumol's law; this was Herscovici's starting point (see especially 1990, p. 120–126). For a critical analysis of Baumol, see also Le Pen, 1982.
28. Given that productivity in the sector is not necessarily stagnant, and that widespread wage increases occurs only very partially in artistic professions.
29. Herscovici makes a distinction between the traditional advertising market and what he calls "new wave advertising markets": patronage, product sponsoring, corporate sponsorship and other forms that have been rapidly developing in the European audiovisual market since the wave of privatization at the start of the 1980s.

5 From Production to Competition: Towards the Reconstruction of the Communication and Culture Economy

1. Martin (1988) speaks of decreasing costs for the corpus of the culture industries and, using the example of television, concludes that this characteristic of the production of cultural goods implies "a tendency towards economic concentration, which translates to the risk of a restriction in the variety of the content broadcast" (p. 114). In fact, there are two completely different

conventional viewpoints on the issue of costs in cultural production. The first viewpoint is expressed in a classic text by Samuelson (1964), to which Kopp declares his loyalty, : "this structure of natural monopoly was partially identified in television's case by P. A. Samuelson [that] ... demonstrates the existence of increasing income ... [he] does not explicitly indicate that there is a natural monopoly, but gives all of its characteristics". (p. 65). The other approach breaks from Baumol's seminal work (1968) on the economy of the live performing arts, to which I had occasion to make reference above, when I discussed Alain Herscovici's contribution to the French school of the communication and culture economy.

2. From this viewpoint, the formation of "equilibrium" pricing ceases to be the central object of the theory, which turns towards profit margins as a more general variable, although no longer satisfying postulates of static or dynamic equilibrium, but as a synthesized expression of the conditions of competition and its potential transformation of the market structure – this being the main theoretical interest. Barriers of entry, on the other hand, enter into the equation not as one of the components of the market structure, but rather as the synthesis of the nature and determinants of competition in a given oligopolistic market, encompassing both potential and internal competition.

   (Possas, 1985, p. 172)

3. Kopp's interest is in making a distinction between "regulatory barriers", imposed by the state, and "barriers erected by the companies (technology, patents, growth of capital requirements, publicity, etc.)", which he also refers to as "traditional barriers", the characteristic of which is that of being the "product of market strategy" (Kopp, 1990, p. 52). It begs the question: how are "regulatory barriers" not also the product of the (political) strategies of the large oligopolistic enterprises (the Brazilian market, since its creation in 1950, shows us interesting examples of strategies of this type – see Bolaño, 2004)? Whatever the answer may be, the distinction is a fair one to make. The problem lies in the objective of this distinction: to show that "the difference between the two types of barriers lies in the fact that the 'regulatory barriers' may have a positive effect" (idem). Thus we wander from the field of economy to that of value judgments, more or less acceptable, more or less Manichaean, but always completely in line with the neoclassical tradition in which everything can be reduced to a question of the maximization of utility for the consumer.
4. Competition is therefore defined as

   a process of confrontation between different capitals, that is, the units of valorisation and economic expansion power conferred as a function of the ownership of capital. It should be thought of in this sense as an integrated, inseparable part of the global movement of capital accumulation, in its different forms, and which imprints upon it, as its primary motivation and essential quality, a determined direction and rhythm and historically specific content. In other words, this is the basic engine of the capitalist dynamic, in the tradition of Schumpeter who, in this matter, bases his ideas on Marx.

   (Possas, 1985, p. 174)

5. Here in each instance I am citing the second edition, revised and expanded, from 2004.
6. Even fairly "confidential" programming strategies are possible (within the limits of a mass vehicle such as television, of course), in contrast to Kopp's opinion, for independent broadcasters in an important local market and even for certain networks in well-defined time slots. It cannot be forgotten, as well, that competition in commercial systems financed by advertising is not based on the audience *tout court*, but rather on the share of the advertising pie that that audience could bring in. The Brazilian case is a telling example (see Bolaño, 1987, 2004).
7. Two clarifications should be made, however. First, that the programme and audience products do not always have a market price. In a commercial television system, the audience always has a price and is always the most important product from the point of view of capital valorization. The programme, in this case, may have a price, as is the case in the USA, where the networks (or stations) buy them from independent producers, or as in the case of pay TV, consumers themselves pay for the right to use the cable or receive the codified programme directly from the satellite. But the programme may also be distributed freely by the company that produced it, as in Brazil, where production and transmission are both done by the networks. In any case, in a purely commercial system, leaving aside the case of pay TV, the programme is always free for the consumer. In a state system, such as the one put in place in Argentina under military rule (see Portales, 1986, Bolaño, 2005), where the state purchased the programmes from independent producers, the situation approaches that of the USA. Second, a situation may arise, in a non-commercial state system, in which neither the programme nor the audience has a price (but the programme may always acquire a price on the international market). In a situation such as this, the dual nature of use values is maintained, but it can no longer be thought of as a product, and the artist's labour acquires a purely ideological character, in the service of the state and the symbolic reproduction of the *Lebenswelt*. This last organizational structure of communications systems is obviously not the most interesting from the point of view of capital, although it may be useful to it in specific situations. We could engage in a whole taxonomy, all the more complex if we do not confine ourselves to television, considering the whole gamut of culture industries. From this point onward, however, I will limit myself to the most general case of a complex commercial television system as defined above.
8. Even affirming that this determination is not as important in Europe as in North America – and also South America – a distinction that used to be more important than it is today.
9. When I say imposition, I am thinking, for example, of the critique of the concept of need Baudrillard made (1972, 1973) in his first critiques of Marxism. But the term is a strong one. Micro-sociological analyses on the spread of new communications technologies have shown that, for example, even if the introduction of a new object into the daily life of its users proves that we are completely immersed in a so-called consumerist society, that is, that "the consumerist model has been generalised, trivialised so easily that it is no longer really a model; it is there, almost naturalised in what is ordinary

within everyday life" (Toussaint & Mallein, 1990, p. 40), "This does not mean that any object of consumption ... has use value. Its consumption must also be meaningful, that is, that this practice of consumption can have meanings of use of the machine in congruence with the evolution of lifestyles associated with it" (ibid., p. 41). It is of a relationship of this type, rather than in one of a simple imposition, that I am thinking here.

10. I make an abstraction here, purely for the sake of convenience, of the entire fundamental discussion presented above on the specificity of creative work and the degrees of freedom of artistic creation; in short, of the limits of the real subsumption of labour under capital in the culture industries. I hope to have previously made my position (which otherwise does not differ in essence from my position on the rest of the communication and culture economy) sufficiently clear to avoid any possible misinterpretation.
11. Less and less, it should be said, in the function of the general aestheticization of our society and the production of material goods itself, as well as the invasion of all possible spaces, even the human body, by advertising.
12. It is interesting to note here, in relation to the quality of the audience, the importance of the notion of the "credibility" of the medium. In fact, the advertiser hopes, among other things, that the TV broadcaster, for example, has the capacity to transfer to them the credibility they have achieved with the audience. Thus, the broadcasters must demonstrate to the advertiser that not only do they have access to certain audience members, but the audience members have a sufficiently favourable view of them to ensure that they will feel receptive, without prejudice, to the advertising message produced, more or less competitively, by the hired agency. And this is not just the vehicle, but rather each specific broadcast must be viewed favourably to remain viable in the advertising market. Thus, pornographic broadcasts are generally not of interest to advertisers, despite the audiences they can capture. An example of this was provided in Brazil with the on-air release of SBT's striptease programme *Coquetel*, an audience success in its time slot that, nevertheless, could not be made viable in the advertising market. The coverage of the Gulf War in Europe also demonstrated a phenomenon of this type. It is clear that everything depends on strategic options that must be analysed on a case-by-case basis. Thus, the sensationalist news magazines *Aquí Agora* and *Telediario Brasil*, both on SBT, can boast two different audiences for advertisers, in qualitative and quantitative terms, and two different types of relationships with those audiences (or two different views among the audience captured by each). The advertiser, for its part, will evaluate all of these elements, along with others such as the price of the advertising space and the product offered by other broadcasters, before deciding on a determined distribution of its media budget among different media and vehicles, with the objective of reducing the risk that the desired response is not achieved. I should mention that the basic concept of this note (the quality of the relationship between the audience and the programme as a fundamental element for determining the use value of the audience product) was suggested to me by Professor Pierre Alain Mercier, who is obviously not in any way responsible for anything stated here.
13. It is based on this conclusion that Smythe extrapolates, in my opinion erroneously, the concept of labour.

14. This point must be proved via an historical analysis of the genesis of industrialized cultural production, which obviously could not be done in the current context. It should be noted that the second form of expropriation refers essentially to the work of the popular culture producer, since erudite culture remains linked to restricted consumer circles, possibly even benefiting from capitalist expansion, due to the incorporation of new middle-class consumers, the development of new materials and new techniques derived from technological progress (responsible as well for the emergence of new disciplines, such as video art, for example) and the constitution of the world market in the field. In these non-industrialized sectors of cultural production, the subsumption of labour under capital is extremely limited. The power structure established in these sectors is described in full by Bourdieu (1977).
15. This has an effect on negotiation in the primary market, without necessarily altering the proposed relationship between value and price. The consideration of these effects simply adds an element of audience expectation that the neoclassic economy of television has not managed to incorporate, following the logic of the lecture in Kopp's work cited (p. 179), which is not surprising.
16. Garnham also refers to this, explaining that in an economy increasingly focused on the satisfaction no longer of material or subsistence needs, but rather of other symbolic or psychological ones, an interaction takes place between "competition for status and the search for self-definition by the consumer, on one side, and niche marketing and flexible specialisation in production on the other" (Garnham, 1990, p. 12).
17. An interesting example was provided through the debate over the socioeconomic classification criteria for the Brazilian population in the early 1990s (Bolaño, 2004, p. 219–224).
18. When I say "in excess", I obviously refer to the strategy that in my opinion should be followed in this specific case, in which a position recently captured by an enterprise with the ambition of disputing at least the second place in the national market must be consolidated. The excess of experimentation would be better recommended for less disputed programme time slots, for smaller enterprises with smaller ambitions or for Globo itself, which can afford the luxury of experimenting in prime time, as was the case with *TV Pirata*, which revolutionized the comedy genre in Brazilian television.
19. The definition of the techno-aesthetic structure is presented by Leroy (1980) to oppose the techno-economic structure:

    > we understand this concept to mean data, datasets or relationships that are strictly aesthetic and essentially qualitative in nature. These structures are distinguished from the techno-economic structures by the fact that they are aesthetically neutral. In techno-economic structures, the theatrical system finds general technology (methods of transportation, types of energy, management IT, etc.), and the impact of this on the "para-aesthetic" aspects of production (deploying the troupe, mechanisation in a strict sense, administrative management proper, etc.) Oppositely, techno-aesthetic structures take into account the aesthetic

> data in its material packaging (scenery, stage lighting, management of artistic personnel, etc.), that is to say, the "projection" onto the material infrastructure of the aesthetic production proper. (p. 242)

A little further along, Leroy defines the techno-aesthetic system as a combination of "numerous types of techno-aesthetic structures" and techno-economic and socioeconomic structures, which form "a coherent set the globalness of which constitutes a techno-aesthetic system, defined by a particular 'style' or a 'genre' " (p. 243). Leroy continues:

> thus, it is a specific and coherent organisation of "differentiated" and "complementary" techno-aesthetic structures that create the operetta "genre", the opera genre or the "boulevard theatre" genre. The system can also define a "style", and mentioned are baroque, classical, mythological systems, etc. In a certain way the star system can also be defined as a techno-aesthetic system, etc. (p. 243)

The dynamic that can be deduced from these conceptions is completely adapted to the conventional structuralist perspective:

> techno-aesthetic structures are simultaneously autonomous and interdependent with other structures, principally economic structures, but also political, religious, moral structures, etc. From that point onward, a type of structural dynamic or, more precisely, a cultural dialect can be conceived that takes into account the "progression" of techno-aesthetic structures. This "progression" (evolution) operates, in reality, on different levels of autonomy: intrastructural dialectics (techno-aesthetic progression) but also interstructural dialectics (dialectic interaction of techno-economic, socioeconomic structures, etc., with techno-aesthetic structures). (p. 246)

Leroy also suggests, as concerns this evolutionist dynamic, the existence of "techno-aesthetic regimes" (p. 247), but does not further develop the idea.

20. Kopp makes the following differentiation between the bargaining power, before television, held by independent producers and sporting organizations:

> the producers of series suffer . . . for having television as their only option. Networks are, therefore, in an oligopolistic position vis-à-vis producers, which justifies a study of the effects of the imperfection of the competition within the market. In the case of sports, television is only one outlet, sometimes substantial, for activities that receive a portion of direct ticket sales. Sporting organisations, teams or federations, therefore have nothing to fear . . . from the networks' excess "bargaining power". In fact, as the Anglo-Saxon literature points out, it is television that is more beholden to bargaining terms that are very advantageous to the sporting organisations.
>
> (Kopp, 1990, p. 196)

Even without dissenting from Kopp's observations, it should be added that these two are not the only cases of asymmetries between event production and organization on one side, and television on the other: let us not forget the worldwide oligopoly of film distribution, nor let us confuse a world football championship, an Olympics, or Carnival in Rio de Janeiro, for example (which are already specially produced for televised transmission, to the point that the standards of the sports themselves evolve to ensure the event) with an indoor football championship in São Paulo or a beach volleyball tournament (it is clear that even these suffer the influence of the evolution of sporting standards as a function of the event characteristic of sports and the consequences of professionalization on young athletes and on the business organization of the teams, etc.) The specific power distribution situations are extremely varied, along with the possibilities to exploit synergies (such as the use of film or television stars by large theatrical enterprises – and vice versa – which also relates to the asymmetries that exist in the arts and live events sector). In sporting events, it is interesting to cite the case of the French cycling tournament as an example of a sporting activity the economic organization of which finds similarities with that of television: the event is free to the public and the organizers sell advertising space on each leg of the tour, as well as, of course, television transmission rights.

21. Another extremely interesting case, in addition to sports, which I cited in the previous note, is that of so-called live performing arts (theatre, ballet, opera, but also rock festivals and music hall events).

> The question is generally posed in terms of transmission, transposition and adaptation; from this perspective, the audiovisual is required to release a work created entirely outside of it on a mass scale and the relationship between the two instances are limited to a negotiation (on equal footing) of secondary exploitation rights [and here it should be made clear that the authors are referring to the case of European public TV, the resources of which are dwindling, but with strong bargaining power. In this case, they doubt the capacity of these broadcasters to provide real conditions for the capitalisation of live performing arts. In the case of a TV commercial] ... it is important to ask whether the audiovisual industries will be ... incentivised to broadcast live performing arts productions. Only they can offer new valorisation conditions ... In each case, they will be specific productions, rewrites and not simple adaptations.
>
> (Miége et al., 1986, p. 77)

With the experience that familiarity with Brazilian television affords me, I can confirm the suspicions of these French authors, whose predictions are based on their knowledge of discographic production, which "developed from the moment in which albums, for both cultural and technical reasons, stood out from broadcasts of concerts or music hall shows" (idem, p. 78). In fact, dramaturgy on television, a sector in which Brazil occupies a leading role worldwide, demands its own language, different from that of theatre, such that the transposition of a work originally written for the latter is a case of rewriting more than just adaptation. But this does not resolve, as the authors of the segments cited seem to hope, the valorization problems of live performing arts productions. In my opinion the question is really one of taking advantage of synergies, as I cited in the previous note, which means the show has to be re-shown, taking advantage not only of the television (or film) star system, but also of the artifices of language that television has created and popularized. If, from the economic perspective, this translates into an accentuation of the asymmetries present in the live performing arts sector, productions that are marginal, directed at more specific audiences, experimental, etc., are not eliminated in any way; they represent an important element, as we saw in the discussion of the French school of communication and culture economy, for the renewal of the mass culture itself, by assuming the risks of innovation that large capitals in the sector are not willing to take on.

22. Through television in the case in point, or by television and radio in the case of the audiovisual in the broad sense, which includes the discographic production sector, as can be observed in the simplified model presented in the second diagram.
23. It is the legitimisation of another form of state intervention that the institutionalisation of the *Independent Administrative Authorities* represents. Instead of intervening concretely in the set of policy determinations for the audiovisual…the state intervenes only as an explicit and competent, but politically neutralised, partner in sectoral regulation. The relationship between the sector and the state thus "rationalised" releases the political burden of direct sectoral management from the shoulders of governmental authorities. Now, the forms of the failure of the CNCL simultaneously demonstrate the perverse effects this has on executive power itself…It is, symbolically and in practice, the government that must take on the social demands concerning the sector…and the critiques…[of] regulation itself. (Négrier, 1989b, p. 98)
24. As far as television is concerned, the issue of intermedia competition touches on three different levels. The first is the more immediate level of the competition for a place in programming for the different sectors of audiovisual production, for which TV is one of the possible exhibition spaces. To this competition for access to the home TV set is added today, on an intermediate level, shall we say, the expansion of the new uses of the screen, among the most important of which, from the viewpoint of their current mass penetration, are video games and videocassettes. On a more general level, this entire set participates in the competition for the distribution of media budgets (along with other forms of advertising communications such as outdoor or mail). In addition to this, on a more fundamental level, this entire set competes for the free time of individuals, along with other ways to spend that time, such as any kind of recreation, including sex, and participation in social, political, religious and philanthropic activities, etc. But this is no longer strictly a matter of intermedia competition. On that subject, it is also interesting to cite Herscovici's discussion on competition. Herscovici recognizes that cultural markets are characteristically monopolistic or oligopolistic, with strong barriers to entry and competition centred on the differentiation of products. However, he affirms that "price competition operates on an intermediatic level and on the level of certain intermediary markets", referring more clearly, in the latter case, to publicity. On the intermediate level, price competition is responsible for important "effects of substitution that can be measured in terms of cross elasticity", which

caused, for example, the substitution of theatre for film and, later, of the latter for television as the dominant medium. "In this sense, such markets could be assimilated into undifferentiated oligopolies, where price effects are of greater importance." In publicity, he refers to the issue, fairly well known, of the interest of advertisers in more segmented or more massified media, in criteria that favour total cost or cost per thousand in price setting, etc., remaining thus, therefore, in the issue of intermedia competition (Herscovici, 1988, p. 127).

25. It is interesting to take the three diagrams together and verify that the intersectoral relationships, in each case, point towards a general model of the publishing/distribution-distribution/small-scale type, and distribution can be substituted in some cases by a direct relationship between distributors and independent producers. In others, the editors themselves control distribution networks. In the case of radio and television, the small-scale sector disappears and is substituted by telecommunications systems, which function in general in monopolistic or near-monopolistic regimes and the relationship of which with the system is of another nature: there is no real intermediation performed by telecommunications enterprises; rather they just grant channels for direct communication or, better still, mediated only technically by content industries with the audience. This difference tends, however, to blur into the development of teledistribution systems (which must be analysed as an intermediate case between small-scale distribution of culture products and traditional broadcasting, pointing as well, as several authors from the French school of the communication and culture economy note, to an approximation of the *flot* industries of the editorial logic) and with the latest technological developments moving networks and programming industries closer together.
26. This also encompasses a fundamental element of the symbolic order, evident, for example, in the quite current idea of a "combinatorial society".
27. Thus, the rigid prohibition of any mention of Luis Inácio da Silva in all of Globo Television Network's programming, for eight long years, until the municipal elections in 1988, did not prevent him, the next year, from reaching the second round of the presidential elections, before being defeated by a small margin by the candidate strongly supported by the network, as its proprietor, Roberto Marinho, would admit almost three years later (Bolaño, 2004, p. 211–214).
28. It would be necessary, in order to elucidate the theme of dominance between the oligopoly of cinematographic distribution and that of broadcasting, to define in which precise terms the connection is made between the national and the international in the sector, taking into account that the television industry itself has become significantly internationalized, above all since the 1980s, presenting alterations in the flow of programmes, expansion of the exportation of capitals, development of new technologies in the field of cable and satellite systems, etc.
29. We can, however, imagine an insurrectional situation in which no attention is given to any sector of the Culture Industry, a situation in which, using Habermas' terms, the symbolic reproduction of the *Lebenswelt* would be exclusively ensured by internal forms of solidarity.

6 Subsumption of Intellectual Work and the Political Economy of the Internet

1. To clarify, I have spoken here of national popular culture only for convenience, as in reality I very much agree with the idea, defended by Renato Ortiz (1994), of the establishment of an "international popular culture"; however, I will not go into this point here so as not to deviate excessively from the fundamental issue.
2. For a more in-depth discussion on the issue of the relationship between intellectual and manual labour, see Sohn-Rethel (1989). See also Galván (2001). For an analysis of the problem in the perspective of the current capitalist restructuring, see Bolaño (2002).
3. See Bolaño (1997) (Org). Also see Bolaño (2000a).
4. On the subject of digital TV, see Bolaño and Brittos (2007).
5. The biotechnology sector is the best example of this current movement, heavily subsidised by the expansion of information technology and communication, explaining the advanced stage of socialization of the production achieved by capitalism today and therefore the objective possibility of exceeding it. (Bolaño, 2004b).
6. White goods could also be considered in this category under the concept of "time compressors" (Pilatti, 1990). The digital revolution is increasingly promoting articulation between the different domestic interfaces of communication systems that are the basis for the convergence, referring to issues such as changes in lifestyle in capitalism today, colonization of the life-world, expansion of market logic and the contradictions that it entails, etc, reinforcing the trends discussed throughout this study. See also Bolaño (2000b).
7. The creation of these economic indicators fulfils an empirical need explained in the following paragraphs:

   > In spite of the excitement and optimism surrounding the Internet Economy, few comprehensive efforts have successfully measured the economic growth and jobs created by this emerging economy. Estimates of the dollar volume of Web-based business are often based on the consideration of fifty or one hundred pure Internet based companies, and can seriously underestimate the size of Internet based transactions. Further, electronic transactions are only one component of the Internet Economy, which should also include infrastructure related activities. A foundation for metrics and measurement is the key to understanding and analyzing issues involving this Internet Economy. For example, what business sectors, products and services should be included in this Internet Economy? What methodologies are appropriate for measuring activities in this new world? How large is this Internet Economy? How fast is it growing? The Internet Economy Indicators (...) seek to fill this void by providing a foundation for conceptualizing and measuring the various components of the Internet Economy. (...) These Internet Economy Indicators are based on the premise that the level of Internet commerce activity hinges on the underlying Internet infrastructure and applications, as well

> as on the presence of electronic intermediaries to facilitate interactions between buyers and sellers.
>
> (University of Texas at Austin, 1999b)

8. A complete and detailed overview of the methodology adopted by the Center for Research in Electronic Commerce at the University of Texas can be found in the second part of the paper on which this analysis is based. To summarize, we can highlight some of the main methodologies adopted by the group, in addition to the already addressed division of the internet economy into four layers: empirical research in 3,138 SMEs linked to one or more layers of the economy, based on telephone interviews and in-depth investigation in 350 major companies operating in the internet economy, with annual revenues equal to or greater than US$25 million and with the use of fairly rigorous exclusion criteria (e.g. companies are only considered part of the internet economy if they carry out their network business using encryption security systems for transmitting data, and additionally, the range of companies investigated consists only of those that are based in the USA); comparison of quarterly results from 1998 of income and jobs produced by this sector; monitoring of annual reports; informational literature and information from the sites of the 300 largest companies with internet business; various methods to avoid overlap in accounting in the case of companies operating in more than one layer and also within the same layer in order to avoid inflation of the results.
9. Levels, strata or layers.
10. In relation to companies acting in more than one layer, note: "For instance, Microsoft and IBM are important players at the Internet infrastructure, applications, and Internet commerce layers, while AOL (before the acquisition of Netscape) is a key player in the infrastructure, intermediary and commerce layers" (University of Texas at Austin, op. cit.). The authors continue:

    > Even though the four-layer Internet Economy framework makes it difficult to separate revenues for multi-layer players, the framework presents a more realistic and insightful view of the Internet Economy than a monolithic conceptualization that does not distinguish between different types of activities. Further, the multi-layered approach lets us analyze how companies choose to enter one Internet layer, choosing later to extend their activities to the other layers.

    In fact, the argument is important because the classification, in the way it is proposed, allows description of the different market structures, social logics and financing models belonging to the larger universe of the internet economy. However, that does not eliminate interest in cross-sectional analyses that allow us to understand the phenomena of significant vertical integration in the economy.
11. Note that the authors of the report make a single distinction in any layer, but mainly in Layer 4, between traditional companies that use the network to increase the potential for marketing their products (bricks and mortar becoming clicks and mortar), citing the case of the bookshop Barnes & Noble that changed from a traditional physical bookshop to one of the largest

in e-commerce, and companies that from the beginning have arisen in the internet sphere, as in the classic case of Amazon.com.

12. According to the authors, this is explained by reasons that are "technical (it would require making the full range of routers equal), social (the navigators are used to not paying for transport and accept some congestion), economic (moving images could not be conveyed at a reasonable price to the end user) and without doubt political" (idem, p. 105). The authors also later cite the limitations of the conventional telephone network for IP transport (limited bandwidth and wasteful use of the switch plus costly infrastructure), citing technical alternatives, such as ADSL networks, in which the American Regional Bell Operating Companies (RBOCs) such as Bell Atlantic and US West have advantages, or cable TV networks. In the case of the latter, they cite interactivity limitations of the "tree" architecture systems which require relatively major investment to upgrade, citing AT&T and France's Lyonnaise Communications as two cases of such strategy. The first, which lost all its local loop with its dismemberment in 1984, invested heavily in cable distribution, taking control of TCI, the largest company in the industry in the USA, of Media One and ISP At Home. In total, today it can offer fast Internet access and IP transport to 25 million users, in addition to controlling an important portal such as Excite (idem, p. 107 and ff.). In addition, mobile telephony systems are beginning to allow access to the net, thus eliminating the need for a computer. This is similar to the relaunch of the Palm tops or PDA (Palm Digital Assistants) or "other equipment, especially domestic, that can connected to the internet" (idem, p. 112, ♣ all quotes).
13. Thus the super valuation of internet company stock traded on the stock exchange may not just be the result of a mere "speculative bubble", but may be well-founded expectations with regard to the threat they pose to the already established telecommunication companies, which as a result could be interested in acquiring them at inflated prices.
14. The authors go on to state that in other countries like Germany, France or the UK the situation is more ambiguous, but make it clear that, even in such cases, the trend is towards concentration and internationalization of the ISP business, citing for example the acquisition of the British company Compuserve by AOL and its alliances with the Bertelsmann and Cegetel groups (German & French respectively).
15. The explanation given by the authors for this difference is that "written information is easily digitised and more easily transportable than animated images and the forms of sale and valuation of Internet assets seems closer to those found for written media than those that can be seen for the audiovisual". (op. cit., p. 113).
16. The authors cite the success of American start-ups: Amazon (8 million customers), CD Now (1.6 million), E-Bay (online auction) and Expedia (real estate and tourism) (idem, p. 114).
17. Exploration costs relate primarily to marketing and promotion (54%). Production is only 15%. The Brazilian magazine *Internet Business* suggests that values for the development of a website in 2000, with a secure server and depending on the degree of complexity, could range from 150,000 to BRL 1 million (*Internet Business*, 2000), values that have certainly been affected by the crisis.

18. This is obviously a graphic simplification of a very complex evolving social phenomenon. There are, for example, two phenomena that cannot be displayed in the chart but influence the definition of social logics and funding models that will exist in the internet economy if they are widely established, as seems to be happening today: namely free internet (essentially altering the position of the ISP, making them more like portals and other pure internet players) and the Internet Data Center (IDC). The IDC, according to information released by the 25 April 2000 edition of the *Gazeta Mercantil*, are literally bunkers of about 20,000 m2 designed to host sites, corporate networks and corporate providers. According to the newspaper, the investments in the IDC in 2000 in Brazil was as follows (in US$): Hewlett Packard, 50 million; Matrix, 25 million; Optiglobe, 160 million; PSINet, 60 million; Telefónica, 50 million; Telemar, 300 million.
19. From the beginning, these gift relations of production were hardwired into the technological structure of the Net. Although funded by the military, scientists developed computer-mediated communications to facilitate the distribution and manipulation of their own research data. Working at universities, they never conceived of this information as a commodity. On the contrary, these academics were advancing their careers by giving away the results of their labour. [...] When online, every connection involves copying material from one computer to another. Once the first copy of a piece of information is placed on the Net, the cost of making each extra copy becomes almost zero. The architecture of the system presupposes that multiple copies of documents can easily be cached around the network. Although most of its users are now from outside the academy, the technical design of the Net still assumes that all information is a gift.

    (Barbrook, 1999)

20. In this regard, Barbrook says he is not interested in broadcasting as a means of communication to resolve specific ethical issues, even though that was what his listeners expected of him, and broadcasters are interested in "selling art through their equipment. But to be on sale, the art has to be buyable today. And I would rather not sell anything, but just make the proposal that broadcasting in principle be a communication apparatus in public life", adding: "if you consider this utopian, I beg you to ask why it is utopian" (ibid, p. 14♣).
21. The next paragraphs of this chapter are taken from Bolaño and Castañeda (2004). For a deeper analysis, see Bolaño and Herscovici (2005). From the perspective of the political economy also see Söderberg (2002). See also Bower (2002). See also Benkler (2002–2003). By the same author, see Benkler (n.d.). A thank you for these references to Dr. Imre Simon, author of, among other things, of *A propriedade intelectual na era da internet*. Available at: http://www.ime.usp.br/~is. For a more complete view on the subject of intellectual property, see Barbosa (1999), Sherwood (1992). On Linux, Pritchard (1999) should also be mentioned.
22. The FSF is dedicated to the development and distribution of free software in all areas of computing and also contribute to the development of the GNU operating system.

23. Message sent by Linus Torvalds to his Usenet discussion group "com.archives".
24. GPL is the licence that accompanies the distribution packets for the GNU project that covers a variety of software including the Linux operating system kernel. It ensures that the software produced under this licence does not become owned for any reason. It is based on international copyright law that gives legal cover to GPL licensed software. In a play on the word "copyright", the GPL is known as "copyleft". (The full official version of the GPL is available at: http://www.gnu.org/licenses/gpl.html).
25. According to the Free Software Foundation (FSF), the free software is based on four freedoms: (a) to run the program for any purpose, (b) to study how the program works and adapt it to the needs of the user, for which access to the source code is required, (c) redistribute copies "so that you can help your peers" and (d) improve the program and release the improvements so that the whole community benefits, for which access to the source code is also fundamental. Full text available at: http://www.fsf.org/philosophy/free-sw.pt.html.
26. This section is taken from Bolaño and Mattos (2004).
27. See Bolaño (2003c).
28. The success of Linux led to Microsoft promising to open the source code for Windows, but, as argued throughout the report, what the company divulges is in fact not the code but access to its site, where it is possible to view the code, but not to analyse it because the operation does not allow copy and paste (Rodrigues, 2003, p. 54). Rodrigues goes on to cite the case of resolution 465 of 2000 of the French Senate, prohibiting the use of software that cannot be audited by the government on the grounds of possible industrial espionage and Microsoft's ties to US intelligence services. The resolution was abandoned with the promise of open access to the Windows source code. According to Pedro de Rezende, one of those interviewed, the senators have been fooled because "they have not received the original source code, but a copy where the programme variables have unrecognizable names, indicating that they had been replaced. Comments accompanying the lines of code seem to have been removed" (idem, p. 56♣).

Bibliography

NOTE: Items marked in this study with the symbol ♣ are translated into English from the Spanish versions of the bibliographical/reference material.

Adorno, T. & M. Horkheimer (1969) *Dialética do Iluminismo.* Excerpts published in Brazil in Lima, L. C. (1978) and in the collection *Os Pensadores.* São Paulo: Abril Cultural, 1980.

Althusser, L. (1969) *Para leer El Capital Biblioteca dei Pensamiento Socialista.* Espanha: Siglo Veintiuno, 1974.

Althusser, L. (1987) *A crise de 1929 e o debate marxista sobre a teoria da crise.* In Hobsbawn (1987).

Altvater, E. (1972) *Remarques sur quelques problèmes posés par l'intervention étatique.* In Vincent (1975).

Altvater, E. (1970) *Ideologia e aparelhos ideológicos do Estado.* São Paulo: Martins Fontes. Anuário Brasileiro de Mídia, 1991–1992.

Arriaga, P. (1980) *Publicidad, economía y comunicación masiva (México—Estados Unidos).* Mexico: Ceesten/Nueva Imagen.

Arruda, M. A. N. (1985) *A embalagem do sistema: a publicidade no capitalismo brasileiro.* São Paulo: Duas Cidades.

Ávila, C. R. A. (1982) *A teleinvasão: a participação estrangeira na televisão do Brasil.* São Paulo: Cortez.

Baran, P. & P. Sweezy (1966) *Capitalismo monopolista.* Rio de Janeiro: Zahar, 1978. (1963) Teses sobre a publicidade. In Cohn (1975).

Barbosa. A. (1999) *Sobre a propriedade do trabalho intelectual: uma perpectiva crítica.* Rio de Janeiro: UFRJ.

Bareinboim, E. O. (2004) *O que é Linux? Primeiros passos.* Available in: <http://olinux.uol.com.br/artigos/248/1.html>. Accessed on: 5 January 2004.

Barbrook, R. (1999) *Cybercomunism: How the Americans Are Superseding Capitalism in Cyberspace.* Available in: <http://www.nettime.org/nettime.w3 archive/199909/msg00046.html>.

Baudrillard, J. (1968) *O sistema dos objetos.* São Paulo: Perspectiva.

Baudrillard, J. (1972) *Pour une critique de Véconomiepolitique du signe.* Paris: Gallimard.

Baudrillard, J. (1973) *Le miroir de la production.* Paris: Casterman.

Baumol, W. (1968) *Performing Arts: The Economic Dilemma.* Cambridge, MA: M. I. T. Press.

Beaud, R, P. Flichy & M. Sauvage (1984) *La télévision comme industrie culturelle—Géomètre contre saltimbanque: La prédominance de la programmation dans la TV française.* In: *Sociologie de la télévision*, p. 187. France: CNET, 1990.

Beaud, R, P. Flichy & M. Sauvage (1991) *Géomètre contre saltimbanque: la prédominance de la programmation dans la télévision française.* In: *Réseaux Hors Séries, Sociologie de la Télévision*: France. Paris: CNET.

Beltrán, L. R. & E. F. Carmona (1980) *Comunicação dominada.* São Paulo: Paz e Terra, 1982.

Benjamin, W. (1936) *A obra de arte na era de sua reprodutibilidade técnicaI*. In: "Obras escolhidas". São Paulo: Brasiliense, 1985.

Benkler, Y. (2002–2003) *Coase's Penguin, or, Linux and the Nature of the Firm*. Forthcoming, Yale, n. 112, Winter 2002–03.

Benkler, Y. (s.d.) The Battle over the Institutional Ecosystem in the Digital Environment. *Communications of the ACM*, v. 44, n. 2, New York.

Bernstein, R. J., org. (1988) *Habermasy la modernidade*. Madrid: Cátedra.

Bettetini, G. (1991) *Réalités et tendances de la télévision européene*, apresentado ao colóquio Sociologie des Télévisions en Europe, Paris, 24 and 25 January.

Blanke, B., U. Jürgens & H. Kastendiek (1977) *On the Current Discussion on the Analysis, Form and Function of the Bourgeois State*. In Holloway & Picciotto (1977).

Bolaño, C. R. S. (1987) *O público brasileiro de televisão*. In: Revista Brasileira de Comunicação, 56. São Paulo: Intercom. Republished in *Cadernos UES/Comunicação, 1*, Aracaju, 1995.

Bolaño, C. R. S. (1987b) *Keynes e os caminhos da síntese neoclássica*. In: ECOS 7(1). Aracaju: INEP/Seplan.

Bolaño, C. R. S. (1991) *O enfoque neo-schumpeteriano concorrência e o mercado de televisão*. In: Revista Brasileira de Comunicação, 65. São Paulo: Intercom.

Bolaño, C. R. S. (1993) *Capital, Estado, Indústria Cultural*. UNICAMP, Campinas, mimeo.

Bolaño, C. R. S. (1994a) *Da derivação à regulação: para uma abordagem da Indústria Cultural*. Aracaju, mimeo.

Bolaño, C. R. S. (1994b) *Considerações sobre a Teoria da Ação Comunicativa de Habermas*. Aracaju: UFS, mimeo.

Bolaño, C. R. S. (1995) *Economia política, globalización y comunicación*. In: Nueva Sociedad, 140, Caracas.

Bolaño, César (1996) Da Derivção à Regulação: Para Uma Abordagem da IC. Aracaju: UFS, mimeo.

Bolaño, C. R. S., org. (1997) *Privatização das Telecomunicações na Europa e na América Latina*. Aracaju: EDUFS, 1997. (1997b) *La génesis de la esfera pública global*. In: Nueva Sociedad, 147, Caracas.

Bolaño, C. R. S. (2000a) *Notas sobre a Reforma das Telecomunicações na Europa e nos EUA até 1992*. EPTIC On Line, Texts for Discussion 1, 2000. Available in: <http://www.eptic.com.br>.

Bolaño, C. R. S. (2000b) *Sociedade da Informação: reestruturação capitalista e esfera pública global*. Revista Estudos de Sociologia, Araraquara/São Paulo, v. 8, n.00, p. 93–128, 2000.

Bolaño, C. R. S. (2002) *Trabalho intelectual, comunicação e capitalismo*. In: Revista da Sociedade Brasileira de Economia Política, Rio de Janeiro, n. 11, dez. 2002, p. 53 a 78.

Bolaño, C. R. S. (2003) *Elementos Teóricos para a construção da Cadeia Produtiva das Comunicações em Aracaju*. In: Falcón, Maria Lúcia de Oliveira; Hansen, Dean Lee; Júnior, Edison Rodrigues Barreto. Cenários de desenvolvimento local: estudos das cadeias produtivas de Aracaju – vol. II. Aracaju: PMA, 2003, p. 217–235.

Bolaño, C. R. S. (2003a) *Da derivação à regulação: para uma abordagem da Indústria Cultural*. In: Eptic On Line V(3), set.-dez. Available in: <http://www.eptic.com.br>.

Bolaño, C. R. S. (2003b) *Duas teses sobre a teoria marxista do Estado*. Revista Tomo, VI(6), Aracaju: UFS-NPPCS (p. 81–106).

Bolaño, C. R. S. (2003c) *Políticas de Comunicação e Economia Política das Telecomunicações*. Available in: <http://www.eptic.com.br>.

Bolaño, C. R. S. (2003d) *Economia Política do Conhecimento e o Proj eto Genoma Humano do Câncer de São Paulo*. Aracaju: UFS, mimeo.

Bolaño, C. R. S. (2004) *Productive restructuring, subsumption of intellectual labor, and the contradictory dynamics of development*. In: Abagli, Sarita, Maciel, Maria Lucia (2010). Information, power, and politics. Technological and institutional mediations. New York: Lexington Books, p. 147–168.

Bolaño, C. R. S., M. Guillermo, S. Francisco (2004) *A Latin American perspective for the political economy of communications*. In: The public, vol. 11, 3, p. 47-58.

Bolaño, C. R. S. (2004a) *Mercado brasileiro de televisão*. 2. ed. São Paulo: Editora Educ.

Bolaño, C. R. S. (2004b) *Economia Política e Conhecimento e o projeto genoma humano do câncer de São Paulo*. In: Eptic on Line, vol. VI, n. 3, set-dez, 2004. Available in: <http://www.eptic.com.br>.

Bolaño, C. R. S. (2005) *Mercado e políticas de comunicação no Brasil e na Argentina*. Situação na primeira metade da década de 2000 em perspectiva histórica. In: Redes.Com, n. 2 Sevilla: Instituto Europeo de Comunicación y Desarrollo.

Bolaño, C. R. S. (2012) Intellectual work, communication and capitalism: The reconfiguration of the subject factor in the current productive reorganization. In: Bolaño, C. R. S., M. Guillermo, S. Francisco (2012). Political economy, communication and knowledge. A Latin American perspective. New York: Hampton Press, p. 11–34.

Bolaño, C. R. S. & V. Eloy (2014) *The political economy of the Internet: social networking sites and a reply to Fuchs*. In: Television and new media JCR, vol. 15, p. 101–117.

Bolaño, C. E Brittos, V. (2007) *A televisão brasileira na era digital: exclusão, esfera pública e movimentos estruturantes*. Aracaju and Porto Alegre.

Bolaño, C. E. Castañeda, M. (2004) *Economia Política da Internet e o modelo GNU/Linux*. Apresentado ao CIBERCOM 2004, UFBa, Salvador, mimeo.

Bolaño, C. E. Herscovici, A. (2005) *A crítica da Economia Política da Info rmação e do Conhecimento*. In: CD-Rom do X Encontro Nacional de Economia Política – SEP. UNICAMP, Campinas, 2005.

Bolaño, C. E. Mattos, F. (2004) *Conhecimento e Informação na atual Reestruturação Produtiva: para uma crítica das teorias da Gestão do Conhecimento*. In: Datagramazero. Revista de Ciência da Informação, vol. 5, n. 3, article 3 June 2004. Rio de Janeiro. Available in: <http://www.dgz.org.br>.

Bonefield, W. (1987) *Reformulation of State Theory*. Capital and Class, 33, London.

Bonnell, R. (1989) *La vingtcinquième image: une économie de Vaudiovisuel*. Paris: Gallimard.

Bourdieu, P. (1977) *La production de la croyance*. In: Actes de la Recherche en Sciences Sociales, 13, Paris.

Bower, D. (2002) *Reclaiming the Commons*. Boston Review, Summer 2002, article based on the book by the same author, *Silent Theft: The Private Owner of Our Common Wealth*. New York: Routledge.

Boyer, R. (1986) *La théorie de la régulation: une analyse critique*. La Découverte, Paris.

Brecht, B. (1932) *Teorias de la radio.* In: El compromiso en literatura y arte. Barcelona: Península, 1973.

Caparelli, S. (1984) *Televisão e capitalismo no Brasil.* Porto Alegre: LPM.

Cardoso, F. H. (1971) *Teoria da dependência ou análises concretas de situações de dependência?* In: Estudos Cebrap, 1, São Paulo.

Cardoso De Mello, J. M. (1977) *O Estado brasileiro e os limites da estatização.* In: Ensaios de Opinião, Rio de Janeiro.

Casetti, E. & R. Odin (1990) *De la paléo à la néo-télévision: approche sémio-pragmatique.* In: Communications, 51. Paris: Seuil.

Cesáreo, G. (1974) *La televisione sprecata: verso una quarta fase dei sistema delle comunicazioni di massa?* Milão: Feltrinelli.

Cesáreo, G. (1979) *La "forma aparato" en los mass media.* In Richeri (1983).

Cesáreo, G. (1988) *De la télévision à la culture de 1'écran: sur quelques transformations de la consommation.* In: Le Debat, 52, November–December. Paris: Gallimard.

Chambat, P. & A. Ehrenberg (1986) *Télévision: essai d'identification d'un objet.* Íris T.S., Un. Paris-Dauphine, mimeo.

Cohn, G. (1975) *Comunicação e indústria cultural.* São Paulo: Nacional.

Collins, R., N. Garnham & G. Locksley (1988) *The Economics of Television: The UK Case.* Londres: Sage.

Collins, R., J. Curran, N. Garnham, P. Scannell, P. Schlessinger & C. Sparks (1986) *Media, Culture and Society: A Critical Reader.* Londres: Sage.

Conceição Tavares, M., J. C. Assis & A. Teixeira (1982) *A questão da poupanqfe: desfazendo confusões.* In: Conceição Tavares, M. & M. D. David (1982) *A economia política da crise.* Rio de Janeiro: Vozes.

Connor, S. (1969) *Postmodernist Culture.* Oxford: Basil Blackwell.

Costa, P. O. (1986) *La crisis de la televisión pública.* Barcelona: Paidós.

Eagleton, T. (1985) *Capitalism, Modernism and Postmodernism.* In: New Life Review, 152, July–August.

Eco, U. (1979) *A língua, o poder, a força.* In: Eco (1983).

Eco, U. (1983a) *Viagem na irrealidade cotidiana.* Rio de Janeiro: Nova Fronteira, 1984.

Eco, U. (1983b) *Tevê: a transparência perdida.* In: Eco (1983).

Enzensberger, H. M. (1971) *Elementos para una teoria de los médios de comunicación.* Barcelona: Anagrama, 1974.

Esteinou Madrid, J. (1979) *El estúdio materialista de la comunicación de masas.* In: Cuadernos dei Ticom, March. Mexico Disponível em: UAM-Xochimilco.

Esteinou Madrid, J. (1980) *La sobredeterminación de los aparatos dei consenso de masas.* In: Cuadernos dei Ticom, January. México: UAM-Xochimilco.

Esteinou Madrid, J. (1983) *Los médios de comunicación y la construcción de la hegemonia.* México: Ceesten-Nueva Imagen.

Fausto, R. (1983, 1988) *Marx: lógica epolítica.* São Paulo: Brasiliense.

Flichy, P. (1980) *Les industries de Vimaginaire.* Grenoble: P.U.G.

Folha de S. Paulo (2000) Intermediário perde espaço com a internet. *Financial Times,* 14 January 2000, p. B6.

Frankel, B. (1987) *The Post-industrial Utopians.* Cambridge: The Polity Press.

Fuchs, C. (2008) *Internet and Society. Social Theory in the Information Age.* New York: Routledge.

Furtado, C. (FEB) *Formação económica do Brasil.* 17th ed. 1980.

Galván, C. (2001) *Moeda e Ciência. Ensaios sobre a teoria de Sohn-Rethel.* Recife: Centro Josué de Castro.

Garnham, N. (1979a) *La cultura como mercancia.* In: Richeri (1983).

Garnham, N. (1979b) *Contribution to a Political Economy of Mass-Communication.* In: Garnham (1990).

Garnham, N. (1990) *Capitalism and Communication: Global Culture and the Economics of Information.* Londres: Sage.

Golding, P. & M. Graham (1997) *The Political Economy of the Media.* Cheltenham: Elgar Publ.

Granou, A. (1972) *Capitalismo y modo de vida.* Madrid: Alberto Corazón, 1974.

Guillou, B. (1985) *Les stratégies multimédias des groupes de communication en Europe.* Paris: La Documentation Française.

Habermas, J. (1961) *Mudança estrutural da esfera pública.* Rio de Janeiro: Tempo Brasileiro, 1984; and the English language version *The Structural Transformation of the Public Sphere* (First MIT Press paperback edition, 1991, translated in 1989 by Massachusetts Institute of Technology).

Habermas, J. (1976) Para *a reconstrução do materialismo histórico.* São Paulo: Brasiliense, 1990.

Habermas, J. (1980) *Modernidade versus pós-modernidade.* In: Arte em Revista, 5(7), São Paulo, August 1983.

Habermas, J. (1981) *Teoria de Laacción comunicativa.* Madri: Taurus, 1987, 2 vols; and *The theory of communicative action*, 2 vols. Boston: Beacon Press 1984–1987.

Habermas, J. (1984) *Teoria de laacción comunicativa: complementos y estúdios prévios.* Madrid: Cátedra, 1989.

Habermas, J. (1987) *A nova intransparência.* In: Novos Estudos Cebrap, 18, São Paulo, September 1987.

Habermas, J. (1989) *Soberania popular como procedimento.* In: Novos Estudos Cebrap, 26, São Paulo, March 1990.

Harvey, D. (1989) *The Condition of Posmodernity.* Cambridge: Basil Blackwell, Cambridge University Press.

Heidemann, H. D. (1983) *O Estado burguês: um conceito básico da geografia política.* In: Revista de Geografia, 7(1), September–December. Recife: UFPE.

Herscovici, A. (s.d.) *Demandes culturelles etpolitique communale.* Original provided by the author.

Herscovici, A. (1988) *Unité économique du secteur de la communication.* In: Médias Pouvoirs, 12, November and December.

Herscovici, A. (1989) *Éléments pour une analyse économique du secteur de la communication.* In: Médias Pouvoirs, 18, October.

Herscovici, A. (1990) *Elementos teóricos para uma análise económica das produções culturais.* In: Análise e Conjuntura, 5(3). Belo Horizonte: Fundação João Pinheiro, September–December.

Herscovici, A. (1991) A *nova dimensão ideológica da cultura no capitalismo avançado: uma releitura do conceito gramsciano de hegemonia cultural.* Caxambu: Anpocs.

Hilferding, R. (1910) *O capital financeiro.* São Paulo: Nova Cultural, 1985.

Hirsch, J. (1974) The state apparatus and social reproduction. In: Holloway and Picciotto (1977).

Herscovici, A. (1983) The Fordist Security State and new social movements. *Kapitalstate*, 10–11.

Hobsbawn, E. (1987) *Mundos do Trabalho.* Rio de Janeiro: Paz e Terra.

Hobsbawn, E. (1987) *História do marxismo*. vol. 8, Rio de Janeiro: Paz e Terra.

Holloway, J. & S. Picciotto (1977) *State and Capital: A Marxist Debate* Londres: Edward Arnold.

Huet, A., J. Ion, A. Lefebvre, B. Miège & R. Peron (1978) *Capitalisme et industries culturelles*. Grenoble: P.U.G.

Jameson, F. (1982) *Pós-modernidade e sociedade de consumo*. In: Novos Estudos Cebrap, 12, São Paulo, June 1985.

Jameson, F. (1982) (1984) *Postmodernism or the cultural logic of late capitalism*. In New Left Review, 146, July–August.

Jessop, B. (1977) Recent theories of the capitalist state. In: *Cambridge Journal of Economics*, 1.

Jessop, B. (1988) Regulation theory, post Fordism and the state. In: *Capital and Class*, vol. 34, London.

Keynes, J. M. (1936) *Teoria geral da moeda, do juro e do dinheiro*. São Paulo: Abril Cultural, 1983.

Koford, K. (1984) Was free television a price control that increased consumers welfare? In: *Quarterly Review of Economics and Business*, 34(1).

Kopp, P. (1990) *Télévisions et concurrence*. Paris: Anthropos.

Kosik, K. (1963) *Dialética do concreto*. Rio de Janeiro: Paz e Terra, 1976.

Latimer, D. (1984) *Jameson and Post-modernism*. In: New Left Review, 148, November–December.

Lênin, W. I. (1916) *Imperialismo: fase superior do capitalismo*. São Paulo: Global, 1979.

Lepen, C. (1982) *L'analyse microéconomique de la production dramatique et 1'efet des subventions publiques*. In: Révue Économique, 33(4), July.

Leroy, D. (1980) *Économie des arts du spectacle vivant*. Paris: Económica.

Leroy, D. (1990) *Histoire des arts du spectacle en France*. Paris: U'Harmatan.

Lima, L. L., org. (1969) *Teoria da cultura de massa*. Rio de Janeiro: Paz e Terra, 1987.

Lipietz, A. (s.d) *Caractères séculaires et conjoncturels de l'intervention èconomique de l'intervention èconomique de l'Etat*. mimeo.

Lyon, D. (1988) *The Information Society: Issues and Illusions*. Cambridge: Polity Press.

Lyotard, J. F. (1979) *Opós-moderno*. Rio de Janeiro: José Olímpio, 1988.

Marglin, org. (1989) *The Golden Age of Capitalism*. Oxford University Press.

Martin, C. (1988) *L'économie politique des industries culturelles et la prise en compte des auditoires*. In: *Communication et Information*, 9(3), Quebec.

Marx, K. (1867, 1885, 1894) *O capital: crítica da economia política*. Rio de Janeiro: Civilização Brasileira, 1980.

Marx, K. (1857–1858) *Elementos fundamentales para la crítica de la economia política*. México: Siglo XXI, 1980.

Marx, K. (1859) *Para a crítica da economia política. Col. Os Pensadores*. São Paulo: Abril Cultural, 1978.

Matta, F. R., org. (1976) *A informação na nova ordem internacional*. São Paulo: Paze Terra 1980.

Mattelart, A. (1972) *Agresión desde el espado: cultura y napalm en la era de los satélites*. Mexico: Siglo XXI, 1986.

Mattelart, A. (1976) *Multinacionais e sistemas de comunicação*. São Paulo: Ciências Humanas.

Mattelart, A., org. (1984) *La culture contre la démocratie? Laudiovisuel à Vheure transnationale.* Paris: La Decouverte.
Mattelart, A. (2010) *Para un análisis de clase de la comunicación.* Buenos Aires: El Río Suena.
Mattelart, A. (2011) *Para un análisis de las prácticas de comunicación popular.* Buenos Aires: El Río Suena.
Mattelart, A. & A. Dorfman (1976) *Para ler o Pato Donald: comunicação de massa e colonialismo.* Rio de Janeiro: Paz e Terra, 1980.
Mattelart, A. & S. Seth (1979, 1983). *Communication and Class Struggle.* New York: International General.
Mccarthy, T. (1987) *La teoria crítica dejiirgen Habermas.* Madrid: Tecnos.
Miège, B. (1990) *La société conquisepar la communication.* Grenoble: P.U.G.
Miège, B., P. Pajon & J. Salaun (1986) *Lindustrialisation de laudiovisuel.* Paris: Res Babel.
Miglioli, J. (1981) *Acumulação e demanda efetiva.* São Paulo: TA.Queiroz.
Möeglin, P. (1998) *L 'industrialization de la formation: État de la question.* Paris: Centre Nationale de Documentation Pédagogique.
Moragas Spà, M. (2011). *Interpretar la comunicación. Estudios sobre medios en América y Europa.* Barcelona: Gedisa.
Morin, E. (1962) *Cultura de massas no século XX.* Rio de Janeiro: Forense-Universitária, 1984.
Mosco, V. (1996) *The Political Economy of Communication.* London: Sage.
Musso, P. & Pineau, G. (1990) *L'Italie et sa télévision.* Paris: INA.
Narváez, M. A. (2002) *Puentes tecnológicos, abismos sociales.* Colombia: Un. Manizales.
Negri, A. & Hardt, M. (2001) *Império.* São Paulo: Record (translated from the original English edition of 2000).
Négrier, E. (1989a) *Réseau, régulation, territoire.* In: Quaderni, n.° 7. Paris: Credap-Dau-phine.
Négrier, E. (1989b) *Audiovisuel: la régulation sans 1 'Etat.* ibidem.
Nordenstreng, K. & T. Varis (1974) *Inventário internacional da estrutura de programas de televisão e circulação internacional de programas.* In: Werthein (1979).
Nordenstreng, K. & T. Varis (1976) *Circula la television en un solo sentido? Examen y análisis de la circulación de los programas de television en el mundo.* In Paris: Unesco, Estúdios y Documentos de Comunicación, 70.
Offe. C. (1984) *Problemas estruturais de Estado capitalista.* Rio de Janeiro: Tempo Universitário.
Ortiz, R. (1988) *A moderna tradição brasileira.* 2nd ed. São Paulo: Brasiliense.
Ortiz, R. (1994) *Mundialização e Cultura.* São Paulo: Brasiliense.
Phan, D. & N'Guyen, G. (1999) *Economie des télécomunications et de l'internet.* Available in: <http://www-eco.enst-bretagne.fr/biblio/ecotel.pdf>.
Pilatti, A. (1990) *L 'indústria dei media.* Milano: Il Sole.
Portales, D. (1986) *La dificultad de inovar.* Santiago: Ilet.
Possas, M. L. (1983) *Dinâmica e ciclo económico em oligopólio. Tese de doutoramento.* Campinas: Unicamp, mimeo.
Possas, M. L. (1985), *Estruturas de mercado em oligopólio.* São Paulo: Hucitec.
Poulantzas, N. (1974) *Las clases sociales en el capitalismo actual.* Siglo XXI, Mexico, 1978.
Poulantzas, N. (1978) *O Estado, o poder, o socialismo.* Rio de Janeiro: Graal, 1981.

Pritchard, S. (1999) *Dar produtos na internet.* Folha de São Paulo, 25 November 1999, esp. p 4.

Prado, S. (1985) *Teoria do Estado e formas de atividade estatal.* In: Descentralização do aparelho de Estado e empresas estatais. Masters dissertation, UNICAMP, Campinas.

Richeri, G. (1983) *La television: entre servido público y negocio.* Barcelona: G. Gili.

Rodrigues, L. I. (2003) *Esse bando de amalucados e seus programas livres.* Reportagem, Yr.IV, n. 44, May, São Paulo.

Rossi-Landi, F. (1968) *A linguagem como trabalho e como mercado: uma teoria da produção e da alienação linguísticas.* São Paulo: Difel, 1985.

Salama, P. (1979) *El Estado capitalista como abstracción real.* In: Críticas de Economia Política, 12–13.

Salaun, J. M. (1987) *La production de la télévision: structuration du secteur prive de laudiovisuel et ses conséquences.* Grenoble: Un. Stendhal, mimeo.

Salaun, J. M. (1989) *A qui appartient la télévision?* Paris: Res Babel.

Salaun, J. M. (1990) *Las paradojas de la situación francesa.* In: Telos, 27 March–May. Madrid: Fundesco.

Samuelson, P. A. (1964) Public Goods and Subscription TV: A Correction of the Record. In: *Journal of Law and Economics*, 7, October.

Sarti, I. (1979) *Comunicação e dependência cultural: um equívoco.* In: Werthein (1979).

Schiller, D. (2000) *Capitalismo Digitale.* Milano: Università Bocconi, 2000, p. 10 (original in English, 1999).

Schiller, H. I. (1968) *O império norte-americano das comunicações.* Petrópolis: Vozes, 1976.

Schiller, H. I. (1984) *Información y economia en tiempo de crisis.* Madrid: Tecnos, 1986.

Schumpeter, J. (1942) *Capitalismo, socialismo e democracia.* Rio de Janeiro: Zahar, 1984.

Sfez, L. (1988) *Critique de la communication.* Paris: Seuil.

Sherwood, R. (1992) *Propriedade Intelectual e Desenvolvimento Econômico.* São Paulo: EDUSP.

Silva, S. (1980) *Expansão cafeeira e origens da indústria no Brasil.* São Paulo: Alfa-Ômega.

Silveira, S. A. (2003) *Inclusão Digital, Software Livre e Globalização Contra-Hegemônica.* In: Silveira, S. A. and Cassiano, J. (Orgs) *Software Livre e Inclusão Digital.* São Paulo: Conrad Editora Brasil, 2003. p. 17–48.

Smythe, D. W. (1977) *Las comunicaciones: Agujero negro dei marxismo occidental.* In: Richeri, G. (1983).

Söderberg, J. (2002) Copyright vs. Copyright: A Marxist Critique. *First Monday*, v. 7, n. 3, Mar. 2002. Available in: <http://firstmonday.org/issues/issue7_3/soderberg/index.html>.

Sohn-Rethel, A. (1989) *Trabalho Espiritual e Corporal: Para a epistemologia da História Ocidental.* Excerpts translated by Cesare Galvan from the German original of 1989. João Pessoa: UFPb, 1995, mimeo.

Straubhaar, J. D. (1983) *O declínio da influência americana na televisão brasileira.* In: Comunicação e Sociedade, 9. São Paulo: IMS-Cortez.

Tauille, J. R. (1989) *Uma introdução à economia política da informação.* In: Ensaios Fee, 2(2), Porto Alegre.

Theret, B. (1979) *Implicaciones teóricas de uma concepción del Estado capitalista como relación social.* In: Críticas de la Economia Política, 12–13.
Theret, B. (1989) *Regimes économiques de 1 'ordrepolitique.* Doctoral thesis. Universidade de Paris 1. Mimeo.
Theret, B. (1991) *Régulation et topologie du social.* IRIS-TS, Uni. Paris-Dauphine, July. Mimeo.
Theret, B. (1992) *Regimes économiques de 1 'ordre politique.* Paris: PUF.
Thompsom, E. (1981) *A miséria da teoria.* Rio de Janeiro: Zahar. (Originally published in English in 1978).
Thompson, J. B. & Held, D., org. (1982) *Habermas – Criticai Debates.* Londres.
Toussaint, N. (1978) *A economia da informação.* Rio de Janeiro: Zahar, 1979.
Toussaint, Y. & P. H. Mallaein (1990) *Apport pour la prospective de lanalyse micro sociale de la difusion des N.I.C.* Université de Paris/Dauphine: Mimeo.
Tresseras, J. M., Marin (1987) *El regne del subjecte. Per una teoria materialista de la comunicació social.* Barcelona: El Llamp.
University of Texas at Austin (1999) *Measuring the internet economy: On-line report.* Available in: <http://www.internetindicators.com>.
U.S. Government Working Group in Electronic Commerce (1999) *Towards Digital eQuality: 2nd Annual Report.* Executive Summary. Available in: <http://www.ecommerce.gov>, 1999, p. iii–vii.
Vincent, J. M., org. (1975) *L 'Etat contemporain et le marxisme.* Paris: Maspero.
Wasko, J. (2014) *Understanding the political economy of the media.* In: Christians, C. & Nordenstreng, Kaarle (2014). Communication theories in a multicultural world. London: Peter Lang Publ.
Weffort, R C. (1971) *Nota sobre a Teoria da Dependência: teoria de classe ou ideologia nacional?* In: Estudos Cebrap, 1, São Paulo.
Werthein, J., org. (1979) *Meios de comunicação: realidade e mito.* São Paulo: Nacional.
Zallo, R. (1988) *Economia de la comunicación y la cultura.* Madri: Akal.
Zallo, R. (s.d.) *Economia de la comunicación y de la cultura.* In: Telos, 10. Madri: Fundesco.
Zarowsky, M. (2013) *Del laboratorio chileno a la comunicación-mundo. Un itinerario intelectual de Armand Mattelart.* Buenos Aires: Biblos.
Zinser, A. A. (1980) *Médios masivos de comunicación: función ideológica o función económica.* In: Estúdios dei Tercer Mundo, set. 80, vol. 3. México: Ceesten.

Journals cited

Communications, Télévisions Mutations. 1990, n.° 51. Paris: Seuil.
Comunicação e Sociedade, ComunicaçãoTransnacional, Comunicação Brasileira. June 1983, n.° 9. São Paulo: IMS-Cortez.
Eptic. www.eptic.com.br (online).
Internet Business. A. 3, n. 29, January 2000, especially p. 13.

Index

Note: Locators followed by 'n' refer to note number.

CPSIA information can be obtained
at www.ICGtesting.com
Printed in the USA
LVHW080321270420
654475LV00020B/1768